ARIS & PHILLIPS HISPANIC CLASSICS

I0593110

EMILIA PARDO BAZÁN

Sunstroke (A Love Story)

Insolación: Historia amorosa

Translated with an introduction and notes by

Graham Whittaker

LIVERPOOL UNIVERSITY PRESS

First published 2020 by
Liverpool University Press
4 Cambridge Street
Liverpool
L69 7ZU

www.liverpooluniversitypress.co.uk

British Library Cataloguing-in-Publication data
A British Library CIP record is available

ISBN 978-1-78962-114-3 hardback
ISBN 978-1-78962-115-0 paperback

Typeset by Tara Montane

Cover: *La pradera de San Isidro*, Francisco de Goya y Lucientes, 1788.
Copyright © Photographic Archive Museo Nacional del Prado.

CONTENTS

ACKNOWLEDGEMENTS

It is always a pleasure and a privilege to work on a volume for the Aris and Phillips Hispanic classics series. Once again, I would like to thank Jonathan Thacker for reading the book in typescript and making a number of corrections, judicious comments and invaluable suggestions.

I would also like to express my sincere gratitude to all the staff of the renowned Real Academia Galega, especially Ana María Menéndez (Directora da Biblioteca), for granting me permission to reproduce the illustrations by José Cuchy included in this volume.

Graham Whittaker

INTRODUCTION

1. Foreword

I started work on this volume while my previous translation, *La Tribuna*, was in the final stages of preparation. The decision to translate another novel by Emilia Pardo Bazán was not a difficult one. Having spent considerable time and effort preparing a bilingual edition of *La Tribuna*, it seemed a natural progression to move on to a second work by the same author. This would enable me to capitalise on the knowledge I had already acquired, not only in terms of the author and the literary, social, political and historical context in which she was working, but also relating to the difficulties and challenges posed by her prose. In addition, the publication of another work by Emilia Pardo Bazán would complement my urge to make the literary output of this uncelebrated, undervalued writer more well-known and accessible.

Why *Insolación*? The obvious choice would have been *Los pazos de Ulloa*, widely considered to be Pardo Bazán's finest work of fiction, but there were two drawbacks: firstly, it represents the culmination of the Spanish-style naturalism she initiated with *La Tribuna*, rather than the preferred option of representing a different stage of the author's artistic development; more importantly, the recent publication of Lucia Graves and Paul O'Prey's *The House of Ulloa* in the Penguin Classics series has guaranteed that the reading public already has access to a modern translation of her magnum opus. Once that possibility had been discarded, this left an open playing field, because, when it comes to her other novels, the English-speaking world is not in a fortunate position. Very little of her immense oeuvre, in a literary career spanning more than four decades, is available in English, most of the translations being either out of print or very dated and of a questionable standard. Deciding that I would like to work on a different sort of novel from *La Tribuna*, the next choice was *Insolación*. I was disappointed to learn that a translation already existed but a cursory inspection of a few pages of Amparo Loring's *Midsummer Madness*

(1907) was enough to persuade me that it was time for a new version of this fine work.

There has not always been such a dearth of available translations, as many of her great works were translated into English during her lifetime. Pardo Bazán's obituary in the *El Ideal Gallego* edition of 13 May 1921, states that good proof of the reputation she enjoyed is the fact that, in 1891, she signed a contract with a foreign publishing house, granting permission to translate into English all the works she had published and those she would go on to write thereafter.[1] In that year the Cassell Publishing Company in New York published Mary J. Serrano's translations of *Un viaje de novios* (*A Wedding Trip*), *El cisne de Vilamorta* (*The Swan of Vilamorta*), *Morriña* (*Homesickness*) and Mary Springer's translation of *Una cristiana* (*A Christian Woman*). The following year it published Serrano's translation of *La piedra angular* (*The Angular Stone*).

In the late 1890s, the Mershon Company began to publish the books of several bankrupt companies, including Cassell & Co., and in 1900 it published Serrano's translation of *Bucólica* (*A Galician Girl's Romance*). Other publishing companies followed suit, and in 1906 Funk & Wagnalls published Annabel Hord Seeger's translation of *Misterio* as *The Mystery of the Lost Dauphin (Louis XVII)*. In 1907 Amparo Loring's translation of *Insolación* was published as *Midsummer Madness* and in 1908 John Lane Co. published Ethel Harriet Hearn's translation of *Los pazos de Ulloa* as *The Son of the Bondwoman*.

There are various editions of *Insolación*, both in print and on the Internet. The Spanish text for this edition has been referenced against the novel as it appears online in conjunction with the texts edited by Ermitas Penas Varela (Madrid: Ediciones Cátedra, 2001), Marina Mayoral (Madrid: Espasa Calpe, 1987) and José Hesse (Madrid, Taurus, 1970). The footnotes in the Spanish text are my own and

---

1 'De la reputación que ya gozaba en aquellos tiempos es buena prueba el hecho de que en el año 1891 celebró un contrato con una casa editorial extranjera, concediendo autorización para traducir al inglés todas las obras que había publicado y las que escribiera en lo sucesivo' ('Fallecimiento de la Condesa de Pardo Bazán').

these are not translated. The reason is simple: not only do I hope that students will read the original Spanish as much as possible, but also the meaning of the footnotes should be fairly obvious, especially in tandem with the translation of the novel on the opposite page. I have consulted primary and secondary sources in Spanish, Galician, French and English whilst writing this introduction; all the translations of quotations taken from these books and articles are my own. The purpose of this introduction is to help students to discover *Insolación*, the author and the context in which this fascinating writer lived and produced her many works.

2. Emilia Pardo Bazán

The most prolific and influential Spanish female writer of the nineteenth century is indisputably Emilia Pardo Bazán. Always a controversial figure, she was attacked for her defiance of literary and societal expectations, especially her enthusiasm for naturalism and her robust feminist stance. Such views, frequently demonised as an unwholesome and unwelcome legacy of the French Revolution, were seen as abhorrent in a woman and inimical to traditional Spanish values. Emilia Pardo Bazán was indeed an anomaly: an educated woman at a time when around 90 per cent of Spanish women were illiterate; a single mother, separated from her husband, in a reactionary age; and a literary authority in a world of letters dominated by men.

In an era when women were widely perceived as intellectually inferior,[2] she was intent on dispelling the myth of 'dos literaturas, una femenina, que trasciende a brisas de violetas; otra masculina, que apesta a cigarro' (two types of literature, a feminine one that smells

---

2 For example, see Pompeyo Gener, 'De la mujer y sus derechos en las sociedades modernas', *La Vanguardia* (26 Feb. 1889): 'los más distinguidos doctores – los antropólogos más sabios, todos están conformes en declarar la inferioridad física, moral e intelectual de la mujer [...] En sí misma, la mujer, no es como el hombre, un ser completo; es sólo el instrumento de la reproducción, la destinada a perpetuar la especie' (the most distinguished doctors, the wisest anthropologists, all agree on the physical, moral and intellectual inferiority of women [...] In herself, a woman isn't a complete being like a man is; she is only the instrument of reproduction, destined to perpetuate the species).

of violet water, and a masculine one that stinks of cigar).[3] Her so-
called masculinity earned her denigration as well as respect from her
contemporaries: whilst Clarín, in his review of Pardo Bazán's paper
'La educación del hombre y de la mujer; sus relaciones y diferencias'
at a pedagogical convention, found the radicalism and *marimachismo*
with which she defended women's education disagreeable,[4] Menéndez
Pelayo praised her for meeting the standards of 'la literatura más
varonil' (the most manly literature), and José Ortega Munilla, the
editor of the newspaper *El Imparcial*, placed her novels on a par
with her male contemporaries: 'Es Usted uno de los tres novelistas
contemporáneos españoles y mi juicio sincero la coloca entre Galdós
y Pereda' (You are one of the three contemporary Spanish novelists
and my honest judgement places you between Galdós and Pereda).[5]
This is why she should be considered not so much the greatest female
author of her time as one of the greatest Spanish authors of all time,
irrespective of sex.

Pardo Bazán was born on 16 September 1851 in La Coruña, the
only child of affluent, educated parents. Her principal home was in
the aristocratic 'upper town' of La Coruña and she received a formal
education that went far beyond the customary training for girls of
her class at that time. Her mother, Amelia de la Rúa, taught little
Emilia to read and her father was a prominent political figure whose
vigorous defence of Catholicism as the state religion earned him the
pontifical title of 'count'. Believing in the intellectual equality of men
and women, her beloved father elaborated his ideas on education from
Rousseau's *Émile*. He opened his considerable library to his daughter
and allowed her to read anything she wanted, except for the works of
Dumas, Sue, George Sand, Victor Hugo and other leaders of French
Romanticism which tempted her from the top shelf. She became a
voracious reader – 'de esos niños que se pasan el día quietecitos en un

---

3   'Carta Magna', *Obras completas, Tomo III* (Madrid: Aguilar, 1973), p. 657.
4   Leopoldo Alas, *Obras completas IV Crítica (Segunda parte)* (Oviedo: Nobel,
2003), p. 1853.
5   Ana María Freire López, *Cartas inéditas a Emilia Pardo Bazán* (La Coruña:
Conde de Fenosa, 1991), p. 123.

rincón cuando se les da un libro' (one of those children who spend the day quietly in a corner when they are given a book)[6] – with *Don Quijote de la Mancha*, the Bible and the *Iliad* among her favourites. She went on to fill the pages of her novels with the encyclopaedic knowledge she had acquired concerning philosophy, science, literature, social and political thought, and history. Nevertheless, none of this excluded a lively interest and expertise in the world of clothing and fashions, the culinary arts and other aspects of homemaking.

When Pardo Bazán was a girl her family spent the winters in Madrid, where she attended a French boarding school sponsored by the royal family, acquiring a high level of linguistic proficiency, reading La Fontaine's *Fables*, Fénelon's *Les aventures de Télémaque* and various other classics. Later, when the family began to spend the winters in La Coruña, she received private tuition. In *Apuntes autobiográficos* Emilia Pardo Bazán makes a reference to the three events of 1868, which occurred in quick succession and symbolise her initiation into adulthood: 'me vestí de largo, me casé y estalló la revolución de septiembre' (I put on a long skirt, got married and the Revolution of 1868 broke out).[7] A year later, following her marriage,at the age of 16 to José Quiroga, an 18-year-old law student from an eminent family in Galicia, and the September Revolution which had precipitated the abdication of the queen, her father, an erstwhile Carlist representative in the National Assembly, was elected deputy to the Cortes as a member of Salustiano Olózaga's Progressive Party. The whole family moved to Madrid, where Doña Emilia happily found herself in a position to relish the many pleasures and benefits of aristocratic society. The following year, after Amadeo's abdication and the collapse of the Progressive Party, her father decided to take the family abroad, initiating a brief but enriching period of travel for Pardo Bazán. On her return to Spain, she became intrigued by the ideas of the German philosopher Karl Christian Friedrich Krause and, thanks to the curious phenomenon of Krausism, she gained a liking

---

6 Emilia Pardo Bazán, *Apuntes autobiográficos*, in *Obras completas, Tomo III*, p. 702.
7 Ibid., p. 706.

for systematic, methodical and reflective reading, which goes beyond reading for pleasure and becomes study.

Emilia Pardo Bazán was a woman of immense energy who devoted most of her life to fulfilling the life plan which, according to Carmen Bravo-Villasante, she had jotted down as a young girl in a notebook: 'to study, to work, to think'.[8] During her lifetime she wrote countless articles on a variety of topics, travelogues, literary criticism, volumes of poetry, plays, 19 novels, 20 or so novellas and over five hundred short stories. Although she had already published poems in the *Almanaque de Galicia* at the age of 16, her first serious publication was a critical monograph on the work of Benito Jerónimo Feijóo, an eighteenth-century Benedictine monk from Galicia whom she admired for his strong attachment to the region, despite its antiquated superstitious beliefs, but primarily for his pioneering feminist outlook. Emilia Pardo Bazán played a crucial role in bringing the discussion of feminism to the forefront of intellectual and popular debate, through her fiction as well as her essays. *Insolacíon* and her seminal essay 'The Women of Spain', in which she is very critical of the education received by Spanish women, were published within a couple of months of each other.

In all of her works Pardo Bazán incorporated her ideas on the need for women to have access to all the rights and opportunities that men already enjoyed. Despite the patent sexism in the intellectual circles of her era, she became the first woman to preside over the literature section of the Ateneo de Madrid in 1906, and the first to occupy a chair of neo-Latin literature at the Central University of Madrid (former name of The Complutense University of Madrid). She inherited the title of countess on her father's death in 1908, and in 1910 was appointed a member of the Council of Public Instruction. In 1921 she was appointed to the Senate but never formally took up her seat. Much to her frustration, she was repeatedly refused a seat at the Spanish Royal Academy, purely on the grounds of her gender.

---

8   Carmen Bravo-Villasante, *Vida y obra de Emilia Pardo Bazán* (Madrid: Ediciones Castilla, 1962), p. 33.

3. The Social and Historical Background

Insolación is not an historical novel, but there are many references to people and events that were of great significance during the author's life: Alfonso XII, La Infanta Isabel, the Carlist wars, General Espartero, the Restoration, the reign of Amadeo I and a number of contemporary politicians including Martos, Sagasta, Castelar and Cánovas del Castillo. The nineteenth century was a very turbulent time for Spain, a period of decline, unrest and instability, a battlefield between the *ancien régime* of absolute monarchy, supported mainly by the clergy and the aristocracy, and the liberal movements and progressive ideals that filtered through to Spain from the French Revolution. This conflict led to the six-year War of Spanish Independence (1808–14), ending with the victory of the Spanish troops and the abdication of Joseph Bonaparte. The throne returned to Ferdinand VII, whose hatred of the French induced him to abolish the new Constitution, censor the press and persecute the liberals. Apart from a brief period of government, when General Rafael del Riego managed to overcome the monarchists and bring back the Constitution, Spain was once again a traditional absolutist monarchy.

As Ferdinand's health failed, he abolished the Salic Law so that his daughter Isabel could accede to the throne. The court was divided into two groups: the *carlistas* wanted the king's pious and reactionary brother, Carlos María Isidro, to reign, while the more liberal *cristinos* wanted the king's wife, María Cristina de Borbón-Dos Sicilias, to hold the title of queen until Isabel came of age. Although Machado's 'las dos Españas' – one Catholic, absolutist and reactionary, the other secular, constitutional and progressive – is a rather oversimplified categorisation, the deep divisions within Spanish society created a difficult situation of political stagnation and led to the three Carlist Wars between 1833 and 1876.

Ferdinand died in 1833 and the three-year-old Isabel was proclaimed Queen of Spain. Her widowed mother acted as regent from 1833 to 1840, and General Espartero from 1841 until 1843, when Isabel II ascended to the throne. During her reign Spain suffered from numerous

military uprisings, interventions and *pronunciamientos*, until she was eventually toppled from power by the 'Glorious Revolution' of September 1868, led by General Prim. For the next three years Spain was a monarchy in search of a monarch. A European-wide search finally came up with Amadeo of Savoy in 1870, who reigned for just over two years before abdicating and escaping from what he called the 'jaula de locos' (madhouse) of Spanish politics. The First Spanish Republic was declared, but it was ended by a military coup just one year later in 1874, and the monarchy was restored in 1875, with Isabel's son, Alfonso XII, succeeding to the throne. The Bourbons had been restored, thus marking the beginning of the historical period known as the Restoration, which lasted until the proclamation of the Second Republic in 1931.

4. The Intellectual and Literary Context: Romanticism, Realism, *Costumbrismo* and Naturalism

Emilia Pardo Bazán is usually associated with realism and naturalism, but she also experimented with other literary styles and genres. Her novelistic production has routinely been divided into two halves: a naturalistic period and a 'spiritual' period in which, with a greater focus on psychology, she directed her attention more on the middle and upper classes. Her move towards psychology echoes a resurgence of interest amongst French novelists in the inner selves of their characters as a backlash against Zola's naturalistic reductionism. It also reflects the works of Russian novelists like Turgenev, Gogol, Tolstoy and Dostoyevsky, whose translations into French Pardo Bazán began to discover in March 1885, when *Crime and Punishment* fell into her hands.

The term 'realist' began to be used in 1850, but it wasn't until a couple of decades later that it established itself as a literary movement in Spain, the most influential writers being Galdós, Alas and Ibáñez. Instead of presenting a moral vision of society, realist writers saw themselves as objective observers of everyday life, and their literature strove to portray people and society as they are rather than how we would like them to be. Unlike Mme de Staël, Chateaubriand and

Lamartine, the Romantic writers whom Pardo Bazán labelled 'los vencidos' (the vanquished) in *La cuestión palpitante*, Stendhal and Balzac, 'los vencedores' (the victors) spearheading realism, focused on the present rather than a glorious past, and on ordinary people instead of heroic figures.

The terms naturalism and realism have often been used synonymously, even occasionally by Pardo Bazán herself, despite her belief that realism was superior to both naturalism and idealism. There is, however, a clear-cut distinction between the two literary movements: while naturalism shared the realist objective of depicting contemporary life and society, Zola believed the role of the writer was to apply the methods of scientific observation to the novel by observing and recording the chain of cause and effect in a dispassionate and non-judgemental way. The naturalists saw the human animal as a product of nature (biology) and society (environment), and viewed the novel as an experiment in which a hypothesis is tested and proved. Behind this experimental conception are Darwinism, Comte's positivistic adherence to observable phenomena and Hippolyte Taine's famous doctrine, posited in *Histoire de la littérature anglaise* (1864), of 'la race, le milieu, le moment': our lives are inescapably determined by the external factors of heredity, environment and the pressure of immediate circumstances.

In *Apuntes autobiográficos*, Pardo Bazán explains the background to the 20 weekly articles she sent to the Madrid newspaper *La Época* between November 1882 and April 1883. These essays, which shortly after were gathered together in the book *La cuestión palpitante* with a prologue by Clarín, sought to explain, defend and criticise the literary and philosophical movement of naturalism as propounded by its founder, Émile Zola. The Spanish public was shocked that a woman should even be reading Zola, let alone commenting on him without unreservedly opposing a literary movement described by Cañete in his article 'Crítica Dramática' (*Revista de Madrid*, 1881) as 'glorificador del adulterio y destructor de la familia' (glorifying adultery and destructive to the family) and its proponents as a band of pirates invading the Spanish mainland.

Insolación is generally considered an example of naturalism which delves into important contemporary issues such as social class, regional differences and the subordinate status of women. From the title itself to the hymn to the couple's patron deity, the sun, in the very last page, Pardo Bazán explores the notion of environmental determinism, as expounded in the novel itself by the artillery commander Gabriel Pardo de la Lage. The novel certainly incorporates many naturalistic components: a reference to Herbert Spencer; the clearly defined historical framework; the use of what Luis Alfonso called 'palabras de baja estofa' (second-rate words);[9] and the authentic settings (streets, squares, churches and other buildings are all identified, and the topography of different districts like el barrio de Salamanca, el puente de Toledo, las Ventas and el cerro de San Isidro is consistent with el Plano del Ensanche de Madrid by Carlos María de Castro, motivated by the expanding population and influenced by Baron Haussmann's renovation of Paris).

On the other hand, there are notable differences between this novel and naturalistic works like *La Tribuna*, especially in terms of the importance of humour, the unmistakable contribution made by key elements of *costumbrismo* (especially the picture of the Fair of San Isidro and Las Ventas del Espíritu Santo) and the aristocratic background of the female protagonist. Also, where Zola's characters are devoid of free will and therefore 'entraînés à chaque acte de leur vie par les fatalités de leur chair' (drawn into each action of their lives by the inexorable laws of their physical nature),[10] we never feel that Pardo Bazán's protagonists are helpless puppets manipulated by forces beyond their control.

In Chapter 2 of *Insolación*, Gabriel Pardo explains at the Duchess of Sahagún's weekly gathering that civilisation is impotent against nature and that as soon as the sun appears, 'se nos sube a la cabeza, y entonces es cuando se nivelan las clases' (it goes to our heads, and that's when class differences are levelled out). This ineluctable power capable of

---

9   See Bravo-Villasante, *Vida y obra de Emilia Pardo Bazán*, p. 88.
10   Émile Zola, 'Préface de la deuxième édition', *Thérèse Raquin* (Paris: Librairie Hachette, 1962), p. 6.

inducing 'bestialidades de toda calaña' (acts of brutality of every kind) is graphically illustrated, despite Pardo Bazán's opposition to Zola's 'manía de escoger lo más feo' (craze for choosing what is ugliest),[11] by a couple of violent incidents: one involves 'un par de navajas desnudas […] volando por los aires en busca de las tripas de algún prójimo' (a pair of bare knives […] flying through the air in search of a nearby human being's intestines); the other, in the preceding chapter, concerns a fight between two large women, a curiously silent brawl which recalls the vociferous 'bataille formidable' between Gervaise and Virginie in the first chapter of Zola's *L'assommoir*. Asís compares 'las dos amazonas' (the two Amazons) to two big fish, like dolphins or sharks, tearing each other to shreds with bites and swipes of their tail, and this illustration of Pardo's theory of Spanish barbarism is echoed later on in the muted dispute between Asís and Pacheco, observed in the distance by a group of *cigarerras* endeavouring to interpret the lovers' gestures and facial expressions without the benefit of auditory pointers.

If one accepts Pardo's theories as Pardo Bazán's, the story of Asís's sunstroke at the *romería* of San Isidro seems to bear out his hypothesis about the triumph of nature, the power of which is manifested in the sun. Indeed, Gabriel Pardo's condemnation of the fair as an 'aquelarre' (witches' coven) is corroborated by the zoomorphic descriptions of the three female gypsies, especially the young girl with 'la frente, chata como la de una víbora, y los brazos desnudos, verdosos y flacos lo mismo que dos reptiles' (her forehead, as flat as a viper's, and her bare arms, greenish and thin like two reptiles); and Asís's assessment of her own demeanour leads her to agree with her compatriot's analysis, all the more so because of its corollary that gender has no bearing on this disturbing propensity for ignominy:

> Bien dice mi paisano […] Una persona decente, en ciertos sitios, obra lo mismo que obraría un mayoral. Aquí estoy yo, que me he portado como una chula.

---

11   Emilia Pardo Bazán, *La revolución y la novela en Rusia*, in *Obras completas, Tomo III*, p. 877.

(My compatriot is right [...] In certain situations, a respectable person acts the same as a drover would act. Look at me, I've behaved like a common, lower-class woman.)

At the fair, where she has the impression that the law of gravity has been rescinded for her, she feels lost at sea. It comes into her head that she has fallen in the boiling hot sea and is floating inside a little boat like a 'cáscara de nuez' (nutshell), a phrase that recalls Pardo's affirmation that civilisation is 'cosa externa, cáscara y nada más' (something external, a shell and nothing more).

However, the uncharacteristic foolhardiness with which Asís abandons her notions of female protocol and social hierarchy is more a case of sensual overload kindled by a potent combination of too much alcohol, the tumultuous atmosphere of the fair and her repressed sexuality awakened by the seductive charms of Diego Pacheco. Despite Fray Candil's pronouncement that 'los influjos del sol fueron la causa de que la Toboada cediese a los antojos carnales de Pacheco' (the sun's influence was the cause of Toboada yielding to Pacheco's carnal desires), Asís's decision to sleep with her beau and marry him, hasty and surprising though it may initially seem to the narrator and the reader, cannot be attributed to the effects of sunstroke. Although some readers may subscribe to the widespread explanation that the forces of heredity and environment prove too strong for Asís, Pardo Bazán actually divulges very few details about the protagonist's background. There is no evidence that either external stimuli (environment) or genetic predisposition (heredity) could in any way account for her feelings and conduct once the effects of her hangover have abated. It is worth remembering that most of the action in the novel takes place indoors (Asís's house, the Duchess of Sahagún's house, the Cardeñosa aunts' house, the café, the shack on the edge of the Manzanares River, the *Fonda de la Confianza*, the train compartment in Asis's dream), thus discrediting the notion of the sun being solely culpable. Furthermore, the final image is of Asís with her new lover, and the last words in the novel are Pacheco's playful impersonation of the gypsy fortune teller's auspicious prediction at the fair, thereby implying a renunciation of Gabriel Pardo's deterministic thesis and consigning it

to 'la perniciosa herejía de negar la libertad humana' (the pernicious heresy of denying human freedom).[12] The last chapter is undoubtedly the most contentious part of the novel. Whilst Beth Wietelmann Bauer refers to the happy ending as a departure from the standard 'desenlace desgraciado [...] representativo de una sensibilidad moderna manifiesta ya en la novela mayor de los escritores de la generación de Pardo Bazán, Palacio Valdés y Clarín' (unhappy ending [...] representative of a modern sensibility already evident in the great novel of the writers of the generation of Pardo Bazán, Palacio Valdés and Clarín),[13] elsewhere it has been decried as a betrayal of the novel's subversive nature and the complexity of the love affair. Viewing the marriage as too conventional and formulaic, a conscious decision to revoke the perceived immorality of the preceding chapters, the resolution in the epilogue has often been ascribed to Pardo Bazán's fervent Catholicism and denounced as incongruent and inconsistent. Some readers may concur with Daniel S. Whitaker and see the facile restoration of moral order as a parody of the typical happy ending in the sentimental novel.[14] Indeed, the parenthetical annotations accompanying the narrator's decision not to provide details of the couple's reconciliation mock the saccharine style of popular romance:

No entremos en el saloncito de Asís mientras dure el tiroteo de explicaciones (¡cosa más empalagosa!), sino cuando la pareja liba la primera miel de las paces (empalagosísima también; pero paciencia).

(Let's not enter Asís's little salon during the crossfire of explanations (so saccharine!), but when the couple are tasting the sweet taste of reconciliation (also very saccharine, but be patient.)

---

12   Emilia Pardo Bazán, *La cuestión palpitante*, in *Obras completas, Tomo III*, p. 645.
13   Beth Wietelmann Bauer, 'Innovación y apertura: la novela realista del siglo XIX ante el problema del desenlace', *Hispanic Review* 59 (1991), p. 197.
14   'The end of Doña Emilia's text is really a parody of the romantic, idealistic scenes still prevalent in many novels and serialized fiction of her day'. See Daniel S. Whitaker 'Artificial Order: Closure in Pardo Bazán's *Insolación*', *Romance Quarterly* 35.3 (1988), p. 362.

However, even if the excesses of the romantic scenes of serialised fiction are satirised in *Insolación*, Pardo Bazán herself was certainly capable of stooping to the same mawkish hyperboles: Pacheco's honeyed obsequiousness and terms of endearment echo her own exaggerated and romanticised description of Francisco Giner de los Ríos – she claimed that their friendship was born 'del conocimiento de la suma bondad de aquella escogida alma' (from my recognition of the supreme goodness of that exceptional soul)[15] – and the cloying sentimentality of her letters to Galdós, in which she addresses him as 'mi ratón', 'mi vida', 'miquiño', 'mi cariño', 'ratonciño del alma', 'minino', 'miquito', 'amado', 'mi dulce bien', 'querido de mi corazón' or 'amado roedor mío', and signs off as 'tu Peinetita', 'tu Porcia', 'Doña Opas', and 'Matilde'.[16]

The ambiguity of the last chapter is epitomised in the ironic disparity between the hackneyed phrases of melodramatic novels used to convey Asís's emotions – 'Sus pupilas se humedecieron, su respiración se apresuró, y corrió por sus vértebras misterioso escalofrío' (Her eyes filled with tears, her breathing quickened and a mysterious shiver, a draught fanned by the wings of the Ideal, ran down her spine) – and the widow's unsentimental pragmatism, her quixotic epiphany that what she sees in Diego Pacheco's dashing appearance is as much an invention as Dulcinea de Toboso or the ladies praised by most poets: 'algo sublime, que realmente no existía' (something sublime, which did not actually exist).

Close scrutiny of the rest of the novel reveals the extent to which it prepares us for Asís's resolute 'quédate' (stay) in the final chapter. With her unequivocal rejection of Zola's uncompromising application of the scientific method, whereby thought and passion were subjected to the same laws which determine a falling stone,[17] Pardo Bazán

---

15   Bravo-Villasante, *Vida y obra de Emilia Pardo Bazán*, pp. 53–54.

16   See Carmen Bravo-Villasante, *Cartas a Galdós* (Madrid: Turner, 1978).

17   'Someter el pensamiento y la pasión a las mismas leyes que determinan la caída de la piedra' (*La cuestión palpitante*, p. 580). In the same paragraph Pardo Bazán gives the example of Zola's *Une page d'amour*, where the heroine 'manifiesta los grados de su enamoramiento por los de temperatura que alcanza la planta de sus pies' (shows the degrees of her love by the temperature reached by the soles of her feet).

ponders the spontaneous, unfathomable and mysterious nature of human love as advanced by Gabriel Pardo in Chapter 13: 'no hay explicación que valga para los fenómenos del corazón' (there's no worthy explanation for things of the heart). In fact, she subtly paves the way for this putative volte-face as early as Chapter 3, when Asís, having bumped into Pacheco on her way to mass, acknowledges that she finds him very good-looking, despite her assurance that she's not attracted just to external appearance. She even defends her right to show it:

> Señor, ¿por qué no han de tener las mujeres derecho para encontrar guapos a los hombres que lo sean, y por qué ha de mirarse mal que lo manifiesten (aunque para manifestarlo dijesen tantas majaderías como los chulos del café Suizo)? […] En suma, Pacheco, que vestía un elegante terno gris claro, me pareció galán de veras …

> (Indeed, why shouldn't women have the right to find men handsome when they are, and why should it look bad for them to show it (even if they were to show it by coming out with as many irritating remarks as the working-class Madrilenians from the Suizo café)? […] In short, I found Pacheco, who was wearing an elegant, light grey three-piece suit, truly handsome…)

By Chapter 16 we are well aware of the couple's mutual attraction and connection, and the episode when Asís loses one of her slippers as she springs out of her admirer's arms in fits of laughter is not without significance. In her chapter entitled 'The Sartorial Charm of the Modern Man in Pardo Bazán's *Insolación*', Dorotea Heneghan's misapprehension that Pacheco places Asís's slipper on his own foot is her *point de départ* for a misguided analysis of 'the Andalusian's challenging the boundaries of his gender by undermining the core distinction – the feminine versus the masculine – on which the bourgeois system of gender differentiation was/is based' and 'the narrator's part of renegotiating the limits of Pacheco's gender'. Her erroneous contention that 'the southerner puts Asís's slipper on with no intention of wearing it, but to entertain the lady he courts, in other

words, with the purpose of having fun with it',[18] totally devalues the intimacy and sensuality of the incident. It is clear from the text that Pacheco picks up the slipper and puts it back on Asís's foot. Far from being 'a playful teasing act', it is an action which recalls the story of Cinderella with its 'happy-ever-after' ending and signals, with the erotic undertone of a man holding a woman's foot and replacing her footwear 'con mil extremos y zalamerías' (with extreme care and fawning), how much their liaison has already evolved.

The development of the relationship is also hinted at in Asís's hairdo. The many references to her untidy hair, in contrast with her well-attested cleanliness and unostentatious elegance, are indicative of the young *marquesa*'s disregard for patriarchal assumptions about female sexuality as well as the couple's growing intimacy. Her hair is a tangled mass when we first encounter her, and on more than one occasion Pacheco disarranges it by hiding his face in it or running his long fingers through it. When she is packing and opens the door to find herself, much to her surprise, face to face with her suitor, her tousled hair, resembling the work of a hair salon for cats, recalls the unruly coiffure of her hangover and anticipates her unkempt delectation in the epilogue after spending the night with her lover.

Indeed, Asís herself acknowledges the fact that 'me gusta, que me va gustando cada día un poco más, que me trastorna con su palabrería …' (I like him, that I'm getting to like him a bit more every day, that he's driving me crazy with his prattle...). There is a stark contrast between the sober, duty-bound loyalty to her late husband, who, with his dyed moustache, ailments and fistulas, 'supo evitar el delirio de los extremos amorosos' (knew how to avoid the delirium of amorous extremes) and the passion and magnetism of the charismatic Andalusian. She even maintains, reversing Pacheco's allegation that she must have given him love potions, that he's the one who has cast a spell on her: 'Cuando se va, reflexiono y caigo en la cuenta; pero en viéndole … acabóse, me perdí' (When he goes off, I think about it and

---

18 Dorotea Heneghan, *Striking their Modern Pose: Fashion, Gender and Modernity in Galdós, Pardo Bazán and Picón* (West Lafayette, IN: Purdue University Press, 2015), pp. 90–91.

the penny drops; but as soon as I see him … it's finished, I'm lost). This culminates, during the first lunch, in her literal intoxication, and at the second lunch, in her disproportionate jealousy when Pacheco dances and flirts with the young *cigarerras*.

Her growing infatuation is also intimated in less obvious ways throughout the novel, especially the variations in repeated actions within the symmetrical structure of the novel. In Chapter 10, bored with the bland food and dull topics of conversation, Asís imagines what has happened as a kind of nightmare whilst also noticing, contrary to the Cardeñosa spinsters, the nudity of Apollo on the mantel clock, thereby emphasising that her prudish, flat-chested maiden aunts embody a sexless way of life that could never fulfil her. She returns to find Pacheco waiting for her and, when he leaves, he looks up towards Asís's bedroom window but sees no one there. This sequence of events is repeated in Chapter 15 when Asís, during a long afternoon of social visits replete with conversations capable of boring a plaster statue, thinks about her conduct. Meanwhile, Pacheco drops by and waits for her return and, once again, he looks up to her bedroom window as he is leaving, but this time he sees a white shape behind it. The implication is that the protagonist cannot now resist looking at him as he disappears.

Even more pertinent, though, is the dream sequence in Chapter 21. Having decided to escape Pacheco's advances and leave Madrid, Asís is busy preparing for her return to Galicia when she falls asleep. Pardo Bazán wastes no time in flaunting her acquaintance with contemporary scientific thinking concerning the relationship between the formation of dreams and somatic sources of stimulation. However, rather than investigating the possible influence of external stimuli, from gastric activity to the effect of a warm bed, on the lobes of the brain, the novelist prefers to conceive a dream in which most of the ingredients either reflect Asís's previous experiences or adumbrate potential developments. In the dream, she is leaving arid, dusty Castile with its relentless heat, the rocky territory of Ávila and the harsh deserts of León when sherry appears in a glass she thought contained water. This evokes the deleterious effects of the sun and alcohol on her conduct

at the San Isidro Fair the day after she had heard, at the Duchess of Sahagún's get-together, Pardo's theory that the Castilian sun is powerful enough to cause Spaniards to cast off their thin veneer of civilisation and behave primitively.

Although she is soon delighted to see the Galician mountains covered with leafy chestnut trees, springs, waterfalls and streams, feeling herself reviving like a fish returned to its native element, it isn't long before the eternal clouds of the north-east release a thick curtain of rain which she feels on her heart and, drowning with sorrow, she wakes up to find her pillow wet with tears. The unpleasantness of this journey suggests her subconscious realisation that leaving the heat and passion of Madrid will not make her happy, because Galicia will not wash away her moral quandary any more than having a bath can erase her regrets and self-deprecation. Pardo Bazán uses this oneiric prophecy, underlined with a sequence of sexual symbols – the rocking sensation of the train in motion, its penetration into the tunnel, the culmination of the dream with a spurting liquid – in order to prepare the reader for what might otherwise be considered an unrealistic change of heart by the protagonist.[19] Whilst she has resisted previous attempts at seduction, after the dream she submits, showing that her decision in the epilogue is a manifestation of the feelings and desires that have been building up inside her since she first met Pacheco.

5. *Insolación*: Genesis and Reception

Insolación and *Morriña* are companion pieces, both published in 1889 and later issued together in a single volume. Although Emilia Pardo Bazán had already established a name for herself as an important novelist with *Los Pazos de Ulloa* (1886) and *La madre naturaleza* (1887), *Insolación* and *Morriña* were initially dismissed as lightweight pieces, partly no doubt on account of the subtitle 'dos historias amorosas' (two love stories).

---

19   See, however, Marina Mayoral's introduction to *Insolación* (Madrid, Calpe, 1987), p. 32: 'Los símbolos, a mi juicio […] no son sexuales, la autora no ha querido que lo fueran …' (The symbols, in my opinion […] aren't sexual, the author didn't want them to be…).

None of Emilia Pardo Bazán's female characters shocked her contemporaries as much as Asís Taboada, a 32-year-old widow with a young daughter scarcely mentioned either by her or the third-person narrator. Although this beautiful, well-educated and respectable Catholic is presented as 'una señora intachable' (an irreproachable lady), 'una perfecta viuda' (a perfect widow) and a 'madre cariñosa' (affectionate mother), her attraction to a charming philanderer from Cádiz was seen by the reading public as unseemly and unladylike, an infringement of society's standards of propriety. Her so-called promiscuity also scandalised many critics like Fray Candil (Emilio Bobadilla), who complained that 'una *verdadera* señora no va de *juerga*, y menos con un hombre a quien apenas conoce' (a *real* lady doesn't go on a *spree*, and even less so with a man she hardly knows).[20]

Although there are many nineteenth-century storylines featuring women who have committed adultery or been seduced, Leopoldo Alas, a former friend turned enemy who played an active role in obstructing Pardo Bazán's admission into the Real Academia de la Lengua, initially referred to *Insolación* as a '*boutade* pseudoerótica de la ilustre dama' (pseudo-erotic *boutade* from the illustrious lady).[21] Later, in one of his more waspish comments, he qualified it as an 'antipático poema de una jamona atrasada de caricias' (unpleasant poem of a meaty, middle-aged woman lacking affection).[22] Finally, in a more detailed criticism, he writes disparagingly of the novel, calling it 'un episodio de amor vulgar [...] la pintura de la sensualidad más pedestre' (an episode of vulgar love [...] the painting of the most pedestrian sensuality),[23] a pointless story of lust, without poetry or feeling, which makes no attempt to convey an idea or a moral, with an imbecile from Seville and a nobody[24] as the two main characters.

---

20 Fray Candil, '*Insolación* (por Emilia Pardo Bazán)', *Triquitraques* (Madrid: Fernando Fe, 1892), p. 222.
21 Leopoldo Alas, 'Palique', *Madrid cómico* (11 May 1884).
22 Leopoldo Alas, 'Palique', *Madrid cómico* (9 Nov. 1889).
23 Leopoldo Alas, *Folletos literarios* VIII, *Museum (mi revista)* (Madrid: Librería de Fernando Fe, 1890), p. 80.
24 'Asís Taboada no es nadie. Pacheco es un imbécil de Sevilla'. See Leopoldo Alas, 'Emilia Pardo Bazán y sus últimas obras', *Obras completas IV Crítica*

In an article published in *El Imparcial*, Pereda set out to demonstrate that Asís, whom he adjudged an equal of the author's own moral laxity, was far worse than the marchioness in his own novel *La Montálvez*. He considers it reprehensible that Asís should suddenly take off with a man she had only just met and about whom all she had heard was the Duchess of Sahagún's assertion that 'no era sino un calaverón de tomo y lomo' (he was just an out-and-out rake); and at the fair of San Isidro 'se mete con él en figones y merenderos, se emborracha [...] para continuar viviendo amancebados *a la vista* del lector' (she goes into cheap restaurants and snack bars with him, gets drunk [...] to end up cohabiting *in full view* of the reader).[25]

However, in the epilogue to *Insolación*, the narrator states quite clearly that without 'la *idea*', in other words the inspiration behind the couple's decision to marry, 'la cosa', that is to say the prior affair, wouldn't even be worth a mention. What Clarín and Pereda obviously disapprove of is not the fact that Asís ends up sleeping with Pacheco after such a brief acquaintance, a story which belongs to a long tradition of tales of forbidden love; on the contrary, it is the joy, pleasure and optimism which emanates from this supposedly sinful liaison, the two lovers' unabashed effrontery, especially Asís's attitude of defiance instead of repentance: 'No hay pesimismo, no hay sarcasmo implícito en esa historia de aventuras indecentes y frías, sosas y apocadas; hay complacencia, casi alegría' (There's no pessimism, no implicit sarcasm in this story of indecent, cold, tasteless and lowly exploits; there's indulgence, almost joy).[26] This was an opinion with which Pardo Bazán could never have agreed: in a reply also published in *El Imparcial*, she maintains that Asís, 'con su imprudente desliz que acaba en boda, es una niñita de pecho al lado de la Montálvez' (with her imprudent slip, which ends in marriage, is a baby girl compared to la Montálvez).[27]

(Segunda parte) (Oviedo: Ediciones Nobel, 2003), p. 1469.

25   José María de Pereda, 'Las comezones de la señora Pardo Bazán', in *Obras completas, Tomo III*, p. 1009.

26   Leopoldo Alas, *Folletos literarios* VII, p. 81.

27   Emilia Pardo Bazán, 'Una y no más ... Al público y a Pereda', in *Obras completas, Tomo III*, p. 1013.

Nowadays, *Insolación* is universally recognised as an important novel, gradually gaining widespread critical attention as a little masterpiece and one of the best novels of the nineteenth century. The novel draws on many aspects of its author's personal life. Asís, like her creator, is from Galicia, and her daughter attends 'un atildado colegio francés' (an elegant French boarding school). Moreover, it is dedicated to José Lázaro Galdiano, 'en prenda de amistad' (as a token of friendship), a fact which has encouraged the common perception of this work of fiction as an autobiographical adaptation of her *affaire de cœur* with the founding editor of *La España Moderna*, a short-lived dalliance which instigated a long professional association but did not end in marriage. According to this viewpoint, exemplified in Marina Mayoral's introduction to the novel,[28] just as Asís Taboada throws open her bedroom window without fear of being seen by her own social circle, Pardo Bazán is publicly displaying her own experience in 1888 when she visited the Universal Exhibition in Barcelona with Narcís Oller, Ixart and Galdós. Years later, in his *Memòries literàries*, Oller writes about the beginning of the romance between Emilia Pardo Bazán and José Lázaro Galdiano, including an excursion to Arenys de Mar.

Galdós, with whom Emilia Pardo Bazán was romantically involved, was made aware of the matter by Oller, who would have been oblivious to their affair and therefore not have foreseen the potential damage of

---

28   'El gesto de doña Emilia de dedicar la novela a su amigo siempre me ha recordado el gesto del personaje de la novela, de Asís Taboada cuando abre la ventana de su dormitorio y se asoma con su amante para que todos puedan verlos juntos. Es un gesto similar, pero mucho más arriesgado y valiente, porque en la marquesa literaria es preámbulo de matrimonio y en la Pardo Bazán [...] sólo puede interpretarse como un gesto de independencia y de desafío a la hipocresía de la sociedad' (Doña Emilia's gesture of dedicating the novel to her friend has always reminded me of the gesture of the character in the novel, of Asís Taboada when she opens her bedroom window and looks out with her lover so that everyone can see them together. It's a similar gesture, but much riskier and braver, because with the literary marchioness it's a preamble to matrimony, but with Pardo Bazán [...] it can only be interpreted as a gesture of independence and defiance of societal hypocrisy). See Marina Mayoral, 'Estudio introductorio', in Emilia Pardo Bazán, *Insolación* (Madrid: Espasa Calpe, 1987), pp. 12–13.

his account. Pardo Bazán wrote to Galdós, confessing that she had been unfaithful to him in Barcelona in the last few days of March, three days after his departure.[29] Nevertheless, her plea for forgiveness comprises two contradictory strands: one where she refers to her infidelity as 'un error momentáneo de los sentidos' (a momentary lapse of feelings), the other a justification for those feelings: 'me encontré seguida, apasionadamente querida y contagiada' (I was pursued, loved with passion and it rubbed off on me).[30] Careful study of Pardo Bazán's correspondence, however, induced José Manuel González Herrán to contend that she had almost completed *Insolación* before her first meeting with Galdiano. In an unpublished letter, housed in the Casa-Museo Pérez Galdós in Las Palmas de Gran Canaria, which the author wrote to Galdós on 16 June 1887, she states that she is writing a new work entitled *Insolación* and that the idea behind it came to her in a train from Madrid to Galicia. If this was indeed the case, we would have to conclude that the subsequent affair was in fact a coincidence and not the main source of inspiration, despite claims that both novelists made use of the incident, Pardo Bazán in *Insolación* and Galdós in both *La incógnita* and *Realidad*.

Publication was delayed by various complications, not least of which was the addition of illustrations by José Cuchy. In a letter she sent to José Yxart on 24 January 1889, Pardo Bazán qualifies her initial reservations about Cuchy's work as mere caricatures, and maintains that she finds his work 'muy aceptable, bastante graciosa y fina' (very acceptable, quite clever and subtle).[31] However, in a letter from 3 June 1889, she says that she found Cabrinety's illustrations for *Morriña* 'más bonita y *réussi* que la de *Insolación*' (prettier and more effective than those for *Insolación*).[32] Fourteen of the original 100 illustrations have been included in this edition. This sample should

---

29   'Mi infidelidad material no data de Oporto, sino de Barcelona, en los últimos días del mes de marzo –tres después de tu marcha' (Bravo-Villasante, *Cartas a Galdós*, p. 23).
30   Ibid., p. 24.
31   David Torres, 'Veinte cartas inéditas de Emilia Pardo Bazán a José Yxart (1883–1890)', *Boletín de la Biblioteca de Menéndez Pelayo* LIII (1977), p. 400.
32   Ibid., p. 405.

give an idea of the character of the original publication and enable readers to decide for themselves whether Cuchy's pictures enhanced or detracted from the novel.

6. Structure and Narrative Viewpoint

The plot of *Insolación* is very simple. Francisca de Asís Taboada, a 32-year-old widow of noble status, falls in love with the son of a wealthy Andalusian landowner. Although a self-confessed profligate whom her friend Gabriel Pardo describes as 'célula ociosa en el organismo social' (an idle cell in the social body), everything about him – hair, hands, eyes, sartorial elegance, refined demeanour, cologne, comical accent and formulaic *piropos* – enthrals Asís with ever-increasing intensity, and, unable to banish him from her mind, she ends up sleeping with him and making wedding plans.

The novel is divided into 22 chapters numbered with Roman numerals, the last of which is entitled 'epílogo'. Its plot follows the classical tripartite organisation of exposition, crisis and dénouement. One of Pardo Bazán's favourite writers as a child, according to her own words in *Apuntes autobiográficos*, was Homer, the name ascribed by the ancient Greeks to the legendary author of the *Iliad* and the *Odyssey*. Both of these epic poems are fine examples of *in medias res*, the technique of beginning a narrative in the middle and then doubling back to the same point by filling in the past with dialogue, flashbacks or descriptions of events. In his *Ars poetica*, the Latin poet and critic Horace argues that the main advantage of this gambit is the ability to arouse interest immediately, plunging the reader in the middle of a crucial situation that is part of a sequence of events.

Insolación makes effective use of this procedure. In the first chapter the reader discovers Francisca de Asís Taboada emerging from the limbo of sleep with a thumping migraine, her cheeks burning and her veins throbbing furiously. Her general biliousness and discomfort seem to be a physical manifestation of a spiritual and emotional distress which becomes palpable as she recalls, in the silence and semi-darkness of her bedroom, the background to this malaise, beginning with a soirée at the Duchess of Sahagún's house where the

widow meets Diego Pacheco, a captivating and handsome womaniser. Although Pardo Bazán approved of Zola's aim of uniting science and art, the Cuban writer Fray Candil, prompted by what he perceived as an improbable discrepancy between Asís's debilitating condition and her long, lucid flashback teeming with ratiocinative introspection, complained about 'la ausencia de conocimientos científicos' (the absence of scientific knowledge) in *Insolación*.[33]

The following morning, Asís bumps into Pacheco, and he asks her to accompany him to the Fair of San Isidro, on the outskirts of town, rather than go to mass as she had planned. She accepts his offer, but ends up intoxicated by a heady cocktail of 'tropical' sun, noise, confusion, crowds, food and copious amounts of wine. The rest of the novel examines her concern for 'el qué dirán' (what people might say), her self-recrimination and her futile efforts to quash the irrepressible, intrusive feelings fomenting inside her. Even though it is clear that Pacheco did not take advantage of the situation, her fear of being seen by someone from her social circle, along with the worry that her servants will start to gossip, prompt her decision to rebuff the lothario from Cádiz, a determination which weakens under his persistent wooing, charm and sexual appeal.

Her guilty conscience at what she deems 'un pecado gordo en frío' (a grave sin, calm and collected) is a reflection of her dismay at having mixed with hordes of lower-class roisterers and behaved in an indiscreet manner, totally inappropriate for a lady of her standing, rather than a belief that her actions themselves are intrinsically heinous or morally reprehensible. She consents to have lunch with Pacheco before leaving for her annual vacation, relieved at their anonymity in a working-class neighbourhood. Although they part on bad terms, Pacheco gains access into Asís's home, unintentionally revealing what has been going on to Gabriel Pardo. Asís, who had been arranging her luggage in order to leave the following day, sleeps with Pacheco and, contrary to Pardo's certitude that marriage isn't a possibility ('casarse no lo creo posible'), the couple discuss wedding plans.

---

33   '*Insolación* (por Emilia Pardo Bazán)', *Triquitraques* (Madrid: Fernando Fe, 1892), p. 220.

The simplicity of this storyline is deceptive, because the narrative techniques employed by the author combine to produce a more subtle, complex and ambivalent picture. The novel has a symmetrical structure and can be divided into four sections. The first part, Chapter 1, consists of Asís waking up with a terrible hangover. This is followed by the second part encompassing chapters 2–9, a flashback in which she relives both the conversation at the Duchess of Sahagún's social function and the next day at the fair. Chapters 10–16, the third part, return to the present and examine Asís's mental and moral turmoil after the fateful outing of the previous section. The fourth part, which begins with Chapter 17, repeats the lunch with Pacheco in a popular setting, interrupted by a lower-class, marginalised woman seeking alms for her children. It closes with Asís, having just woken up after spending the night with Pacheco; the nausea of her awakening in Chapter 1 has blossomed into euphoria; the throbbing pains in her body, burning like Saint Lawrence on his gridiron, have been replaced by pleasure and gratification; her anxiety and mental confusion ousted by clarity of thought and intent; the fear of incurring the opprobrium of her peers and her Jesuit confessor has been superseded by a total lack of apprehension; and the bath to wash away the stains on her reputation has transmuted into 'un baño de claridad solar' (a bath of solar light).

With the exception of her first novel, *Pascual López, autobiografía de un estudiante de medecina* (*Pascual López: Autobiography of a Medical Student*), up to and including 1889, the year *Insolación* was published, Pardo Bazán relied on third-person narrators. Although in her early novels there is a measure of insight into the working of her protagonists' minds, from 1886 onwards there is a notable increase in the amount of attention given to the motivation and psychological reaction of principal characters, especially Julián in *Los Pazos de Ulloa* and Gabriel Pardo in *La madre naturaleza*. However, from 1890 onwards, Pardo Bazán's full-length novels mainly employ a first-person narrator. *Insolación*, published at the crossroads of this technical shift, alternates between two different points of view: that of a third-person narrator, who vacillates between sympathy for and

condemnation of the protagonist, which accounts for about two-thirds of the novel; and that of an unreliable first-person narrator, Asís, torn between her obligation to conform to society's mores and her nascent sexuality.

These shifts in narrative perspectives, which convey the protagonist's moral dilemma, materialise at the very beginning of the flashback as Asís makes her way to church 'con mi eucologio y mi mantillita hecha una santa' (like a saint with my euchologion and my *mantilla*). The incongruity between her saintly appearance and her undeniable enjoyment of the string of absurd compliments directed at her by 'dos o tres de esos chulos de pantalón estrecho' (two or three of those working-class Madrilenian men in tight trousers) encapsulates the opposing drives of a woman simultaneously upholding and overturning the patriarchal gender boundaries and ideals of femininity. This inner conflict is identified by the narrator who, at the end of Chapter 18, describes women as 'un péndulo continuo que oscila entre el instinto natural y la aprendida vergüenza' (a continuous pendulum swinging between natural instinct and a learned sense of shame).

Occasionally, it is unclear whether certain observations are the comments of a supposedly dispassionate narrator or the innermost thoughts of Asís. Whilst Pardo Bazán made no secret of her admiration for Flaubert's notion of *impassibilité* (impersonality), she frequently deviates from the French author's principle that the artist should be invisible like God. At times she seems unable to resist making her presence felt, especially in comments relating to the narrative process or judgements and opinions expressed by the third-person narrator. However, there is no prediction from the narrator concerning the likelihood of long-term happiness for the couple; consequently, even if the novel ends on a positive note, with Asís 'más fresca que el amanecer' (fresher than the dawn), we are in the dark about who came up with the 'idea' and we cannot know for sure that the wedding actually ever takes place.

Despite the fact that there is nothing scandalous about her comportment at the fair, Asís's acute awareness of having transgressed the rules of feminine decorum makes for an account riddled with

ambiguity, obfuscation, reticence, circumlocution and prevarication. Ellipses, euphemisms and inconsistencies combine to hint rather than state, and her adventure with Pacheco is vaguely referred to as 'eso', 'aquello', 'la cosa', 'lo que', 'la historia' and 'las circunstancias inesperadísimas en que me he visto' (the unexpected circumstances in which I found myself). In fact, Asís's intentions are immediately called into question by the omniscient narrator. Even before the protagonist's guilt-ridden monologue begins, the reader is advised that, whilst the first-person narrator is not necessarily deliberately misleading, we should certainly be cautious about the impartiality and objectivity of her story:

> ... Asís, en la penumbra del dormitorio, entre el silencio, componía mentalmente el relato que sigue, donde claro está que no había de colocarse en el peor lugar, sino paliar el caso: aunque, señores, ello admitía bien pocos paliativos.

> (...Asís, in the silence and semi-darkness of her bedroom, mentally composed the following story, in which obviously she was not going to show herself in the worst light, but gloss over the affair, although, ladies and gentlemen, it allowed very few palliatives.)

When the 'omniscient' narrator picks up the mantle again at the beginning of Chapter 9, the impossibility of vouching for the absolute sincerity of Asís's account is stated emphatically:

> No afirmamos que, aun dialogando con su conciencia propia, fuese la marquesa, viuda de Andrade, perfectamente sincera, y no omitiese algún detalle, que agravara su tanto de culpa en el terreno de la imprevisión, la ligereza o la coquetería.

> (We cannot guarantee that, even in this dialogue with her own conscience, the widowed Marchioness of Andrade was completely sincere and didn't omit some detail that might exacerbate her level of guilt in the matter of lack of foresight, levity or coquetry.)

At times the third-person narrator appears untrustworthy, either echoing Gabriel Pardo's viewpoint that women are torn between natural instinct and a learned sense of shame, or deliberately refraining

from filling in or counterbalancing Asís's self-preservatory omissions. The impression of complicity in an elaborate cover-up comes to a head with the pendulum swinging from a third-person indirect discourse that cannot know information beyond the protagonist's consciousness or the narrator's feigned ignorance (to whom the idea first occurred, for example) to the no-nonsense stance that honesty forbids the exclusion of certain bits of information. Whilst acknowledging the possibility of skilfully disguising authorial disapprobation, a discreet silence is kept regarding the couple's meeting, even though it contravenes Asis's earlier promise of 'puerta cerrada, esquinazo, mutis' (door shut, cold shoulder, silence). The fact that the man who leaves the house at seven o'clock is unnamed seems designed to arouse suspicion and fuel speculation, but also undermines the reader's trust in the narrator's neutrality and even implies a tacit endorsement of the protagonist's premarital transgression.

The tension between revelation and dissimulation is an integral part of *Insolación*. Asís is constantly wrestling with her conscience: sometimes she balks at the prospect of confessing to Father Urdax, 'un jesuita tan duro de pelar y tan largo de entendederas' (a Jesuit who's so hard to deceive and so intelligent), about 'aquella cosa inaudita y estupenda' (that unheard of and spectacular thing); sometimes she subdues her true feelings, despite her insistence that 'no hay nada más peligroso que lo reprimido y oculto, lo que se queda dentro' (there's nothing more dangerous than what is repressed and hidden, what stays inside). No sooner has she adopted a confessional tone in which she vows to avoid Pacheco than she meets him in her private quarters and contrives to hide his comings and goings from her servants. These subterfuges, which cast doubt on her integrity as a disinterested narrator of plain facts, are mirrored by the third-person narrator's tactics, 'procurando con maña que no lastimen tanto como si apareciesen de frente, insolentonas y descaradas, metiéndose por los ojos' (craftily ensuring that they don't offend as much as if they appeared head-on, haughty and shameless, right before your eyes). The reader, confronted with this dynamic ambivalence, is encouraged to question the protagonist's rectitude as well as the veracity of the narrative.

Near the beginning of Chapter 10, Asís performs frantic ablutions while waiting for her bath to be ready, believing that with soap and *eau de cologne* her 'fricciones mitad morales, mitad higiénicas' (half moral, half hygienic chafing) will not only remove the dust and dirt of the fair and wash away the memories and shame of the previous day's aberrations but also overcome her erotic impulses. This episode recalls both *L'assommoir*, when Gervaise starts her adulterous relations with Lantier and washes her hands and shoulders frantically 'comme pour enlever son ordure' (as if to remove her filth), and Lady Macbeth seeking to remove the 'damned spot' from her hand. However, the novel focuses on the psychological reactions of Asís, and the author uses first-person rather than third-person narration in order to probe the protagonist's febrile ruminations and protracted self-analysis.

The narrative web is further entangled by the presence of Gabriel Pardo. Not only is he misleading about his ulterior motives, especially where Asís is concerned, but also, in his ambition to ensure that his version of the gossip involving his niece puts him in a favourable light, evasive about 'ese misterio' (that mystery) from his life. His surname and Galician provenance encourage us, initially, to trust his opinions and view him as a mouthpiece for the author, because he shares a number of Bazán's preoccupations, especially the lack of educational opportunities for women and the double standards of a society that expects of men the very thing it denigrates in women:

> ... es vergonzoso para el hombre no tener aventuras, y [...] hasta queda humillado si las rehúye ... De modo, que lo mismo que a nosotros nos pone muy huecos, a ustedes las envilece.

> (...it's shameful for a man not to have any flings, and even [...] humiliating if he avoids them... So, the very same thing that makes us proud degrades you.)

However, when Asís asks him in after their stroll in the area around the Museo del Prado, he declines the invitation, seemingly more at home in the masculine environment of the Military Club and the Café de Fornos.

In Chapter 2, when he champions the notion of environmental

stimuli as determining factors in individual behaviour, he uses the San Isidro Fair to substantiate his contention, thereby unwittingly foretelling Asís's fate:

> Aquí está nuestra amiga Asís, que a pesar de haber nacido en el Noroeste, donde las mujeres son reposadas, dulces y cariñosas, sería capaz, al darle un rayo de sol en la mollera, de las mismas atrocidades que cualquier hija del barrio de Triana o del Avapiés ...

> (Take our friend Asís here, who, in spite of having been born in the north-west, where the women are calm, sweet and affectionate, would be capable, with a ray of sun beating on the top of her head, of the same atrocious behaviour as any daughter of the neighbourhoods of Triana or Avapiés...)

Although Gabriel Pardo is often referred to as a vehicle for the author's ideas, it is difficult to subscribe to this view and see him as a progressive male. Firstly, Pardo is described in Chapter 2 as 'un poquillo inocentón, y sobre todo muy estrafalario y bastante pernicioso en sus ideas' (a little bit naïve, but above all very eccentric and with rather pernicious ideas), and his opinions and observations regarding the widowed marchioness's suitor are clearly not disinterested. In fact, there is a rumour that Pardo 'hacía tiro al decente caudal y a la agradable persona de Asís' (was attracted by the honest wealth and the agreeable person of Asís) and had intended to make a proposal of marriage to her. Although many of Pardo's remarks in chapters 13 and 14 are rather cagey or vague, there is the suggestion that Asís's marriage to her uncle makes him think of her as a substitute for his own niece, especially when, instead of the graceful silhouette of the Prado Museum, he sees

> las verdosas tapias del convento santiagués, las negras rejas de trágicos recuerdos, y tras de aquellas rejas comidas de orín una cara pálida, con obscuros ojos, muy semejante a la de cierta hermana suya que había sido el cariño más profundo de su vida.

> (the greenish walls of the Santiago convent, the black bars of tragic memories, and behind those rusted bars a pale face with dark eyes

very similar to those of a certain sister of his who had been the most profound love of his life.)

Another important consideration in any appraisal of Pardo as a forward-thinking paragon of bourgeois respectability is his inability to hide his jealousy when, hearing at the *tertulia* that the only thing Pachecho had done so far was to turn women's heads, he mutters: 'Buen ejemplar de raza española' (A fine example of our Spanish race). He betrays his enlightened principles and exposes his deep resentment when the identity of the owner of the English leather card case is revealed and Asís's expressive glances disclose her true feelings towards the Andalusian gallant. Not only does Pardo lay bare his dislike of Pacheco – 'raro es que el amigo de una dama, en caso semejante, no desapruebe la elección' (rarely, in any such case, does a lady's friend not disapprove of her choice) – but he also complains hypocritically about Asís's duplicity: 'me ha engañado la viuda' (the widow has deceived me). Seeing Pacheco and Asís together, he rails against the fickleness of women with an exasperated, anti-feminist outburst: '¡Y decir que no hará dos semanas que se conocieron en casa de Sahagún! ¡¡Mujeres!! …' (And to think that it won't be two weeks since they first met at the Duchess of Sahagún's house. Women!!).

7. Language and Translation

There have not been any changes in the Spanish language over the last 150 years which in themselves impede comprehension of Pardo Bazán's novel. It is, however, worth pointing out two features which may unsettle some students of Spanish. The novel begins with the following sentence: 'La primer señal por donde Asís Taboada se hizo cargo de que había salido de los limbos del sueño …' (The first sign which made Asís Taboada realise that she had emerged from the limbo of sleep…). In modern Spanish, a number of adjectives lose their final vowel when placed before a masculine singular noun, or combination of adjective and masculine noun, but not before a feminine noun. However, popular speech sometimes uses these apocopated forms of adjectives before feminine nouns, such as 'la señal', and this convention is also found in a number of good Spanish writers in the

past. Secondly, up to the early twentieth century the enclitic pronoun, the placing of an object pronoun on the end of a conjugated verb, was common practice in literary Spanish. An example of this can be found in the first chapter of the novel: 'Intentólo en efecto; mas si por un lado era soporífera la operación, por otro agravaba las inquietudes y resquemazones morales de la señora' (And indeed she tried; but if on the one hand the action was soporific, on the other it increased the lady's moral concerns and misgivings). In modern Spanish, of course, 'intentólo' would be 'lo intentó'.

In the prologue to *La dama joven*, Pardo Bazán states that writers should not alter or correct popular speech forms even at the risk of incurring critical censure. This is why she praises Cervantes, whose realist nature drove him to make Sancho speak very badly, and criticises Valera, all of whose characters, she professes, merely emulate the way their creator talks.[34] The way each individual speaks in a novel is an important part of the author's attempt to create an illusion of real people. Everyday conversation, with all its hesitations, pauses, mistakes, interruptions, deviations and filler words, is so far removed from the speech in most novels that if an author presented us with a transcript of typical dialogue, the end result would usually be tedious and sometimes border on unreadable. The novelist thus walks a fine line between a desire to mirror the real world and the need to produce an intelligible and interesting text.

Pardo Bazán makes a consistent effort throughout *Insolación* to strike a balance between representing the way people really speak and using dialogue to enhance the reader's understanding and appreciation of the novel. When I translated *La Tribuna* I was conscious of the difficulties caused by Pardo Bazán's determination to ensure that her characters speak 'como realmente se habla en la región en donde los saqué' (as people really do speak in the region whence I took them).[35] In *Insolación*, however, the difficulty of the task is magnified by the

---

34 *La cuestión palpitante*, in *Obras completas*, p. 640: 'no hay Sanchos, todos son Valeras' (there are no Sanchos, they are all Valeras).

35 *La Tribuna*, ed. and trans. Graham Whittaker (Liverpool: Liverpool University Press, 2017), p. 68.

variety of speech patterns she endeavours to replicate. Whilst Asís, Gabriel Pardo and the Duchess of Sahagún speak a correct, standard form of Castilian throughout the novel, Pardo Bazán tries to capture the essential characteristics of the *chulo* slang and demotic speech of Madrid, *caló* (gypsy dialect), Galician and Andalusian Spanish with almost all the other characters, no matter how minor their role. The novel, set in Madrid, transcribes working-class Madrilenian communication, from the string of corny *piropos* unleashed by the men outside the Suizo café in Chapter 3 and the phonetic vulgarisms of 'el tipo perfecto del rata' (the perfect example of a thief) in Chapter 4 to the dry, clipped accent of the women working at the tobacco factory in Chapter 19. In chapters 5 and 6 the Andalusian gypsies' dialogue is riddled with rhotacism (the sound change converting a consonant into an *r*-sound), elision of the consonant *d* (for example, *nombre e Dios* and *icir*), *seseo* (pronunciation of *c* before *e* and *i* and of *z* as *s*) and *ceceo* (the pronunciation of *s* as *th*, such as *Zanto* instead of *Santo*). Although Asís is from Galicia, it is only with Diabla and the *guinduilla* in Chapter 4 that we encounter any *gallegüismos*.

Pacheco, from Cádiz in Andalusia, is the main character with whom linguistic idiosyncrasies are fully exploited, a fact which can be clearly seen in the orthographical changes implemented by Pardo Bazán. In Chapter 4, when trying to persuade Asís to go for lunch with him, Pacheco's original 'maldito' is emended to 'mardito'. This confirms that the author designated rhotacism, a phenomenon often associated with Andalusian Spanish, as a key element of Pacheco's idiolect, as well as that of the gypsy fortune tellers. In Chapter 20, however, he says, '¡Maldita sea hasta la hora en que te vi!' (Cursed be the hour I set eyes on you!). Pardo Bazán's neglects to apply this particular aspect of Pacheco's pronunciation with any consistency in the novel: in Chapter 4 he says, 'lo que vamos a haser es almorsá en una fondita de aquí' (what we'll do is have lunch in a small restaurant here) before, in the very next utterance, talking about 'el gran armuerso del siglo' (the great lunch o' the century).

In fact, the author is prone to other discrepancies and confusion where Pacheco's dialogue is concerned. Firstly, she refers to 'el

ceceo mimoso y triste de su pronunciación' (the affectionate, sad lisp of his pronunciation), even though this mannerism, a less common trait of Andalusian Spanish, never features in his discourse. Secondly, although Pacheco's dialogue is strewn with examples of *seseo*, there are many times when this aspect of his pronunciation is seemingly forgotten. He says both 'hase' and 'hace', 'cabesa' and 'cabeza', and whilst he calls calls Asís 'terrón de azúcar' and 'terroncito de sal' (Chapter 16), the night air, mimicking his accent, whispers 'terronsito e asúcar' in the lady's ear. Pacheco's *yeísmo* (the pronunciation of *ll* as *y*) is equally sporadic. In Chapter 5 he orders 'una boteya e mansaniya' and in Chapter 19 tells Asís 'ajogo las peniyas'; elsewhere, however, he appears to differentiate between the *ll* and *y* sounds, calling Asís 'chiquilla' (chapters 11, 15, 16, 18, 20 and 22) and, in Chapter 18, telling her to keep quiet ('Que te calles') and mentioning 'el puente de Vallecas'. The same unpredictability applies to the metathesis found in certain words Pacheco uses: he refers to himself as 'este probetico' in Chapter 4, but addresses Asís as 'pobrecita' in Chapter 7.

Pardo Bazán is also erratic in the elision of the consonants *d* and intervocalic *r* in Pacheco's conversation: he usually says 'too' or 'toa' instead of 'todo' and 'toda', but in Chapter 11 he informs Asís that he hasn't slept 'en toda la noche'; 'lata de sardinas' and 'boteya e mansaniya' exist side by side. However, if Pardo Bazán's rendering of dialect is seemingly selective and unreliable, any shortcomings reflect the difficulty of formulating an adequate and appropriate orthography to reproduce dialect. A written form of everyday dialogue can only be an approximation of the actual sounds that any individual actually produces. When Pacheco says 'too', the sound is nothing like the word 'too' in English. In reality, even the way a simple, monosyllabic word like 'too' is pronounced by different native English speakers can vary greatly. Since any literary dialect is an invented language, an effective means of imparting nuances in characterisation, the crux of the matter is not so much whether the dialect is accurate, but rather if it is realistic within the context of the fictional world of the novel. Does it serve a discernible purpose in the novel, does it help the reader

to hear a unique voice for specific characters, thereby bringing variety into the cast of the novel?

What we see immediately is that the use of dialect in *Insolación*, achieved primarily through variant spellings and non-standard grammar, serves to make the gulf in background and temperament between Asís and Pacheco more tangible. This plays an important role in accentuating the ostensible unsuitability of their union. If there are inconsistencies in Pacheco's dialect this does not detract from the impression we have of his speech and our ability to hear his voice in our head. Pacheco is, in fact, a sort of linguistic chameleon and part of his originality and charm, for Asís as well as the reader, lies in his 'rara mezcla de espontaneidad popular y cortesía hidalga' (rare mixture of popular spontaneity and noble courtesy), his fascinating ability to adapt to his surroundings and adopt a variety of formal and informal registers:

> En el meridional no era sorprendente este salto desde las ternezas más moriscas al más prosaico de los incidentes callejeros: estaba en su modo de ser la transición brusca, la rápida exteriorización de las impresiones.

> (In the southerner this jump from tender words to the most prosaic of street incidents was not surprising. Sudden change was part of his being, the rapid externalisation of impressions.)

Sometimes, perhaps, the author fails to distinguish accordingly between different characters' dialects with the result that they lack a unique voice, and the desired panoply of 'substandard' speech merges into one generic *koine*. With this in mind, I have not worried unduly about the impossible task of producing a consistent and convincing English equivalent. If handled clumsily, using colloquial accents to hone individual character delineation can be counterproductive, especially if the reader has to work hard at tuning into the different voices and deciphering dialogue. This would almost certainly be the case with the gypsy fortune teller, the *guindilla* and the *cigarreras* if they were major characters in the novel.

Unsurprisingly, it is Pacheco whose particular mode of expression offers the greatest challenge. It soon became apparent that his plethora

of dropped aitches, glottal stops, elisions and contractions in the first draft of this translation hindered communication and detracted from the empathy of his portrayal by conjuring up the image of a gauche country bumpkin rather than an urbane, charismatic and socially adept libertine. Consequently, in an attempt to make sure that his accent doesn't violate his dialogue, either visually or aurally, and obfuscate the fact that he is struggling to come to terms with unfamiliar feelings just as much as Asís, a decision was made to scale down misspellings and dialectal clichés. The various comments in the text should be sufficient to convey his Andalusian accent – 'que era cerrado y sandunguero sin tocar en ordinario' (which was thick and amusing without sounding common) – and readers will be able to use their own imagination to hear what he is saying. Likewise, the difficulty of bringing Pacheco's humour alive on the page is pre-empted by Asís's comment at the beginning of Chapter 4:

> ... es indudable que si se escribiesen las ocurrencias de los andaluces, no resultarían tan graciosas, ni la mitad, de lo que parecen en sus labios; al sonsonete, al ceceíllo y a la prontitud en responder, se debe la mayor parte del salero.'

> (…it is undeniable that, written down, the witty remarks of Andalusians wouldn't be even half as funny as they sound, most of the wit being due to the mocking undertone, the little lisp and the speed of response.)

A foreign text from a bygone age, featuring a large variety of accents, dialects and slang, will inevitably prove demanding for modern English speakers. This should not, however, become an excuse for introducing what Anton Popovič called shifts of intellectual and aesthetic values or for adding supplementary remarks and information which reflect the translator's vision rather than 'carrying across' the writer's thoughts and ideas into the target language. When they have been strolling around Saint Isidro for a while, Pacheco says he can guess what is wrong with Asís. The fact that his choice of vocabulary fazes her is shown by her monosyllabic response:

> –Lo que usted tiene ya lo adivino yo, sin necesidad de ser sahorí …
> Usted tiene ni más ni menos que … gasusa.
> –¿Eh?

This was translated in *Midsummer Madness* as follows:

'I can guess what is the matter with you, without being a mind-reader, either. You are suffering from inanition.'
'What in the world is that?' asked I, surprised at the queer word.

The word 'gasusa' (*gazuza* spoken with Pacheco's *seseo*) might be unusual, but Asís's puzzled reaction in the original Spanish text does not warrant her expansive response or the ensuing narratorial explanation. By disregarding the integrity of the source, the essence of the original text is adulterated, the flavour lost. Paradoxically, there is no need to elaborate because the esoteric colloquialism 'inanition', a 'queer word' for exhaustion caused by lack of nourishment, is enough on its own in conjunction with Pacheco's subsequent definition.

The many difficulties posed by the dialogue in *Insolación* are compounded by the author's eclectic phraseology. In his homage to Emilia Pardo Bazán, Manuel Gálvez praises her enormous lexicon: 'Su vocabulario era de una vastedad que a nosotros, escritores americanos y harto afrancesados, nos produce asombro' (We American writers, very pro-French, are amazed by the vastness of her vocabulary).[36] This 'riqueza de vocabulario' (richness of vocabulary)[37] is evident throughout *Insolación*, where a mine of vernacularisms coexists harmoniously with an impressive array of erudite vocabulary. In Chapter 19 Pacheco is described as 'camelador'. This adjective, derived from *camelar*, a verb which is described by Ivo Buzek in *El léxico gitano en la lexicografía española* as 'uno de los gitanismos españoles más emblemáticos' (one of the most characteristic Spanish gypsy words), didn't appear in the *Diccionario de la Real Academia Española* until 1936, 15 years after Pardo Bazán's death, when it was defined as 'que camela'. Elsewhere, she uses more highbrow, academic words such as 'el epigastrio' (epigastrium) and 'el occipucio' (occiput).

In Chapter 11 of *La cuestión palpitante* Pardo Bazán discusses the Goncourt brothers and her admiration of the way they harness

---

36   Manuel Gálvez, 'Emilia Pardo Bazán', *Nosotros, Año 15 – Tomo 38* (Buenos Aires, 1921), p. 29.
37   Bravo-Villasante, *Vida y obra de Emilia Pardo Bazán*, p. 158.

language to mirror observable reality, including their willingness to resort to tautology, invent new words and nominalise adjectives in their quest for perfection. She goes on to postulate that they were 'los más osados neologistas del mundo' (the most daring neologists in the world),[38] extending, enriching and dislocating the French language in order to create the desired effect.

In *Insolación*, Pardo Bazán shows a propensity for inventing words in the interests of precision, refinement and incisive nuances. Her neologisms include 'trasegaduras' and 'galeotismo' (Chapter 1), 'boquifrescas' (Chapter 6), 'gedeonadas' (Chapter 13), 'ilogismo' (Chapter 15) and 'muequera' (Chapter 18). In addition, she is willing to make use of a variety of other means to achieve her ends. The novel contains a host of words characteristic of speech imported from other languages. The influence of *gallego* can be seen in words like 'soleado' in Chapter 1, but particularly in Chapter 4, where the policeman's conversation is imbued with *gheada* ('justan' for *gustan*, 'Lujo' for *Lugo*), the 'castilianisation' of Galician words ('vusté' for *vostede*) and the use of the Galician definite article ('o coche' for *el coche*). The influence of French can be found in Gallicisms like 'antucá' (for *en tout cas*, Chapter 3) and 'ambigú' (Chapter 5), and Anglicisms in the novel include 'sherry' (Chapter 2), 'flirtación' (Chapter 6), 'milord' (Chapter 10) and 'puf' (Chapter 16).

As a consummate author, Emilia Pardo Bazán obviously selected all of these words for a specific reason and to achieve a particular effect. The translator's role is to fathom the reason behind all of these choices and endeavour to recreate the same effect. However, when it comes to translating a word with several meanings, one has to compromise and settle for an English equivalent which usually only covers one or two of those different meanings. Hence, when people talk about 'loss' in translation, what is most frequently lost is ambiguity. Gabriel García Márquez, who consistently expressed his respect for translators, praised Gregory Rabassa for placing intuitiveness above intellectualism, and considered his English translation of *Cien años de soledad* a separate work of art in its own right that was clearer than the

---

38   *La cuestión palpitante*, in *Obras completas, Tomo III*, p. 613.

original Spanish. Paradoxically, then, the pay-off of disambiguation sometimes engendered by translation can be beneficial, especially if it leads to a sharper focus.

Since the translator's task is creative as well as interpretative, his or her writing ability is just as important as linguistic prowess. Literature has been translated for thousands of years, but the fundamental challenge has never changed: how to stay faithful to the original whilst recreating its unique atmosphere, all without drawing attention to the fact that the new work is a translation. As well as ambiguity, humour and irony, an obvious difficulty that comes with fiction is the sheer length of the content. At just under forty-three and a half thousand words, *Insolación* is a short novel, especially when compared to other nineteenth-century Hispanic classics like *Fortunata y Jacinta* or *La Regenta*. Nevertheless, the size of the task is still problematic when, as anyone involved in literary translation will confirm, even one word or phrase can prove extremely difficult to translate, requiring hours of research, deliberation, reconsideration and redaction.

Without the translation of literature, we would not be able to access the vast majority of literary works available in archives and libraries around the world. Although fiction translated from other languages only makes up about three per cent of English publishers' output, the newly evolved Man Booker International Prize of 2016 represents a significant development by acknowledging the importance of literary translation: Deborah Smith, the translator of the winning novel, *The Vegetarian*, shared the award with the author, Han Kang. For most native English speakers, who have no knowledge of Korean, a bilingual edition of this book would serve no purpose. Anybody wanting to discover a foreign novel of this sort will want a translation that, despite the many different cultural references, reads like it was written in English.

Expectations and requirements are bound to be different when approaching a bilingual text. Because the Aris and Phillips Hispanic Classics series will appeal primarily to readers who, depending on their level of linguistic ability, either need or want to read the Spanish text in conjunction with an English translation, I have veered more

towards the end of the spectrum embracing fidelity to the original. If one has an intermediate knowledge of the source language the main purpose of the parallel translation will undoubtedly be to provide help with the more difficult aspects of the text. On the other hand, if one has a very high command of the source language, the choice of a bilingual edition will probably reflect a desire to scrutinise the translation process as much as an interest in the text itself. I hope this edition, for all its shortcomings, can be of use to anyone interested in great literature, from readers with little or no knowledge of Spanish to Hispanists lacking the confidence to tackle the novel unaided and people with an excellent command of Spanish who want to discover the novel and evaluate the translation at the same time.

BIBLIOGRAPHY

Emilia Pardo Bazán, 'Una opinión sobre la mujer', *Nuevo Teatro Crítico* 2 (March 1892).

Emilia Pardo Bazán, *Obras completas, Tomo II* (Madrid: Aguilar, 1947).

Emilia Pardo Bazán, *Insolación*, ed. José Hesse (Madrid: Taurus, 1970).

Emilia Pardo Bazán, *Obras completas, Tomo III* (Madrid: Aguilar, 1973).

Emilia Pardo Bazán, *Insolación*, ed. Marina Mayoral (Madrid: Espasa Calpe, 1987).

Emilia Pardo Bazán, *Insolación*, ed. Benito Varela Jácome (Madrid: Editorial Espasa Calpe, 2002).

Emilia Pardo Bazán, *La Tribuna*, ed. and trans. Graham Whittaker (Liverpool: Liverpool University Press, 2017).

Leopoldo Alas, 'Palique', *Madrid cómico* (11 May 1884).

Leopoldo Alas, 'Palique', *Madrid cómico* (9 Nov. 1889).

Leopoldo Alas, *Folletos literarios VIII, Museum (mi revista)* (Madrid: Librería de Fernando Fe, 1890), p. 80.

Leopoldo Alas, *Obras completas IV Crítica (Segunda parte)* (Oviedo: Nobel, 2003).

Elizabeth Amann, 'Nature and Nation in Emilia Pardo Bazán's *Insolación*', *Bulletin of Spanish Studies* LXXXV.2 (2008), pp. 175–92.

Beth Wietelmann Bauer, 'Innovación y apertura: la novela realista del siglo XIX ante el problema del desenlace', *Hispanic Review* 59 (1991), pp. 187–203.

Carmen Bravo-Villasante, *Vida y obra de Emilia Pardo Bazán* (Madrid: Ediciones Castilla, 1962).

Carmen Bravo-Villasante, *Cartas a Galdós* (Madrid: Turner, 1978).

D. F. Brown, *The Catholic Naturalism of Emilia Pardo Bazán* (Chapel Hill: University of North Carolina Press, 1957).

Fray Candil, '*Insolación* (por Emilia Pardo Bazán)', *Triquitraques* (Madrid: Fernando Fe, 1892).

Nelly Clémessy, *Emilia Pardo Bazán, romancière (la critique, la théorie, la pratique)* (Paris: Centre de Recherches Hispaniques, 1973).

Maria Colbert, 'Rules of Gender, Reserve, and Resolution in Pardo Bazán's *Insolación*', *Hispanic Review* 77.4 (Oct. 2009), pp. 427–48.

Pilar Faus, *Emilia Pardo Bazán: su época, su vida, su obra* (La Coruña: Fundación Pedro Barrié de la Maza, 2005).

Ana María Freire López, *Cartas inéditas a Emilia Pardo Bazán* (La Coruña: Conde de Fenosa, 1991).

Pompeyo Gener, 'De la mujer y sus derechos en las sociedades moderna', *La Vanguardia* (26 Feb. 1889).

Mary E. Giles, 'Feminism and the Feminine in Emilia Pardo Bazán's Novels', *Hispania* 63.2 (May 1980), pp. 356–67.

Anne W. Gilfoil, 'The Construction of the "New Woman" in Pardo Bazán's *Insolación*', *Confluencia* 16.2 (2001), pp. 83–91.

Maurice Hemingway, *Emilia Pardo Bazán: The Making of a Novelist* (Cambridge: Cambridge University Press, 1983).

Dorota K. Heneghan, 'Fashion and Femininity in Emilia Pardo Bazán's *Insolación*', *Hispanic Review* 80.1 (Jan. 2012), pp. 63–84.

Dorotea Heneghan, *Striking their Modern Pose: Fashion, Gender and Modernity in Galdós, Pardo Bazán and Picón* (West Lafayette, IN: Purdue University Press, 2015).

David Henn, *The Early Pardo Bazán* (Liverpool: Francis Cairns, 1988).

Susan Kirkpatrick, *Las Románticas: Women Writers and Subjectivity in Spain, 1835–1850* (Berkeley, CA: University of California Press, 1989).

María Laffitte, *La mujer en España* (Madrid: Aguilar, 1964).

Lisa Nalbone, '*Insolación* by Emilia Pardo Bazán (Review)', *Anales Galdosianos*, 49 (2014), pp. 137–38.

Robert E. Osborne, *Emilia Pardo Bazán su vida y sus obras* (Mexico City: Ediciones de Andrea, 1964).

W. Pattison, *Emilia Pardo Bazán* (New York: Twayne Publishers, 1971).

Janet Pérez, *Contemporary Women Writers of Spain* (Boston, MA: Twayne Publishers, 1988).

Elizabeth Scarlett, *Under Construction: The Body in Spanish Novels* (Charlottesville, VA: University Press of Virginia Press, 1994).

Ruth A. Schmidt, 'A Woman's Place in the Sun: Feminism in *Insolación*', *Revista de Estudios Hispánicos* 8 (1974), pp. 69–81.

Jennifer Smith, 'Sexual Desire and the Nautical and Solar Motifs in Emilia Pardo Bazán's *Insolación*', *Anales Galdosianos* 49 (2014), pp. 93–105.

Joyce Tolliver, *Cigar Smoke and Violet Water: Gendered Discourse in the Stories of Emilia Pardo Bazán* (Lewisburg, PA: Bucknell University Press, 1998).

David Torres, 'Veinte cartas inéditas de Emilia Pardo Bazán a José Yxart

(1883–1890)', *Boletín de la Biblioteca de Menéndez Pelayo*, LIII (1977), pp. 383–409.

Daniel S. Whittaker, 'Artificial Order: Closure in Pardo Bazán's *Insolación*', *Romance Quarterly* 35.3 (1988), pp. 359–66.

SUNSTROKE (A LOVE STORY)

INSOLACIÓN: HISTORIA AMOROSA

INSOLACIÓN
(HISTORIA AMOROSA)

Emilia Pardo Bazán

Ilustración de J. Cuchy

A José Lázaro Galdiano
en prenda de amistad

La Autora

I

La primer[1] señal por donde Asís Taboada se hizo cargo de que había salido de los limbos del sueño, fue un dolor como si le barrenasen las sienes de parte a parte con un barreno finísimo; luego le pareció que las raíces del pelo se le convertían en millares de puntas de aguja y se le clavaban en el cráneo. También notó que la boca estaba pegajosita, amarga y seca; la lengua, hecha un pedazo de esparto; las mejillas ardían; latían desaforadamente las arterias; y el cuerpo declaraba a gritos que, si era ya hora muy razonable de saltar de cama, no estaba él para valentías tales.

Suspiró la señora; dio una vuelta, convenciéndose de que tenía molidísimos los huesos; alcanzó el cordón de la campanilla, y tiró con garbo. Entró la doncella, pisando quedo, y entreabrió las maderas del cuarto-tocador. Una flecha de luz se coló en la alcoba, y Asís exclamó con voz ronca y debilitada:

–Menos abierto … Muy poco … Así.

---

1 Antiguamente era aceptable la forma apocopada de *primera* ante un sustantivo femenino, pero hoy es considerada como un arcaísmo.

SUNSTROKE
(A LOVE STORY)

Emilia Pardo Bazán

Illustrations by J. Cuchy

To José Lázaro Galdiano
as a token of friendship

The Author

1

The first sign which made Asís Taboada realise that she had emerged from the limbo of sleep was a sensation of pain, as if a very fine drill were boring from one side to the other through her temples; then the roots of her hair seemed to turn into thousands of needle points and stick into her skull. She also noticed that her mouth was sticky, bitter and dry, her tongue like a piece of esparto grass, and her cheeks were burning. Her veins were throbbing furiously and, whilst this was a very reasonable time to jump out of bed, her whole body was shouting out that it wasn't up to such acts of bravery.

The lady sighed, and in turning over came to the conclusion that every bone ached; she reached for the bell cord, and pulled it gracefully. The maid entered quietly and half-opened the dressing room shutters. A ray of sun shot into the bedroom, and Asís exclaimed in a weak and husky voice:

'Not so wide… Just a little… That's it.'

−¿Cómo le va, señorita? −preguntó muy solícita la Ángela (por mal nombre *Diabla*)−. ¿Se encuentra algo más aliviada ahora?

−Sí, hija …, pero se me abre la cabeza en dos.

−¡Ay! ¿Tenemos la maldita de la jaquecona?

−Clavada … A ver si me traes una taza de tila …

−¿Muy cargada, señorita?

−Regular …

−Voy volando.

Un cuarto de hora duró el vuelo de la Diabla. Su ama, vuelta de cara a la pared, subía las sábanas hasta cubrirse la cara con ellas, sin más objeto que sentir el fresco de la batista en aquellas mejillas y frente que estaban echando lumbre.

De tiempo en tiempo, se percibía un gemido sordo.

En la mollera suya funcionaba, de seguro, toda la maquinaria de la Casa de la Moneda, pues no recordaba aturdimiento como el presente, sino el que había experimentado al visitar la fábrica de dinero y salir medio loca de las salas de acuñación.

'How are you doing, madam?' asked Ángela (known to everyone as "Diabla"),[1] in a very solicitous manner. 'Are you feeling a bit better now?'

'Yes ... but my head's splitting.'

'Oh dear! Have we got a bad headache?'

'Thumping... Would you bring me a cup of lime flower tea?'

'Very strong, madam?'

'Normal.'

'I'll be back in a jiffy.'

Diabla's jiffy lasted a quarter of an hour. Her mistress, facing the wall, pulled up the sheets until they covered her face, with the sole purpose of feeling the cool batiste on those burning cheeks and forehead.

From time to time a muffled groan could be heard.

In her head the whole machinery of the Mint must surely be working, because she couldn't remember bewilderment like this, except what she had experienced when visiting the money factory and coming out of the coining rooms half mad.

---

1 Her name, meaning 'she-devil', is also a term used for an astute, shrewd person.

Entonces, lo mismo que ahora, se le figuraba que una legión de enemigos se divertía en pegarle tenazazos en los sesos y devanarle con argadillos candentes la masa encefálica.

Además, notaba cierta trepidación allá dentro, igual que si la cama fuese una hamaca, y a cada balance se le amontonase el estómago y le metiesen en prensa el corazón.

La tila. Calentita, muy bien hecha. Asís se incorporó, sujetando la cabeza y apretándose las sienes con los dedos. Al acercar la cucharilla a los labios, náuseas reales y efectivas.

–Hija … está hirviendo … Abrasa. ¡Ay! Sostenme un poco, por los hombros. ¡Así!

Era la Diabla una chica despabilada, lista como una pimienta: una luguesa que no le cedía el paso a la andaluza más ladina. Miró a su ama guiñando un poco los ojos, y dijo compungidísima al parecer:

–Señorita … Vaya por Dios. ¿Se encuentra peor? Lo que tiene no es sino eso que le dicen allá en nuestra tierra un *soleado* …² Ayer se caían los pájaros de calor, y usted fuera todo el santo día …

–Eso será … –afirmó la dama.

–¿Quiere que vaya enseguidita a avisar al señor de Sánchez del Abrojo?

–No seas tonta … No es cosa para andar fastidiando al médico. Un meneo a la taza. Múdala a ese vaso …

Con un par de trasegaduras³ de vaso a taza y viceversa, quedó potable la tila. Asís se la embocó, y al punto se volvió hacia la pared.

–Quiero dormir … No almuerzo … Almorzad vosotros … Si vienen visitas, que he salido … Atenderás por si llamo.

Hablaba la dama sorda y opacamente, de mal talante, como aquel que no está para bromas y tiene igualmente desazonados el cuerpo y el espíritu.

---

2 Sustantivo gallego que significa *insolación*.
3 Neologismo: cambios de una bebida de un lugar a otro.

Then, like now, it seemed as though a legion of demons were amusing themselves by pounding her brains with a pair of pliers and winding up her encephalic mass on white-hot reels.

Moreover, she felt a certain inner shaking, as if the bed were a hammock, with every roll making her stomach turn and her heart become constricted.

The lime flower tea. Nice and hot, very well prepared. Asís sat up, holding her head and pressing her temples with her fingers. Bringing the teaspoon to her lips, a sudden wave of real nausea.

'Why … it's boiling … I've burnt myself. Ow! Give my shoulders a bit of support. That's it.'

Diabla was sharp, as bright as a button, a native of Lugo who was the equal of even the most cunning Andalusian girl. Squinting a little, she looked at her mistress and, to all appearances full of remorse, asked:

'Madam… Oh dear. Are you feeling worse? What you've got is nothing other than what's called a *solar hangover* in our region… Birds were dropping with the heat yesterday, and you being out the whole blessed day…'

'It must be that,' declared the lady.

'Do you want me to go right away and tell Señor Sánchez del Abrojo?'[2]

'Don't be silly… It isn't something to go bothering the doctor with. A shake of the cup. Put it into that glass…'

By pouring it back and forth between glass and cup a couple of times, the tea became drinkable. Asís swallowed it all, and turned immediately towards the wall.

'I want to sleep… I won't have anything to eat… Have your meal… If there are any visitors, say I've gone out… Be ready when I ring.'

The lady spoke bad-temperedly in the muffled, lifeless tone of someone in no mood for jokes and whose mind and body are equally out of sorts.

---

2   Señor Sánchez del Abrojo also appears in Pardo Bazán's *Morriña* (1889) as a famous doctor. Recurring characters are a common feature in the fiction of several nineteenth-century novelists, including Balzac, Zola, Pereda and Galdós.

Se retiró por fin la doncella, y al verse sola, Asís suspiró más profundo y alzó otra vez las sábanas, quedándose acurrucada en una concha de tela. Se arregló los pliegues del camisón, procurando que la cubriese hasta los pies; echó atrás la madeja del pelo revuelto, empapado en sudor y áspero de polvo, y luego permaneció quietecita, con síntomas de alivio y aun de bienestar físico producido por la infusión calmante.

La jaqueca, que ya se sabe cómo es de caprichosa y maniática, se había marchado por la posta desde que llegara al estómago la taza de tila; la calentura cedía, y las bascas iban aplacándose ... Sí, lo que es el cuerpo se encontraba mejor, infinitamente mejor; pero, ¿y el alma? ¿Qué procesión le andaba por dentro a la señora?

No cabe duda: si hay una hora del día en que la conciencia goza todos sus fueros, es la del despertar. Se distingue muy bien de colores después del descanso nocturno y el paréntesis del sueño. Ambiciones y deseos, afectos y rencores se han desvanecido entre una especie de niebla; faltan las excitaciones de la vida exterior; y así como después de un largo viaje parece que la ciudad de donde salimos hace tiempo no existe realmente, al despertar suele figurársenos que las fiebres y cuidados de la víspera se han ido en humo y ya no volverán a acosarnos nunca. Es la cama una especie de celda donde se medita y hace examen de conciencia, tanto mejor cuanto que se está muy a gusto, y ni la luz ni el ruido distraen. Grandes dolores de corazón y propósitos de la enmienda suelen quedarse entre las mantas.

Unas miajas de todo esto sentía la señora; sólo que a sus demás impresiones sobrepujaba la del asombro. –«¿Pero es de veras? ¿Pero me ha pasado *eso*? Señor Dios de los ejércitos, ¿lo he soñado o no? Sácame de esta duda»–. Y aunque Dios no se tomaba el trabajo de responder negando o afirmando, *aquello* que reside en algún rincón de nuestro ser moral y nos habla tan categóricamente como pudiera hacerlo una voz divina, contestaba: –Grandísima hipócrita, bien sabes tú cómo fue: no me preguntes, que te diré algo que te escueza.

–Tiene razón la Diabla: ayer atrapé un *soleado*, y para mí, el sol ... matarme. ¡Este chicharrero de Madrid! ¡El veranito y su alma! Bien empleado, por meterme en avisperos. A estas horas debía yo andar por mi tierra ...

Finally the maid withdrew and Asís, finding herself alone, sighed more deeply and pulled up the sheets again, snuggling down in a shroud of linen. She arranged the folds of her nightdress, taking care to cover her feet, threw back her tangled mass of hair, drenched in perspiration and rough with dust, and then stayed still, with signs of relief and even physical comfort produced by the calming herbal tea.

The migraine, and we know only too well how volatile and stubborn they can be, had gone as soon as the lime flower tea reached her stomach; the fever abated and the nausea was subsiding… Yes, as far as her body was concerned she felt better, infinitely better. But what about her mind? What was going on inside the lady?

There's no doubt that if there's a time of day when awareness enjoys all its powers it's on waking up. Colours are readily distinguished after a night's rest and the interval of sleep. Ambitions and desires, affections and resentment have faded away in a kind of foggy confusion. The excitement of external life is absent and, as after a long journey it seems that the town we set out from a while ago doesn't really exist, we usually imagine when we wake up that the cares and troubles of the previous day have vanished in smoke and will never hound us again. The bed is a kind of cell where we meditate and examine our conscience, all the better for being very comfortable, and neither light nor noise is a distraction. Great heartache and intentions to mend our ways usually remain between the blankets.

The woman felt a tiny bit of all this, only amazement surpassed her other impressions. "But is it true? Has *that* really happened to me? Good God, have I dreamt it or not? Take this doubt from me." And although God didn't trouble Himself to answer in the negative or affirmative, *that* which resides in some corner of our moral being and speaks to us as decisively as a divine voice, answered: "You big hypocrite, you know full well what happened. Don't ask me, or I'll say something that may upset you."

'Diabla is right: I've got *a solar hangover* from yesterday, and for me, the sun … oh my goodness. This furnace Madrid! Lovely summer weather! Serves me right for getting myself in a mess! At this time of year I should stick to my own neck of the woods…'

Doña Francisca Taboada se quedó un poquitín más tranquila desde que pudo echarle la culpa al sol. A buen seguro que el astro-rey dijese esta boca es mía protestando, pues aunque está menos acostumbrado a las acusaciones de galeotismo[4] que la luna, es de presumir que las acoja con igual impasibilidad e indiferencia.

–De todos modos –arguyó la voz inflexible–, confiesa, Asís, que si no hubieses tomado más que sol … Vamos, a mí no me vengas tú con historias, que ya sabes que nos conocemos … ¡como que andamos juntos hace la friolera de treinta y dos abriles! Nada, aquí no valen subterfugios … Y tampoco sirve alegar que si fue inesperado, que si parece mentira, que si patatín, que si patatán … Hija de mi corazón, lo que no sucede en un año sucede en un día. No hay que darle vueltas. Tú has sido hasta la presente una señora intachable; bien: una perfecta viuda; conformes: te has llevado en peso tus dos añitos de luto (cosa tanto más meritoria cuanto que, seamos francos, últimamente ya necesitabas alguna virtud para querer a tu tío, esposo y señor natural, el insigne marqués de Andrade, con sus bigotes pintados y sus alifafes, fístulas o lo que fuesen); a pesar de tu genio animado y tu afición a las diversiones, en veinticuatro meses no se te ha visto el pelo sino en la iglesia o en casa de tus amigas íntimas; convenido: has consagrado largas horas al cuidado de tu niña y eres madre cariñosa; nadie lo niega: te has propuesto siempre portarte como una señora, disfrutar de tu posición y tu independencia, no meterte en líos ni hacer contrabando; lo reconozco: pero … ¿qué quieres, mujer?, te descuidaste un minuto, incurriste en una chiquillada (porque fue una chiquillada, pero chiquillada del género atroz, convéncete de ello), y por cuanto viene el demonio y la enreda y te encuentras de patitas en la gran trapisonda … No andemos con sol por aquí y calor por allá. Disculpas de mal pagador. Te falta hasta la excusa vulgar, la del cariñito y la pasioncilla … Nada, chica, nada. Un pecado gordo en frío, sin circunstancias atenuantes y con ribetes de desliz chabacano. ¡Te luciste!

Ante estos argumentos irrefutables menguaba la acción bienhechora

---

4 Neologismo derivado de Galeoto, caballero de la Tabla Redonda, mediador en amores entre Lanzarote y la reina Ginebra.

Doña Francisca Taboada felt a little bit calmer as long as she could blame the sun. The king of the sky would certainly not open his mouth to protest because, although less accustomed than the moon to accusations of meddling, he no doubt receives them with equal impassiveness and indifference.

'Anyway, Asís,' the inflexible voice argued, 'admit that if it were just the sun... Come on, don't go telling me stories, you know we're well acquainted ... we've been together for no less than thirty-two summers! Subterfuges don't count for anything here... And nor is it any use claiming that it was unexpected, that it seems untrue, or this, that and the other... My darling, you never know what's round the corner. You don't have to think too deeply about it. Up until now you've been irreproachable; good, a perfect widow, agreed. You carried the burden of your two years of mourning (all the more to your credit, let's be honest, because in the end it really needed some virtue to love your uncle, husband and natural lord, the distinguished Marquis of Andrade, with his dyed moustache and his ailments, fistulas or whatever they were); in spite of your lively disposition and your love of fun, in twenty-four months no one has caught so much as a glimpse of you, other than in church or at your close friends' houses. Agreed, you've dedicated a lot of time to looking after your daughter and you're an affectionate mother; nobody denies it. You're intent on always behaving as a lady, enjoying your position and independence, getting into no trouble or doing anything forbidden; I recognise this. But what do you expect? You dropped your guard for one minute, committed a childish act (because it was a childish act, but of a terrible kind, believe you me), so along comes the devil and casts his net and you find yourself ensnared... Let's not blame the sun here and the heat there. Those are feeble excuses. You haven't even got the common excuse of a caprice, a passing whim... Nothing, my girl, nothing! A grave sin, calm and collected, without extenuating circumstances and adorned with vulgar indiscretion. You excelled yourself!'

Faced with these irrefutable arguments, the beneficial effect of the

de la tila y Asís iba experimentando otra vez terrible desasosiego y sofoco. El barreno que antes le taladraba la sien, se había vuelto sacacorchos, y haciendo hincapié en el occipucio,[5] parecía que enganchaba los sesos a fin de arrancarlos igual que el tapón de una botella. Ardía la cama y también el cuerpo de la culpable, que, como un San Lorenzo en sus parrillas, daba vueltas y más vueltas en busca de rincones frescos, al borde del colchón. Convencida de que todo abrasaba igualmente, Asís brincó de la cama abajo, y blanca y silenciosa como un fantasma entre la penumbra de la alcoba, se dirigió al lavabo, torció el grifo del depósito, y con las yemas de los dedos empapadas en agua, se humedeció frente, mejillas y nariz; luego se refrescó la boca, y por último se bañó los párpados largamente, con fruición; hecho lo cual, creyó sentir que se le despejaban las ideas y que la punta del barreno se retiraba poquito a poco de los sesos. ¡Ay, qué alivio tan rico! A la cama, a la cama otra vez, a cerrar los ojos, a estarse quietecita y callada y sin pensar en cosa ninguna …

Sí, a buena parte. ¿No pensar dijiste? Cuanto más se aquietaban los zumbidos y los latidos y la jaqueca y la calentura, más nítidos y agudos eran los recuerdos, más activas y endiabladas las cavilaciones.

–Si yo pudiese rezar –discurrió Asís–. No hay para esto de conciliar el sueño como repetir una misma oración de carretilla.

Intentólo[6] en efecto; mas si por un lado era soporífera la operación, por otro agravaba las inquietudes y resquemazones morales de la señora. Bonito se pondría el padre Urdax cuando tocasen a confesarse de aquella cosa inaudita y estupenda. ¡Él, que tanto se atufaba por menudencias de escotes, infracciones de ayuno, asistencia a saraos en cuaresma, mermas de misa y otros pecadillos que trae consigo la vida mundana en la corte! ¿Qué circunloquios serían más adecuados para atenuar la primer impresión de espanto y la primer filípica? Sí, sí ¡circunloquios al padre Urdax! ¡Él, que lo preguntaba todo derecho y claro, sin pararse en vergüenzas ni en reticencias! ¡Con aquel geniazo

---

5 Parte de la cabeza por donde esta se une con las vértebras del cuello (RAE).
6 Uso arcaico del pronombre enclítico utilizado muy a menudo por la autora, al igual que muchos escritores de su tiempo.

lime flower tea diminished and once again Asís went through terrible anxiety and suffocation. The drill that before was piercing her temples had become a corkscrew and, focusing on her occiput,[3] seemed to hook her brain in order to pull it out like the cork from a bottle. The bed was burning, as was the culprit's body, which, like Saint Lawrence on his gridiron, tossed and turned in search of a cool place on the edge of the mattress.[4] Convinced that every spot was equally hot, Asís jumped out of bed and, as white and silent as a ghost in the semi-darkness of the room, headed for the washbasin, turned the tap of the water tank and, dipping her fingertips in the water, wet her forehead, cheeks and nose; then she refreshed her mouth, and lastly bathed her eyelids for a long time with great relish. With this accomplished, her ideas seemed to become clearer, and the point of the drill gradually withdrew from her brain. Oh, what a blessed relief! To bed, to bed again, to close her eyes, to be still and quiet and think of nothing…

Yes, easily said. Did you say stop thinking? The more the buzzing, the throbbing, the headache and the burning calmed down, the clearer and sharper were her memories, the more active and diabolical her cogitations.

'If I could pray!' reflected Asís. 'There's nothing like reciting the same prayer by heart for getting to sleep.'

She did indeed try, but if on the one hand the action was soporific, on the other it increased her moral concerns and misgivings. Father Urdax would have a fit when the time came to confess to that unheard of and spectacular thing. He who would get so angry at trifles relating to décolletage, failure to observe a fast, attendance at soirées during Lent, absence from mass and other peccadilloes which everyday life in Madrid entails! What circumlocutions would be most suitable for toning down his first impression of horror and his first philippic? Yes indeed, circumlocutions for Father Urdax! He who asked everything straightforwardly and clearly, without embarrassment or reticence stopping him! With that explosive temperament and tight-laced

---

3   The back of the head.
4   Saint Lawrence was one of the seven deacons of Rome martyred in the persecution of Christians ordered by the Roman emperor Valerian. According to legend, he was roasted alive on a gridiron.

de pólvora y aquella manga estrechita que gastaba! Si al menos permitiese explicar la cosa desde un principio, bien explicada, con todas las aclaraciones y notas precisas para que se viese la fatalidad, la serie de circunstancias que … Pero, ¿quién se atreve a hacer mérito de ciertas disculpas ante un jesuita tan duro de pelar y tan largo de entendederas? Esos señores quieren que todo sea virtud a raja tabla y no entienden de componendas, ni de excusas. Antes parece que se les tachaba de tolerantísimos: no, pues lo que es ahora …

No obstante el triste convencimiento de que con el padre Urdax sería perder tiempo y derrochar saliva todo lo que no fuese decir *acúsome, acúsome,* Asís, en la penumbra del dormitorio, entre el silencio, componía mentalmente el relato que sigue, donde claro está que no había de colocarse en el peor lugar, sino paliar el caso: aunque, señores, ello admitía bien pocos paliativos.

rigidity! If he would at least allow things to be explained from the beginning, well explained, with all the clarifications and precise details so the inevitability could be seen, the train of circumstances which... But who'd dare proffer excuses when faced with a Jesuit who's so hard to deceive and so intelligent? Those people want virtue at any cost and they don't countenance compromise or excuses. Apparently they were once branded as extremely tolerant; no, as for now...

In spite of a melancholy conviction that with Father Urdax it would be a waste of time and breath to say anything except *I accuse myself, I accuse myself*, Asís, in the silence and semi-darkness of her bedroom, mentally composed the following story, in which obviously she was not going to show herself in the worst light, but gloss over the affair, although, ladies and gentlemen, it allowed very few palliatives.[5]

---

5   The final paragraph of this first chapter makes it clear to the reader that Asís is going to take over from the third-person narrator and provide the background to her indisposition from her own point of view.

II

Hay que tomarlo desde algo atrás y contar lo que pasó, o por mejor decir, lo que se charló anteayer en la tertulia semanal de la duquesa de Sahagún, a la cual soy asidua concurrente. También la frecuenta mi paisano el comandante de artillería don Gabriel Pardo de la Lage, cumplido caballero, aunque un poquillo inocentón, y sobre todo muy estrafalario y bastante pernicioso en sus ideas, que a veces sostiene con gran calor y terquedad, si bien las más noches le da por acoquinarse y callar o jugar al tresillo, sin importársele de lo que pasa en nuestro corro. No obstante, desde que yo soy obligada todos los miércoles, notan que don Gabriel se acerca más al círculo de las señoras y gusta de armar pendencia conmigo y con la dueña de la casa; por lo cual hay quien asegura que no le parezco saco de paja a mi paisano, aun cuando otros afirman que está enamorado de una prima o sobrina

2

We must go back a bit and remember what happened, or rather what was discussed, the day before yesterday at the Duchess of Sahagún's weekly social gathering which I usually attend. Also a regular is my fellow Galician, Don Gabriel Pardo de la Lage,[6] an artillery commander, a model gentleman, although a little bit naïve, but above all very eccentric and with rather pernicious ideas, which he sometimes backs up with great passion and stubbornness, although most nights he is subdued and quiet or plays *tresillo*[7] without concerning himself about what is going on in our circle. Nevertheless, since my presence has been mandatory every Wednesday, it has been observed that Don Gabriel veers more towards the ladies' group and likes stirring up trouble with me and the hostess. This is why some say I'm not without significance to my compatriot, even if others declare that he is in love with a cousin or niece, who is the subject of God knows what strange

---

6   Another example of recurring characters in Pardo Bazán's novels, Don Gabriel Pardo de la Lage also features in *Los Pazos de Ulloa* (1886), *La madre naturaleza* (1887) and *Morriña* (1889).
7   Tresillo is a trick-taking card game for three players which originated in Spain at the beginning of the seventeenth century.

suya, acerca de quien se refieren no sé qué historias raras. En fin, el caso es que disputando y peleándonos siempre, no hacemos malas migas el comandante y yo. ¡Qué malas migas! A cada polémica que armamos, parece aumentar nuestra simpatía, como si sus mismas genialidades morales (no sé darles otro nombre) me fuesen cayendo en gracia y pareciéndome indicio de cierta bondad interior ... Ello va mal expresado ..., pero yo me entiendo.

Pues anteayer (para venir al asunto), estuvo el comandante desde los primeros momentos muy decidor y muy alborotado, haciéndonos reír con sus manías. Le sopló la ventolera de sostener una vulgaridad: que España es un país tan salvaje como el África Central, que todos tenemos sangre africana, beduina, árabe o qué sé yo, y que todas esas músicas de ferrocarriles, telégrafos, fábricas, escuelas, ateneos, libertad política y periódicos, son en nosotros postizas y como pegadas con goma, por lo cual están siempre despegándose, mientras lo verdaderamente nacional y genuino, la barbarie, subsiste, prometiendo durar por los siglos de los siglos. Sobre esto se levantó el caramillo que es de suponer. Lo primero que le repliqué fue compararlo a los franceses, que creen que sólo servimos para bailar el bolero y repicar las castañuelas; y añadí que la gente bien educada era igual, idéntica, en todos los países del mundo.

–Pues mire usted, eso empiezo por negarlo –saltó Pardo con grandísima fogosidad–. De los Pirineos acá, todos, sin excepción, somos salvajes, lo mismo las personas finas que los tíos; lo que pasa es que nosotros lo disimulamos un poquillo más, por vergüenza, por convención social, por conveniencia propia; pero que nos pongan el plano inclinado, y ya resbalaremos. El primer rayito de sol de España –este sol con que tanto nos muelen los extranjeros y que casi nunca está en casa, porque aquí llueve lo propio que en París, que ese es el chiste ...–.

Le interrumpí:

–Hombre, sólo falta que también niegue usted el sol.

–No lo niego, ¡qué he de negarlo! Por lo mismo que suele embozarse bien en invierno, de miedo a las pulmonías, en verano lo tienen ustedes convirtiendo a Madrid en sartén o caldera infernal, donde nos achicharramos todos ... Y claro, no bien asoma, produce una fiebre y

stories. Anyway, the fact is that the commander and I, even though we're forever arguing and fighting, don't get on badly. Not get on! Every controversy we cause seems to increase our mutual affection, as though his moralistic nature (I don't know what other name to give it) were beginning to appeal to me as a sign of a certain inner goodness... That is very badly expressed ... but I know what I mean.

Well, the day before yesterday (to get to the point), from the word go the commander was very amusing and very excited, making us laugh with his obsessions. He suddenly decided to maintain something offensive: that Spain is a country as uncivilised as Central Africa, that we've all got African, Bedouin, Arabic or whatever blood, and that all this paraphernalia of railroads, telegraph lines, factories, schools, cultural centres, political freedom and daily papers is artificial and glued on, as it were, with gum, hence forever coming unstuck, whilst the genuine, national part – our barbarism – survives, promising to endure forever more. This sparked off the commotion you would expect. My first retort was to compare him to the French, who think that all we're good for is dancing the bolero and clicking castanets; and I added that well-educated people are exactly the same in all countries of the world.

'Now look, that's what I'll begin by denying!' Pardo piped up with great spirit. 'This side of the Pyrenees we are all, without exception, savages, refined people as much as ordinary folk; what happens is that out of shame, social convention and convenience we hide it a little better. But let them put a downward slope before us, and we'll soon slip into bad habits. At the first ray of Spanish sun (this sun that foreigners dwell on so much, and which is seldom around, since it rains here as much as in Paris, that's the joke of it...).'

I interrupted him:

'The only thing left is for you to deny that we have any sun at all!'

'I don't deny it. How could I deny it? Just as we usually muffle up in winter for fear of pneumonia, in summer Madrid turns into a frying pan or a seething cauldron, where we all roast in the heat... And of course, as soon as it appears it produces a diabolical fever and

una excitación endiabladas … Se nos sube a la cabeza, y entonces es
cuando se nivelan las clases ante la ordinariez y la ferocidad general …
  –Vamos, ya pareció aquello. Usted lo dice por las corridas de toros.
En efecto, a Pardo le da muy fuerte eso de las corridas. Es uno
de sus principales y frecuentes asuntos de sermón. En tomando la
ampolleta sobre los toros, hay que oírle poner como digan dueñas a
los partidarios de tal espectáculo, que él considera tan pecaminoso
como el padre Urdax los bailes de Piñata y las representaciones del
Demimonde y *Divorciémonos*. Sale a relucir aquello de las tres fieras,
toro, torero y público; la primera, que se deja matar porque no tiene
más remedio; la segunda, que cobra por matar; la tercera, que paga
para que maten, de modo que viene a resultar la más feroz de las tres;
y también aquello de la suerte de pica, y de las tripas colgando, y de
las excomuniones del Papa contra los católicos que asisten a corridas,
y de los perjuicios a la agricultura … Lo que es la cuenta de perjuicios
la saca de un modo imponente. Hasta viene a resultar que por culpa
de los toros hay déficit en la Hacienda y hemos tenido las dos guerras
civiles … (Verdad que esto lo soltó en un instante de acaloramiento,
y como vio la greguería y la chacota que armamos, medio se desdijo.)
Por todo lo cual, yo pensé que al nombrar ferocidad y barbarie,
vendrían los toros detrás. No era eso. Pardo contestó:
  –Dejemos a un lado los toros, aunque bien revelan el influjo
barbarizante o barbarizador (como ustedes gusten) del sol, ya que es
axiomático que sin sol no hay corrida *buena*. Pero prescindamos de
ellos; no quiero que digan ustedes que ya es manía en mí la de sacar
a relucir la gente cornúpeta. Tomemos cualquiera otra manifestación
bien genuina de la vida nacional …, algo muy español y muy
característico … ¿No estamos en tiempo de ferias? ¿No es mañana

excitement... It goes to our heads, and that's when class differences are levelled out by coarseness and general ferocity...'

'Oh, so that's it. You're saying it on account of bullfighting.'

Indeed, Pardo feels very strongly about bullfights. It is one of the main and most frequent topics of his lectures. Monopolising the conversation about bulls, you should hear him insult supporters of a spectacle he considers as sinful as Father Urdax does *piñata* dances and performances of *Le Demi-monde* and *Divorciémonos*.[8] The thing about the three wild beasts comes out: the bull, the bullfighter and the public! The first, which lets itself be killed because it's got no choice; the second, who is paid to kill; the third, who pays them to kill, so turns out to be the most ferocious of the three; and also about the *picador*'s lance, and the guts hanging out, and the Pope's excommunication on Catholics who attend bullfights, and the damage to agriculture... When it comes to calculating the damage he draws some awe-inspiring conclusions. It even turns out that bullfighting is responsible for the deficit in the Treasury and our two civil wars...[9] (It's true that he unleashed that one in a moment of passion, and seeing the outcry and uproar, he backtracked halfway.) This is why I thought that when he used the words ferocity and barbarism, bullfighting would follow. But it didn't. Pardo answered:

'Let's put bullfighting to one side, even though it clearly shows the barbarising or barbarised (as you wish) influence of the sun, seeing as it's self-evident that without the sun there is no *good* bullfight. But let's do without it; I don't want you to say that it's an obsession of mine to bring up the bullfighting brigade. Let's take any other truly genuine manifestation of our national life ... something very Spanish and very characteristic... Are we not in fiesta time? Isn't tomorrow the

---

8 *Piñata* dances: masked dances celebrated the first Sunday of Lent. People would dance around a ceramic pot containing sweets and gifts hanging from the ceiling. The pot would eventually be broken with a stick by blindfolded guests. *Le Demi-monde* (1855) is a play by Alexandre Dumas and *Divorciémonos* is the Spanish translation of Victorien Sardou's *Divorçons* (1882). Both plays were considered shocking at the time.

9 This is a reference to the first two Carlist Wars, the first of which took place between 1833 and 1839 and the second between 1872 and 1876.

San Isidro Labrador? ¿No va la gente estos días a solazarse por la pradera y el cerro?

–Bueno: ¿y qué? ¿También criticará usted las ferias y el Santo? Este señor no perdona ni a la corte celestial.

–Bueno está el Santo, y valiente saturnal asquerosa la que sus devotos le ofrecen. Si San Isidro la ve, él que era un honrado y pacífico agricultor, convierte en piedras los garbanzos tostados, y desde el cielo descalabra a sus admiradores. Aquello es un aquelarre, una zahúrda de Plutón. Los instintos españoles más típicos corren allí desbocados, luciendo su belleza. Borracheras, pendencias, navajazos, gula, libertinaje grosero, blasfemias, robos, desacatos y bestialidades de toda calaña … Bonito *tableau*, señoras mías … Eso es el pueblo español cuando le dan suelta. Lo mismito que los potros al salir a la dehesa, que su felicidad consiste en hartarse de relinchos y coces.

–Si me habla usted de la gente ordinaria …

–No, es que insisto: todos iguales en siendo españoles; el instinto vive allá en el fondo del alma; el problema es de ocasión y lugar, de poder o no sacudir ciertos miramientos que la educación impone: cosa externa, cáscara y nada más.

–¡Qué teorías, Dios misericordioso! ¿Ni siquiera admite usted excepciones a favor de las señoras? ¿Somos salvajes también?

–También, y acaso más que los hombres, que al fin ustedes se educan menos y peor … No se dé usted por resentida, amiga Asís. Concederé que usted sea la menor cantidad de salvaje posible, porque al fin nuestra tierra es la porción más apacible y sensata de España.

Aquí la duquesa volvió la cabeza con sobresalto. Desde el principio de la disputa estaba entretenida dando conversación a un tertuliano nuevo, muchacho andaluz, de buena presencia, hijo de un antiguo amigo del duque, el cual, según me dijeron, era un rico hacendado residente en Cádiz. La duquesa no admite presentados, y sólo por

festival of Saint Isidro the Farm Labourer?[10] Won't people be going to enjoy themselves in the next few days on the meadow and hills?'

'Well, so what? Are you going to criticise the fairs and patron saint as well? This man won't spare even the Celestial Court.'

'The saint is good, but what a revolting saturnalia his devotees offer him. If Saint Isidro, that honourable and peace-loving farmer, could see it, he would turn the roasted chickpeas into pebbles and attack his admirers from heaven. It is a witches' coven, one of Pluto's pigsties.[11] The most characteristic Spanish instincts run riot there, showing themselves off. Drunkenness, brawling, stabbings, gluttony, crude licentiousness, blasphemy, theft, disrespect and acts of brutality of every kind... A very nice *tableau*, ladies... That's the Spanish people when they're let loose. Just like colts put out to pasture, neighing and kicking to their heart's content.'

'If you're talking about common people...'

'No. I insist that we Spaniards are all the same. The instinct lives in the very depth of our soul; the problem is one of time and place, of being able or not to shake off certain considerations which our upbringing imposes: something external, a shell and nothing more.'

'What theories, merciful God! Don't you allow exceptions even for women? Are we savages too?'

'Certainly, and perhaps more savage than men, because after all you are less and worse educated... Don't be offended, my friend Asís. I will concede that you are as little a savage as possible, for after all our region is the most even-tempered and sensible part of Spain.'

Here the duchess turned round in surprise. From the beginning of our discussion she had been conversing with a new member of the gathering, a good-looking young Andalusian, the son of an old friend of the duke, who, according to what I was told, was a rich landowner residing in Cádiz. The duchess doesn't accept people she

---

10   The festival of Saint Isidro the Farm Labourer, the patron saint of Madrid and of farm labourers, is celebrated on 15 May. The celebration, held in the open-air area known as the Pradera del Santo, usually lasts about nine days and includes fairs, concerts, dances and pilgrimages to the Ermita de San Isidro situated in Carabanchel, Madrid.

11   Pluto was the ruler of the underworld in classical mythology.

circunstancias así pueden encontrarse caras desconocidas en su tertulia. En cambio, a las relaciones ya antiguas las agasaja muchísimo, y es tan consecuente y cariñosa en el trato, que todos se hacen lenguas alabando su perseverancia, virtud que, según he notado, abunda en la corte más de lo que se cree. Advertía yo que, sin dejar de atender al forastero, la duquesa aplicaba el oído a nuestra disputa y rabiaba por mezclarse en ella: la proporción le vino rodada para hacerlo, metiendo en danza al gaditano.

–Muchas gracias, señor de Pardo, por la parte que nos toca a los andaluces. Estos galleguitos siempre arriman el ascua a su sardina. ¡Más aprovechados son! De salvajes nos ha puesto, así como quien no quiere la cosa.

–¡Oh duquesa, duquesa, duquesa! –respondió Pardo con mucha guasa–. ¡Darse por aludida usted, usted que es una señora tan inteligente, protectora de las bellas artes! ¡Usted que entiende de pucheros mudéjares y barreñones asirios! ¡Usted que posee colecciones mineralógicas que dejan con la boca abierta al embajador de Alemania! ¡Usted, señora, que sabe lo que significa *fósil*! ¡Pues si hasta miedo le han cobrado a usted ciertos pedantes que yo conozco!

–Haga usted el favor de no quedarse conmigo suavemente. No parece sino que soy alguna literata o alguna marisabidilla … Porque le guste a uno un cuadro o una porcelana … Si cree usted que así vamos a correr un velo sobre aquello del salvajismo … ¿Qué opina usted de eso, Pacheco? Según este caballero, que ha nacido en Galicia, es salvaje toda España y más los andaluces. Asís, el señor don Diego Pacheco … Pacheco, la señora marquesa viuda de Andrade … el señor don Gabriel Pardo …

El gaditano, sin pronunciar palabra, se levantó y vino a apretarme la mano haciendo una cortesía; yo murmuré entre dientes eso que se murmura en casos análogos. Llena la fórmula, nos miramos con la curiosidad fría del primer momento, sin fijarnos en detalles. Pacheco, que llevaba con soltura el frac, me pareció distinguido, y aunque andaluz, le encontré más bien trazas inglesas: se me figuró serio y no muy locuaz ni disputador. Haciéndose cargo de la indicación de la duquesa, dijo con acento cerrado y frase perezosa:

isn't acquainted with, and only in circumstances like this can a strange face be found at her gatherings. On the other hand, she lavishes lots of attention on old relationships, and is so consistent and affectionate in her manner that everyone praises her perseverance, a virtue I have noticed as being more bountiful in Madrid than people think. I had noticed that, without ceasing to pay attention to the stranger, the duchess was lending an ear to our conversation and was dying to participate in it; she was given the perfect opportunity to do this by involving the man from Cádiz.

'Many thanks, Señor Pardo, in the name of all Andalusians. These Galicians always look after number one. They're so opportunistic! They've casually classed us as savages, as if it were of little importance.'

'Oh duchess, duchess, duchess!' replied Pardo in fun. 'You think I'm referring to you, you who are such an intelligent woman, a patron of the fine arts! You who know about Mudejar cooking pots and Assyrian earthenware tubs! You whose collection of minerals leaves the German ambassador lost for words. You, madam, who know the meaning of the word *fossil*! Yes, some pedants I know have even become afraid of you!'

'Please don't pull my leg. It makes me seem like a woman of letters or a bluestocking… Just because one likes a painting or a bit of porcelain… If you think that this is how we'll draw a veil over the business about savagery… What do you think about that, Pacheco? According to this gentleman, who was born in Galicia, the whole of Spain is savage and those from Andalusia most of all. Asís, Don Diego Pacheco … Pacheco, the Marchioness of Andrade … Don Gabriel Pardo…'

Without saying a word, the young man stood up and shook my hand with a bow; I murmured the things we murmur in such cases. This formality over, we looked at each other with the cold curiosity of first acquaintance, without noticing details. Pacheco, who was wearing his dress coat with an air of confidence, seemed distinguished to me and, although Andalusian, I found his appearance more English. I imagined him as serious and not very talkative or argumentative. Understanding the duchess's signal, he said with a thick accent and lazy expression:

–A cada país le cae bien lo suyo ... Nuestra tierra no ha dado pruebas de ser nada ruda: tenemos allá de too: poetas, pintores, escritores ... Cabalmente en Andalucía la gente pobre es mu fina y mu despabilaa. Protesto contra lo que se refiere a las señoras. Este cabayero convendrá en que toítas son unos ángeles del cielo.

–Si me llama usted al terreno de la galantería –respondió Pardo–, convendré en lo que usted guste ... Sólo que esas generalidades no prueban nada. En las unidades nacionales no veo hombres ni mujeres: veo una raza, que se determina históricamente en esta o en aquella dirección ...

–¡Ay, Pardo! –suplicó la duquesa con mucha gracia–. Nada de palabras retorcidas, ni de filosofías intrincadas. Hable usted clarito y en cristiano. Mire usted que no hemos llegado a sabios, y que nos vamos a quedar en ayunas.

–Bueno: pues hablando en cristiano, digo que ellos y ellas son de la misma pasta, porque no hay más remedio, y que en España (allá va, ustedes se empeñan en que ponga los puntos sobre las íes) también las señoras pagan tributo a la barbarie –lo cual puede no advertirse a primera vista porque su sexo las obliga a adoptar formas menos toscas, y las condena al papel de ángeles, como les ha llamado este caballero–. Aquí está nuestra amiga Asís, que a pesar de haber nacido en el Noroeste, donde las mujeres son reposadas, dulces y cariñosas, sería capaz, al darle un rayo de sol en la mollera, de las mismas atrocidades que cualquier hija del barrio de Triana o del Avapiés ...

–¡Ay, paisano!, ya digo que está usted tocado, incurable. Con el sol tiene la tema.[7] ¿Qué le hizo a usted el sol, para que así lo traiga al retortero?

–Serán aprensiones, pero yo creo que lo llevamos disuelto en la sangre y que a lo mejor nos trastorna.

–No lo dirá usted por nuestra tierra. Allá no le vemos la cara sino unos cuantos días del año.

–Pues no lo achaquemos al sol; será el aire ibérico; el caso es que

---

7   Idea fija que suelen tener los dementes (RAE).

'Everyone thinks his own country best... Our region hasn't provided any evidence of being uncultured: we've got everythin' there: poets, painters, writers... Poor people in Andalusia are actually very refined and very sharp. I object to what was said about ladies. This gentleman'll agree that they're all angels from heaven.'

'If we're talking gallantry,' replied Pardo, 'I'll agree on anything you like... It's just that those generalisations don't prove anything. In each nation I see neither men nor women: I see a race, which tends historically in this or that direction...'

'Ah, Pardo!' implored the duchess with great charm. 'Forget about complicated words and intricate philosophies. Speak in plain, clear Spanish. Just imagine that we're not learned and that we'll miss the point.'

'Fine: well, speaking in plain Spanish, I say that males and females are two of a kind, because there's nothing we can do about it, and that in Spain (here goes, you insist that I dot the i's and cross the t's) women also pay tribute to barbarism, which may not be apparent at first sight because their sex obliges them to adopt smoother manners, and condemns them to the role of angels, as this gentleman has said. Take our friend Asís here, who, in spite of having been born in the north-west, where the women are calm, sweet and affectionate, would be capable, with a ray of sun beating on the top of her head, of the same atrocious behaviour as any daughter of the neighbourhoods of Triana or Avapiés...'[12]

'Oh, my dear compatriot, I say you're wrong in the head, incurable. You're obsessed with the sun. What did the sun do to you that it's so much on your mind?'

'They might be strange ideas, but I think it's dissolved in our blood and that it maybe makes us crazy.'

'You can't say that about our region. We only see its face a few days a year there.'

'Well, then, let's not put it down to the sun. It must be the Iberian

---

12 Triana is a working-class neighbourhood of Seville with a large gypsy population. Avapiés, known today as Lavapiés, is a multiethnic neighbourhood in Madrid. Before the expulsion of the Jews in 1492 it was the Jewish quarter of the city.

los gallegos, en ese punto, sólo aparentemente nos distinguimos del resto de la Península. ¿Ha visto usted qué bien nos acostumbramos a las corridas de toros? En Marineda ya se llena la plaza y se calientan los cascos igual que en Sevilla o Córdoba. Los cafés flamencos hacen furor; las cantaoras traen revuelto al sexo masculino; se han comprado cientos de navajas, y lo peor es que se hace uso de ellas; hasta los chicos de la calle se han aprendido de memoria el tecnicismo taurómaco; la manzanilla[8] corre a mares en los tabernáculos marinedinos; hay sus cañitas y todo; una parodia ridícula; corriente; pero parodia que sería imposible donde no hubiese materia dispuesta para semejantes aficiones. Convénzanse ustedes: aquí en España, desde la Restauración, maldito si hacemos otra cosa más que jalearnos a nosotros mismos. Empezó la broma por todas aquellas demostraciones contra don Amadeo: lo de las peinetas y mantillas, los trajecitos a medio paso y los caireles; siguió con las barbianerías del difunto rey, que le había dado por lo chulo, y claro, la gente elegante le imitó; y ahora es ya una epidemia, y entre patriotismo y flamenquería, guitarreo y cante jondo, panderetas con madroños colorados y amarillos, y abanicos con las hazañas y los retratos de Frascuelo y Mazzantini, hemos hecho una Españita bufa, de tapiz de Goya o sainete de don Ramón de

---

8 Vino blanco que se hace en Sanlúcar de Barrameda y en otros lugares de Andalucía.

air; the thing is that we Galicians differ from the inhabitants of the rest of the peninsula in appearance only. Have you noticed how well we are taking to bullfights? The bullring in Marineda[13] gets full now, and people get as worked up as they do in Seville or Cordoba. Flamenco cafés are all the rage and men go wild over the female flamenco singers. Hundreds of knives have been bought, and the worst thing is that they are used. Even street boys have learnt by heart the technical vocabulary of bullfighting; *manzanilla* sherry flows abundantly in the dwellings of Marineda. There are small glasses and everything; a ridiculous parody, certainly, but a parody that would be impossible in a place where everything wasn't ready and available for such pastimes. You need to understand: here in Spain, since the Restoration, I'll be damned if we do anything more than cheer ourselves on. The farce began with all those demonstrations against Don Amadeo: the business with *peinetas* and *mantillas*, short skirts and wigs. Then came the audacity of the deceased king who took to dressing in typical Madrilenian attire, and of course elegant people imitated him;[14] and now it's an epidemic, and between patriotism and flashiness, the casual strumming of a guitar and flamenco singing, tambourines with red and yellow tassels, and fans adorned with the portraits and exploits of Frascuelo and Mazzantini, we've made a comic opera Spain, like one of Goya's tapestry designs or a burlesque by Ramón de la Cruz.[15] There's nothing for it, it's the fashion and

13　A fictional town in Galicia, based on La Coruña, which appears first in Pardo Bazán's *La Tribuna* (1883) and later in *La piedra angular* (1891), *Doña Milagros* (1894) and *Memorias de un solterón* (1896).

14　The Duke of Aosta, from the Italian House of Savoy, was proclaimed King of Spain, with the name of Amadeo I, by the Cortes in 1870. Although less controversial and divisive than a German or French monarch would have been, some people chose to display their patriotism by wearing typical eighteenth-century Spanish clothing, similar to that seen in Goya's tapestry designs. A *peineta* is an ornamental comb traditionally worn with a *mantilla* (a large light veil or scarf, often of black lace, worn by women over the head and covering the shoulders). The deceased king is Alfonso XII.

15　Francisco Sánchez Povedano (1842–98), known as Frascuelo, and Manzantini (1856–1926) were two well-known bullfighters of the time. Francisco de Goya y Lucientes (1746–1828) was the leading Spanish painter and etcher of the late eighteenth and early nineteenth centuries. He was court painter to Charles III,

la Cruz. Nada, es moda y a seguirla. Aquí tiene usted a nuestra amiga la duquesa, con su cultura, y su finura, y sus mil dotes de dama: ¿pues no se pone tan contenta cuando le dicen que es la chula más salada de Madrid?

–Hombre, si fuese verdad, ¡ya se ve que me pondría! –exclamó la duquesa con la viveza donosa que la distingue–. ¡A mucha honra!, más vale una chula que treinta gringas.⁹ Lo gringo me apesta. Soy yo muy españolaza: ¿se entera usted? Se me figura que más vale ser como Dios nos hizo, que no que andemos imitando todo lo de extranjis … Estas manías de vivir a la inglesa, a la francesa … ¿Habrá ridiculez mayor? De Francia los perifollos; bueno; no ha de salir uno por ahí espantando a la gente, vestido como en el año de la nanita … De Inglaterra los asados … y se acabó. Y diga usted, muy señor mío de mi mayor aprecio: ¿cómo es eso de que somos salvajes los españoles y no lo es el resto del género humano? En primer lugar: ¿se puede saber a qué llama usted salvajadas? En segundo: ¿qué hace nuestro pueblo, pobre infeliz, que no hagan también los demás de Europa? Conteste.

–¡Ay! …, ¡si me aplasta usted! …, ¡si ya no sé por donde ando! *Pietá, Signor*. Vamos, duquesa, insisto en el ejemplo de antes: ¿ha visto usted la romería de San Isidro?

–Vaya si la he visto. Por cierto que es de lo más entretenido y pintoresco. Tipos se encuentran allí, que … Tipos de oro. ¿Y los columpios? ¿Y los tiovivos? ¿Y aquella animación, aquel hormigueo de la gente? Le digo a usted que, para mí, hay poco tan salado como esas fiestas populares. ¿Que abundan borracheras y broncas? Pues eso pasa aquí y en Flandes: ¿o se ha creído usted que allá, por la *Ingalaterra*, la gente no se pone nunca a medios pelos, ni se arma quimera, ni hace barbaridad ninguna?

–Señora … –exclamó Pardo desalentado–, usted es para mí un enigma. Gustos tan refinados en ciertas cosas, y tal indulgencia para lo brutal y lo feroz en otras, no me lo explico sino considerando que con un corazón y un ingenio de primera, pertenece usted a una

---

9   Extranjeras, especialmente inglesas.

to be followed. Here we have our friend the duchess, with all her culture, refinement and her many womanly talents: well, doesn't she just love being told that she's the most charming, back-street wench in Madrid?'

'Indeed I would, if it were true!' exclaimed the duchess with her customary vivacity. 'And proud of it! A working-class wench is worth more than thirty foreign girls. Imitating foreign customs sickens me. I'm Spanish through and through, do you understand? I think it's better to be like God made us than imitating everything from abroad ... These crazes for living like the English and the French ... is there anything more ridiculous? Frippery from France; that's fine, you shouldn't hang around dressed like a fright from a long time ago... From England, roast meat ... and that's all. And tell me, my esteemed sir, how do you make out that we Spanish are savages and not the rest of the human race? In the first place, may we know what you call unmannerly behaviour? Secondly, what does our poor unfortunate country do that the rest of Europe doesn't? Answer that.'

'Ah! You've crushed me! I don't know what I'm saying! *Pietà, Signor.*[16] Well then, duchess, I'll go back to the previous example. Have you seen the Saint Isidro Fair?'

'Of course I have... By the way, it's one of the most interesting and picturesque of sights. The people you meet there... Exquisite characters. And the swings? And the merry-go-rounds? And all that activity, that swarm of people? I tell you, for me there's very little that's as charming as those popular festivals. There's no shortage of drunkenness and fighting? Well that happens here and in Flanders. Or do you believe that over there in *Ingerland* people never get a little tipsy or start a fight or do stupid things?'

'Madam,' exclaimed Pardo, discouraged, 'you're an enigma to me. Such refined tastes in certain things and such indulgence for the brutal and ferocious in others is something I can only explain by bearing in mind that, with your first-class heart and mind, you belong to a

---

Charles IV and Ferdinand VII of Spain. Don Ramón de la Cruz (1731–94) was the author of a large number of one-act farces called *sainetes*, including *Las tertulias de Madrid* and *Manolo*.

16   'Lord, have mercy' (Italian).

generación bizantina y decadente, que ha perdido los ideales ... Y no digo más, porque se reirá usted de mí.

–Es muy saludable ese temor; así no me hablará usted de cosazas filosóficas que yo no entiendo –respondió la duquesa soltando una de sus carcajadas argentinas, aunque reprimidas siempre–. No haga usted caso de este hombre, marquesa –murmuró volviéndose a mí–. Si se guía usted por él la convertirá en una cuákera. Vaya usted al Santo, y verá cómo tengo razón y aquello es muy original y muy famoso. Este señor ha descubierto que sólo se achispan los españoles: lo que es los ingleses, ¡angelitos de mi vida!, ¡qué habían de ajumarse nunca!

–Señora –replicó el comandante riendo, pero sofocado ya–: los ingleses se achispan; conformes: pero se achispan con *sherry*,[10] con cerveza o con esos alcoholes endiablados que ellos usan; no como nosotros, con el aire, el agua, el ruido, la música y la luz del cielo; ellos se volverán unos cepos así que trincan, pero nosotros nos volvemos fieras; nos entra en el cuerpo un espíritu maligno de bravata y fanfarronería, y por gusto nos ponemos a cometer las mayores ordinarieces, empeñándonos en imitar al populacho. Y esto lo mismo las damas que los caballeros, si a mano viene, como dicen en mi país. Transijamos con todo, excepto con la ordinariez, duquesa.

–Hasta la presente –declaró con gentil confusión la dama–, no hemos salido ni la marquesa de Andrade ni yo a trastear ningún novillo.

–Pues todo se andará, señoras mías, si les dan paño –respondió el comandante.

–A este señor le arañamos nosotras –afirmó la duquesa fingiendo con chiste un enfado descomunal.

–¿Y el señor Pacheco, que no nos ayuda? –murmuré volviéndome hacia el silencioso gaditano. Éste tenía los ojos fijos en mí, y sin apartarlos, disculpó su neutralidad declarando que ya nos defendíamos muy bien y maldita la falta que nos hacían auxilios ajenos: al poco rato miró el reloj, se levantó, despidióse con igual laconismo, y fuese. Su marcha varió por completo el giro de la conversación. Se habló de él, claro está: la Sahagún refirió que lo había tenido a su mesa, por ser hijo de persona a quien estimaba mucho, y añadió que ahí donde lo

---

10　Anglicismo: *vino de Jerez*.

Byzantine, decadent generation which has lost its ideals… I won't say any more, because you'll laugh at me.'

'That is a very healthy fear if it means you won't talk to me of philosophical things I don't understand,' replied the duchess with one of her silver-toned laughs, hearty but always repressed. 'Take no notice of this man, marchioness,' she murmured, turning to me. 'If you're guided by him he'll convert you into a Quaker. Go to the Saint Isidro and you'll see how I'm right and that it is very shocking and very amusing. This man has discovered that only the Spanish get tipsy. As for the English, they're little angels who never get drunk!'

'Madam,' retorted the commander with a laugh, but already annoyed, 'the English do get drunk, agreed, but they get drunk with sherry, beer or those diabolical alcoholic drinks they imbibe; not like us, with the air, water, noise, music and light of heaven. They may become idiotic as soon as they drink, but we become wild beasts; a malicious spirit of bravado and bragging is infused into our bodies, and we start doing the most vulgar things, taking pains to imitate the plebs. And this is the same for men and women, should the opportunity arise, as they say in my region. Let's tolerate everything, duchess, except for vulgarity.'

'Up until now,' declared the lady with genteel confusion, 'neither the Marchioness of Andrade nor I have gone out to fight a young bull.'

'Well all in good time, my ladies, if they give you the opportunity,' replied the commander.

'We'll scratch this man,' declared the duchess, disguising her great anger with a jest.

'And Señor Pacheco won't come to our help?' I murmured, turning towards the silent man from Cádiz. He had his eyes fixed on me and, without looking away, excused his neutrality by declaring that we were defending ourselves very well and damn it if we needed other people's help. A short while after he looked at his watch, got up, said goodbye with the same laconic manner and left. His departure completely altered the direction of the conversation. We talked about him, of course: the Duchess of Sahagún explained that she had invited him because he was the son of someone she valued highly, and

veíamos, hecho un moro por la indolencia y un inglés por la sosería, no era sino un calaverón de tomo y lomo, decente y caballero sí, pero aventurero y gracioso como nadie, muy gastador y muy tronera, de quien su padre no podía hacer bueno, ni traerle al camino de la formalidad y del sentido práctico, pues lo único para que hasta la fecha servía era para trastornar la cabeza a las mujeres. Y entonces el comandante (he notado que a todos los hombres les molesta un poquillo que delante de ellos se diga de otros que nos trastornan la cabeza) murmuró como hablando consigo mismo:

–Buen ejemplar de raza española.

added that where we saw a Moor on account of his indolence and an Englishman because he was insipid, he was just an out-and-out rake. Respectable and gentlemanly, indeed, but uncommonly adventurous and amusing, very extravagant and hare-brained. His father couldn't make him be good, nor lead him to the path of reliability and practical sense, because the only thing he'd done so far was to turn women's heads. And then the major (I've noticed that all males are slightly put out when they hear that other men turn our heads) muttered, as if speaking to himself:

'A fine example of our Spanish race.'

III

Bien sabe Dios que cuando al siguiente día, de mañana, salí a oír misa a San Pascual, por ser la festividad del patrón de Madrid, iba yo con mi eucologio y mi mantillita hecha una santa, sin pensar en nada inesperado y novelesco, y a quien me profetizase lo que sucedió después, creo que le llevo a los tribunales por embustero e insolente. Antes de entrar en la iglesia, como era temprano, me estiré a dar un borde por la calle de Alcalá, y recuerdo que, pasando frente al Suizo, dos o tres de esos chulos de pantalón estrecho y chaquetilla corta que se están siempre plantados allí en la acera, me echaron una sarta de requiebros de lo más desatinado; verbigracia: –Ole, ¡viva la purificación de la canela! Uyuyuy, ¡vaya unos ojos que se trae usted, hermosa! Soniche, ¡viva hasta el cura que bautiza a estas hembras con mansanilla e lo fino!–. Trabajo me costó contener la risa al entreoír estos disparates; pero logré mantenerme seria y apreté el paso a fin de perder de vista a los ociosos.

Cerca de la Cibeles me fijé en la hermosura del día. Nunca he visto aire más ligero, ni cielo más claro; la flor de las acacias del paseo de Recoletos olía a gloria, y los árboles parecía que estrenaban vestido

3

God knows only too well that the following morning, when I went to mass at Saint Pascual's for the feast of the patron saint of Madrid, I was like a saint with my euchologion[17] and my *mantilla*, thinking of nothing unexpected or romantic, and I believe I'd take anyone who prophesied what happened afterwards to court for being untruthful and insolent. As it was early, I set off for a stroll along Calle Alcalá before going into church, and I remember that, as I passed by the Suizo café, two or three of those working-class Madrilenian men in tight trousers and short jackets who are always standing around on the pavement directed a string of absurd compliments at me. For example, 'Bravo, long live purified cinnamon! Oyoyoy, what eyes you've got, my beauty! Silence, long live the priest who baptises these women with *manzanilla* sherry!' I found it hard to contain my laughter when I half-heard this nonsense; but I managed to remain serious and I quickened my pace in order to lose sight of these idlers.

Near the Cibeles fountain I noticed what a beautiful day it was. Never have I seen purer air or a clearer sky; the acacia blossom in the Paseo de Recoletos smelt divine, and the trees looked as if they were

---

17 A collection of prayers; a prayer book; also, a book of ritual, primarily that of the Greek Church.

nuevo de tafetán verde. Ganas me entraron de correr y brincar como a los quince, y hasta se me figuraba que en mis tiempos de chiquilla, no había sentido nunca tal exceso de vitalidad, tales impulsos de hacer extravagancias, de arrancar ramas de árbol y de chapuzarme en el pilón presidido por aquella buena señora de los leones ... Nada menos que estas tonterías me estaba pidiendo el cuerpo a mí.

Seguí bajando hacia las Pascualas, con la devoción de la misa medio evaporada y distraído el espíritu. Poco distaba ya de la iglesia, cuando distinguí a un caballero, que parado al pie de corpulento plátano, arrojaba a los jardines un puro enterito y se dirigía luego a saludarme. Y oí una voz simpática y ceceosa, que me decía:

–A los pies ... ¿Adónde bueno tan de mañana y tan sola?

–Calle ... Pacheco ... ¿Y usted? Usted sí que de fijo no viene a misa.

–¿Y usted qué sabe? ¿Por qué no he de venir a misa yo?

Trocamos estas palabras con las manos cogidas y una familiaridad muy extraña, dado lo ceremonioso y somero de nuestro conocimiento la víspera. Era sin duda que influía en ambos la transparencia y alegría de la atmósfera, haciendo comunicativa nuestra satisfacción y dando carácter expansivo a nuestra voz y actitudes. Ya que estoy dialogando con mi alma y nada ha de ocultarse, la verdad es que en lo cordial de mi saludo entró por mucho la favorable impresión que me causaron las prendas personales del andaluz. Señor, ¿por qué no han de tener las mujeres derecho para encontrar guapos a los hombres que lo sean, y por qué ha de mirarse mal que lo manifiesten (aunque para manifestarlo dijesen tantas majaderías como los chulos del café Suizo)? Si no lo decimos, lo pensamos, y no hay nada más peligroso que lo reprimido y oculto, lo que se queda dentro. En suma, Pacheco, que vestía un elegante terno gris claro, me pareció galán de veras; pero con igual sinceridad añadiré que esta idea no me preocupó arriba de dos segundos, pues yo no me pago solamente del exterior. Buena

wearing brand-new green taffeta silk. I got the urge to run and jump like when I was fifteen, and it struck me that even as a little girl I had never felt such vitality, such an impulse to do something outrageous, to tear branches from the trees and to take a dip in the basin presided over by that good lady of the lions…[18] My body was crying out for nothing less than these acts of folly.

I continued down towards Las Pascualas, with my religious fervour half evaporated and my mind distracted. Not far from the church I recognised a gentleman; standing at the foot of a massive plane tree, he threw a freshly lit cigar into the garden and then came to greet me. And I heard a kind, lisping voice say to me:

'At your service… Where are you off to so early and all on your own?'

'Stop it … Pacheco… And you? For sure you're not going to mass.'

'And how do you know? Why shouldn't I be going to mass?'

We exchanged these words whilst shaking hands and with a familiarity which, in view of the formal and superficial nature of our first acquaintance the day before, was very strange. No doubt the transparency and joy of the atmosphere influenced us both, communicating our satisfaction and giving an expansive character to our voice and attitudes. As I am having a dialogue with my conscience and nothing should be hidden, the truth is that the favourable impression the Andalusian's personal qualities made on me played a large part in the cordiality of my greeting. Indeed, why shouldn't women have the right to find men handsome when they are, and why should it look bad for them to show it (even if they were to show it by coming out with as many irritating remarks as the working-class Madrilenians from the Suizo café). If we don't say it we're still thinking it, and there's nothing more dangerous than what is repressed and hidden, what stays inside. In short, I found Pacheco, who was wearing an elegant, light grey three-piece suit, truly handsome; but with equal sincerity I'll add that this idea did not concern me for more than a couple of seconds, because I'm not attracted just to external appearance. I gave good

---

18   The iconic fountain, found in the part of Madrid commonly known as the Paseo de Recoletos, depicts the Roman goddess Cybele riding a chariot pulled by two lions.

prueba di de ello casándome a los veinte con mi tío, que tenía lo menos cincuenta, y lo que es de gallardo ...

Adelante. El señor de Pacheco, sin reparar que ya tocaban a misa, pegó la hebra, y seguimos de palique, guareciéndonos a la sombra del plátano, porque el sol nos hacía guiñar los ojos más de lo justo.

—¡Pero qué madrugadora!

—¿Madrugadora porque oigo misa a las diez?

—Sí señó: todo lo que no sea levantarse para almorsá ...

—Pues usted hoy madrugó otro tanto.

—Tuve corasonada. Esta tarde estarán buenos los toros: ¿no va usted?

—No: hoy no irá la Sahagún, y yo generalmente voy con ella.

—¿Y a las carreras de caballos?

—Menos; me cansan mucho: una revista de trapos y moños: una insulsez. Ni entiendo aquel tejemaneje de apuestas. Lo único divertido es el desfile.

—Y entonces, ¿por qué no va a San Isidro?

—¡A San Isidro! ¿Después de lo que nos predicó ayer mi paisano?

—Buen caso hase usted de su paisano.

—Y ¿creerá usted que con tantos años como llevo de vivir en Madrid, ni siquiera he visto la ermita?

—¿Que no? Pues hay que verla; se distraerá usted muchísimo; ya sabe lo que opina la duquesa, que esa fiesta merece el viaje. Yo no la conozco tampoco; verdá que soy forastero.

—Y ... ¿y los borrachos, y los navajazos, y todo aquello de que habló don Gabriel? ¿Será exageración suya?

—¡Yo qué sé! ¡Qué más da!

—Me hace gracia ... ¿Dice usted que no importa? ¿Y si luego paso un susto?

—¡Un susto yendo conmigo!

—¿Con usted? —y solté la risa.

—¡Conmigo, ya se sabe! No tiene usted por qué reírse, que soy mu buen compañero.

Me reí con más ganas, no sólo de la suposición de que Pacheco

proof of that at the age of twenty by marrying my uncle, who was at least fifty, and as for being dashing…

Moving on. Pacheco, without noticing that the church bells were calling to mass, started a conversation and we carried on chatting, taking refuge in the shade of the plane tree because the sun was making us squint more than necessary.

'What an early riser!'

'Up early because I'm going to mass at ten?'

'Yeah, indeed, any time before lunch…'

'Well, you got up just as early as me today.'

'I had a feeling. The bullfight'll be good this afternoon. Aren't you going?'

'No. The Duchess of Sahagún won't be there today, and I generally go with her.'

'And the horse races?'

'Even less so. They bore me. A showcase for bags and glad rags. Sheer tastelessness. Nor do I understand that betting jiggery-pokery. The only entertaining part is the procession.'

'Well, then, why not go to the Saint Isidro Fair?'

'To Saint Isidro? After what my compatriot preached yesterday?'

'You take good notice of your compatriot.'

'And can you believe that in all the years I've been living in Madrid I haven't even visited the Hermitage?'

'Really? You must see it, then; it'll captivate you. You already know what the duchess thinks, that the fair's worth a visit. I haven't been there either; the truth is I'm an outsider.

And … and what about the drunks, and the knifings, and everything Don Gabriel spoke about? Could he be exaggerating?'

'What do I know? Who cares?'

'You make me laugh… You say it doesn't matter? And what if I get a fright?'

'A fright with me there!'

'With you?' and I burst out laughing.

'Of course with me! You've no reason to laugh, I'm very good company.'

I laughed more heartily, not only at Pacheco's assumption about

me acompañase, sino de su acento andaluz, que era cerrado y sandunguero sin tocar en ordinario, como el de ciertos señoritos que parecen asistentes.

Pacheco me dejó acabar de reír, y sin perder su seriedad, con mucha calma, me explicó lo fácil y divertido que sería darse una vueltecita por la feria, a primera hora, regresando a Madrid sobre las doce o la una. ¡Si me hubiese tapado con cera los oídos entonces, cuántos males me evitaría! La proposición, de repente, empezó a tentarme, recordando el dicho de la Sahagún: –«Vaya usted al Santo, que aquello es muy original y muy famoso»–. Y realmente, ¿qué mal había en satisfacer mi curiosidad?, pensaba yo. Lo mismo se oía misa en la ermita del Santo que en las Pascualas; nada desagradable podía ocurrirme llevando conmigo a Pacheco, y si alguien me veía con él, tampoco sospecharía cosa mala de mí a tales horas y en sitio tan público. Ni era probable que anduviese por allí la sombra de una persona decente, ¡en día de carreras y toros!, ¡a las diez de la mañana! La escapatoria no ofrecía riesgo … ¡y el tiempo convidaba tanto! En fin, que si Pacheco porfiaba algo más, lo que es yo …

Porfió sin impertinencia, y tácitamente, sonriendo, me declaré vencida. ¡Solemne ligereza! Aún no había articulado el *sí* y ya discutíamos los medios de locomoción. Pacheco propuso, como más popular y típico, el tranvía; pero yo, a fin de que la cosa no tuviese el menor aspecto de informalidad, preferí mi coche. La cochera no estaba lejos: calle del Caballero de Gracia: Pacheco avisaría, mandaría que enganchasen e iría a recogerme a mi casa, por donde yo necesitaba pasar antes de la excursión. Tenía que tomar el abanico, dejar el devocionario, cambiar mantilla por sombrero … En casa le esperaría. Al punto que concertamos estos detalles, Pacheco me apretó la mano y se apartó corriendo de mí. A la distancia de diez pasos se paró y preguntó otra vez:

–¿Dice usted que el coche cierra en el Caballero de Gracia?

–Sí, a la izquierda … un gran portalón …

Y tomé aprisita el camino de mi vivienda, porque la verdad es que necesitaba hacer muchas más cosas de las que le había confesado a Pacheco; ¡pero vaya usted a enterar a un hombre …! Arreglarme el pelo, darme velutina, buscar un pañolito fino, escoger unas botas

accompanying me, but also at his Andalusian accent, which was thick and amusing without sounding common, like that of certain young gentlemen who resemble soldier-servants.

Pacheco let me finish laughing, and without becoming less serious calmly explained how easy and amusing it would be to have a little stroll through the fair first thing in the morning, going back to Madrid at around 12 or one o'clock. If my ears had been sealed with wax right then, how many evils I would have avoided. The proposal suddenly began to tempt me, bringing to mind the duchess's remark: "Go to the Saint Isidro Fair, it's so different and amusing". And after all, I thought, what harm was there in satisfying my curiosity? Mass could be heard just as well at the Hermitage of Saint Isidro as in Las Pascualas; nothing disagreeable could happen if I took Pacheco with me, and anyone who saw me with him would suspect nothing bad of me at that hour and in such a public place. And it wasn't likely that any decent person would be walking round there, on a day of horse racing and bullfighting, at ten o'clock in the morning! The escapade offered no risk … and the weather was so inviting! In short, if Pacheco insisted a bit more, well…

He insisted without impertinence, and with a tacit smile I showed I had been won over. Solemn indiscretion! I still hadn't said *yes* and yet we were already discussing means of transport. Pacheco proposed the tram as the most popular and traditional, but I preferred my own carriage so that things wouldn't look at all spontaneous. The coach house wasn't far, in the Calle del Caballero de Gracia; Pacheco would give the order to hitch up and come to pick me up at my house where I needed to drop by before the excursion. I had to pick up my fan, drop off my prayer book, swap my *mantilla* for a hat… I would wait for him at home. As soon as we agreed on these details, Pacheco squeezed my hand and ran off. Ten paces away he stopped and asked again:

'Did you say the carriage is kept in the Caballero de Gracia?'

'Yes, on the left … a large entrance…'

And I quickly took the road home because, if truth be known, I needed to do lots more things than I had confessed to Pacheco; but as for telling a man…! Do my hair, powder my face, look for a delicate handkerchief, choose some new boots that look really good on me,

nuevas que me calzan muy bien, ponerme guantes frescos y echarme en el bolsillo un *sachet* de raso que huele a *iris* (el único perfume que no me levanta dolor de cabeza). Porque al fin, aparte de todo, Pacheco era para mí persona de cumplido; íbamos a pasar algunas horas juntos y observándonos muy de cerca, y no me gustaría que algún rasgo de mi ropa o mi persona le produjese efecto desagradable. A cualquier señora, en mi caso, le sucedería lo propio.

Llegué al portal sofocada y anhelosa, subí a escape, llamé con furia y me arrojé en el tocador, desprendiéndome la mantilla antes de situarme frente al espejo. —«Ángela, el sombrero negro de paja con cinta escocesa ... Ángela, el antucá[11] a cuadritos ..., las botas bronceadas ...»

Vi que la Diabla se moría de curiosidad ... «¿Sí?, pues con las ganas de saber te quedas, hija ... La curiosidad es muy buena para la ropa blanca». Pero no se le coció a la chica el pan en el cuerpo y me soltó la píldora.

—¿La señorita almuerza en casa?

Para desorientarla respondí:

—Hija, no sé ... Por si acaso, tenerme el almuerzo listo, de doce y media a una ... Si a la una no vengo, almorzad vosotros ...; pero reservándome siempre una chuleta y una taza de caldo ..., y mi té con leche, y mis tostadas.

Cuando estaba arreglando los rizos de la frente bajo el ala del sombrero, reparé en un precioso cacharro azul, lleno de heliotropos, gardenias y claveles, que estaba sobre la chimenea.

—¿Quién ha mandado eso?

—El señor comandante Pardo ..., el señorito Gabriel.

—¿Por qué no me lo enseñabas?

—Vino la señorita tan aprisa ... Ni me dio tiempo.

No era la primera vez que mi paisano me obsequiaba con flores. Escogí una gardenia y un clavel rojo, y prendí el grupo en el pecho.

---

11 Galicismo de *en tout cas* (en todo caso): sombrilla grande que se sirve de paraguas.

put on fine gloves and slip into my pocket a satin *sachet* that smells of *iris* (the only perfume which doesn't give me a headache). Because after all, apart from everything else, for me Pacheco was a responsible person; we were going to spend some hours together, watching each other very closely, and I wouldn't like any feature of my clothing or person to have a disagreeable effect on him. The same thing would apply to any woman in my position.

I reached the entrance hall out of breath and panting, rushed upstairs, rang the bell furiously and threw myself into the dressing room, discarded my *mantilla* before positioning myself in front of the mirror. "Ángela, my black straw hat with the plaid ribbon... Ángela, my large, checked parasol ... my bronze-coloured boots..."

I could see that Diabla was dying of curiosity... "Yes? Well, you can remain itching to know, my dear ... curiosity is very good with white linen."[19] But the girl could not hold back and just spat out the question.

'Is madam having lunch at home?'

To muddle her up I answered:

'I don't know ... just in case, have my lunch ready from half past twelve to one ... If I'm not here at one, you eat lunch ... but still save me a chop and a cup of broth ... and my tea with milk and my toast.'

Whilst I was arranging the curls of my fringe under the brim of my hat, I noticed a lovely blue pot filled with heliotropes, gardenias and carnations on the mantelpiece.

'Who's sent that?'

'Major Pardo ... Master Gabriel.'

'Why didn't you point it out to me?'

'Madam came back in such a hurry ... I didn't have time.'

It wasn't the first time my compatriot had sent me flowers. I chose a gardenia and a red carnation, and pinned them on my chest. I

---

19 As well as meaning 'curiosity', the word *curiosidad* in Spanish can mean *limpieza* (cleanliness). Interestingly, fastidiousness in food and clothing is an obsolete meaning of its English cognate, an example of which can be found in James Fordyce's *Sermons to Young Women* (London: S. Crowder, C. Ware and T. Payne, 1775 Vol. 1, Sermon ii), p. 48: 'In affairs of this kind, it is but just to allow to women a degree of curiosity and care'.

Sujeté el velo con un alfiler; tomé un casaquín ligero de paño; mandé a Ángela que me estirase la enagua y volante, y me asomé, a ver si por milagro había llegado el coche. Aún no, porque era imposible; pero a los diez minutos desembocaba a la entrada de la calle. Entonces salí a la antesala andando despacio, para que la Diabla no acabase de escamarse; me contuve hasta cruzar la puerta; y ya en la escalera, me precipité, llegando al portal cuando se paraba la berlina[12] y saltaba en la acera Pacheco.

–¡Qué listo anduvo el cochero! –le dije.

–El cochero y un servidor de usted, señora –contestó el gaditano teniendo la portezuela para que yo subiese–. Con estas manos he ayudao a echar las guarniciones y hasta se me figura que a lavar las ruedas.

Salté en la berlina, quedándome a la derecha, y Pacheco entró por la portezuela contraria, a fin de no molestarme y con ademán de profundo respeto …: ¡valiente hipócrita está él! Nos miramos indecisos por espacio de una fracción de segundo, y mi acompañante me preguntó en voz sumisa:

–¿Doy orden de ir camino de la pradera?

–Sí, sí … Dígaselo usted por el vidrio.

Sacó fuera la cabeza y gritó: «¡Al Santo!»–. La berlina arrancó inmediatamente, y entre el primer retemblido de los cristales, exclamó Pacheco:

–Veo que se ha prevenío usted contra el calor y el sol … Todo hace falta.

Sonreí sin responder, porque me encontraba (y no tiene nada de sorprendente) algo cohibida por la novedad de la situación. No se desalentó el gaditano.

–Lleva usted ahí unas flores presiosas … ¿No sobraba para mí ninguna? ¿Ni siquiera una rosita de a ochavo? ¿Ni un palito de albahaca?

–Vamos –murmuré–, que no es usted poco pedigüeño … Tome usted para que se calle.

Desprendí la gardenia y se la ofrecí. Entonces hizo mil remilgos y zalemas.

---

12   Coche de caballos cerrado y comúnmente de dos asientos.

fastened my veil with a pin, took a short, light jacket made of cloth, told Ángela to straighten my petticoat and flounce, and looked out to see if by some miracle the carriage had arrived. Not yet, because it was impossible, but ten minutes later it came into the end of the street. Then I walked slowly into the antechamber so that Diabla's suspicions wouldn't come to an end. I restrained myself until I had gone through the door, rushed down the staircase and reached the entrance just as the berlin was stopping and Pacheco was jumping out onto the pavement.

'The coachman must have driven quickly!' I said to him.

'The coachman and someone at your service,' replied the native of Cádiz, holding the door open for me to get in. 'With these hands I helped to put on the harnesses and even wash the wheels I reckon.'

I jumped into the berlin, staying on the right, and Pacheco got in through the other door, so as not to disturb me and with a gesture of profound respect ... what a hypocrite! We looked at each other undecidedly for a fraction of a second, and my escort asked me in a submissive voice:

'Shall I tell him to take the Pradera road?'

'Yes, yes ... tell him through the window.'

He stuck his head out and shouted: "To the fair". The berlin set off immediately, and amidst the first shuddering of the windows, Pacheco exclaimed:

'I see you've come prepared for the heat and sun... It'll all be needed.'

I smiled without answering, because I felt, and it's hardly surprising, somewhat ill at ease by the novelty of the situation. The man from Cádiz did not lose heart.

'You've brought some beautiful flowers there ... wasn't there one left for me? Not even a rosebud for a farthing? Nor a sprig of basil?'

'Well,' I murmured, 'you're a real scrounger... Take this to keep you quiet.'

I pulled out the gardenia and gave it to him. He then made a great fuss and many salaams.

–Si yo no pretendía tanto … Con el rabillo me contentaba, o con media hoja que usted le arrancase … ¡Una gardenia para mí solo! No sé cómo lucirla … No se me va a sujetar en el ojal … A ver si usted consigue, con esos deditos …

–Vamos, que usted no pedía tanto, pero quiere que se la prendan, ¿eh? Vuélvase usted un poco, voy a afianzársela.

Introduje el rabo postizo de la flor en el ojal de Pacheco, y tomando de mi corpiño un alfiler sujeté la gardenia, cuyo olor a pomada me subía al cerebro, mezclado con otro perfume fino, procedente, sin duda, del pelo de mi acompañante. Sentí un calor extraordinario en el rostro, y al levantarlo, mis ojos se tropezaron con los del meridional, que en vez de darme las gracias, me contempló de un modo expresivo e interrogador. En aquel momento casi me arrepentí de la humorada de ir a la feria; pero ya …

Torcí el cuello y miré por la ventanilla. Bajábamos de la plazuela de la Cebada a la calle de Toledo. Una marea de gente, que también descendía hacia la pradera, rodeaba el coche y le impedía a veces rodar. Entre la multitud dominguera se destacaban los vistosos colorines de algún bordado pañolón de Manila, con su fleco de una tercia de ancho. Las chulas se volvían y registraban con franca curiosidad el interior de la berlina. Pacheco sacó la cabeza y le dijo a una no sé qué.

–Nos toman por novios –advirtió dirigiéndose a mí–. No se ponga usted más colorada: es lo que le faltaba para acabar de estar linda – añadió medio entre dientes.

Hice como si no oyese el piropo y desvié la conversación, hablando del pintoresco aspecto de la calle de Toledo, con sus mil tabernillas, sus puestos ambulantes de quincalla, sus anticuadas tiendas y sus paradores que se conservan lo mismito que en tiempo de Carlos cuarto. Noté que Pacheco se fijaba poco en tales menudencias, y en vez de observar las curiosidades de la calle más típica que tiene Madrid, llevaba los ojos puestos en mí con disimulo, pero con pertinacia, como el que estudia una fisonomía desconocida para leer en ella los pensamientos de la dueña. Yo también, a hurtadillas, procuraba enterarme de los más mínimos ápices de la cara de Pacheco. No dejaba de llamarme la atención la mezcla de razas que creía ver en

'But I wasn't after that much ... I'd've been happy with the stem, or half a leaf you'd torn from it... A whole gardenia just for me! I don't know how to show it off... It won't stay in place in me buttonhole... Let's see if you can manage with those dainty fingers...'

'I see, you weren't after that much, but you want it fastening on, eh? Turn a bit, I'm going to secure it for you.'

I inserted the false stem of the flower in Pacheco's buttonhole, and taking a pin from my bodice secured the gardenia, whose smell of ointment went to my head, mixing with another fine perfume, coming no doubt from my companion's hair. I felt an extraordinary heat in my face, and when I looked up my eyes met the southerner's, who instead of thanking me looked at me in an expressive and inquisitive way. At that moment I almost regretted my whim of going to the fair; but anyway...

I turned and looked out of the window. We were going down from the small Cebada Square to the Calle de Toledo. A flood of people, also going down towards the Pradera, surrounded the carriage and at times prevented it from moving forward. Standing out amongst that Sunday crowd were the bright colours of an embroidered Manila shawl with a fringe some three centimetres wide. The lower-class women of Madrid turned and with brazen curiosity scrutinised the interior of the berlin. Pacheco put his head out of the window and said something to one of them.

'They think we're newly-weds,' he explained to me. 'Don't go any redder, that's all you need to give the finishing touch to your beauty,' he added half mumbling.

I pretended not to hear his flattery and changed the subject, talking about the picturesque aspect of the Calle de Toledo, with its numerous taverns, the mobile trinket stalls, the old-fashioned shops and inns which look just the same as in the time of Charles IV. I noticed that Pacheco paid little attention to such trifles, and instead of looking at the curiosities of the most typical street of Madrid, he kept his eyes fixed on me, discreetly but persistently, like someone studying an unfamiliar physiognomy in order to read the owner's thoughts. I too, on the sly, managed to discover the tiniest details of Pacheco's face. The mixture of races I thought I could see in it constantly drew my

ella. Con un pelo negrísimo y una tez quemada del sol, casaban mal aquel bigote dorado y aquellos ojos azules.

–¿Es usted hijo de inglesa? –le pregunté al fin–. Me han contado que en la costa del Mediterráneo hay muchas bodas entre ingleses y españolas, y al revés.

–Es cierto que hay muchísimas, en Málaga sobre todo; pero yo soy español de pura sangre.

Le volví a mirar y comprendí lo tonto de mi pregunta. Ya recordaba haber oído a algún sabio de los que suele convidar a comer la Sahagún cuando no tiene otra cosa en que entretenerse, que es una vulgaridad figurarse que los españoles no pueden ser rubios, y que al contrario el tipo rubio abunda en España, sólo que no se confunde con el rubio sajón, porque es mucho más fino, más enjuto, así al modo de los caballos árabes. En efecto, los ingleses que yo conozco son por lo regular unos montones de carne sanguínea, que al parecer se escapa sola a la parrilla del rosbif; tienen cada cogote y cada pescuezo como ruedas de remolacha; las bocas de ellos dan asco de puro coloradotas, y las frentes, de tan blancas, fastidian ya, porque eso de la *frente pura* está bueno para las señoritas, no para los hombres. ¿Cuándo se verá en ningún inglés un corte de labios sutil, y una sien hundida, y un cuello delgado y airoso como el de Pacheco? Pero al grano: ¿pues no me entretengo recreándome en las perfecciones de ese pillo?

¡Qué hermoso y alegre estaba el puente de Toledo! Lo recuerdo como se recuerda una decoración del Teatro Real. Hervía la gente, y mirando hacia abajo, por la pradera y por todas las orillas del Manzanares, no se veían más que grupos, procesiones, corrillos, escenas animadísimas de esas que se pintan en las panderetas. A mí ciertos monumentos, por ejemplo las catedrales, casi me parecen más bonitas solitarias; pero el puente de Toledo, con sus retablazos, o nichos, o lo que sean aquellos fantasmones barrocos que le guarnecen a ambos lados, no está bien sin el rebullicio y la algazara de la gentuza, los chulapos y los tíos, los carniceros y los carreteros, que parece que acaban de bajarse de un lienzo de Goya. Ahora que se han puesto tan de moda los casacones, el puente tiene un encanto especial. Nuestro coche dio vuelta para tomar el camino de la pradera, y allí, en el mismo recodo, vi una tienda rara, una botería, en cuya fachada se ostentaban botas

attention. His jet-black hair and sunburnt skin didn't match up very well with that fair moustache and those blue eyes.

'Are you the son of an English woman?' I asked him finally. 'I've heard that on the Mediterranean coast there are lots of marriages between English men and Spanish women, and the other way around.'

'It's true there are lots, especially in Málaga; but I'm of pure Spanish blood.'

I looked at him again and realised the folly of my question. I remembered having heard from one of those scholars whom the Duchess of Sahagún usually invites to dinner when she has no other form of entertainment, that it is crass to think that Spaniards can't be fair-haired, and that on the contrary the blonde type abounds in Spain, only it is not comparable with the Saxon blonde, being leaner and more delicate like Arabian steeds. Indeed, the English I've met are generally mountains of blood-red meat, not far removed from roast beef, each having napes and throats like slices of beetroot. The sheer redness of their mouths makes you sick and their foreheads, being so white, are disgusting, because a 'pale brow' is fine for women, but not for men. When will you see Pacheco's finely cut lips, sunken temples and slim, graceful neck on any Englishman? But back to the point: am I not amusing myself by taking pleasure in that rogue's qualities?

How beautiful and lively was the Toledo Bridge! I remember it like a set at the Royal Theatre is remembered. It was crowded with people and looking down towards the Pradera and the banks of the River Manzanares all you could see was groups, processions, huddles of people, the sort of very lively scenes that are painted on tambourines. Certain monuments, cathedrals for example, almost seem to me more beautiful in isolation; but Toledo Bridge, with its large altarpieces, or recesses, or whatever those pompous baroque constructions are that adorn it on both sides, is no good without the hustle and bustle of the mob, the lower-class Madrilenians, butchers and wheelwrights who look like they've just stepped out of a Goya painting. Now that greatcoats have become so fashionable, the bridge has a special charm. Our carriage turned into the Pradera road and there, on the same bend, I saw a strange shop, a wineskin workshop whose facade flaunted wineskins of all sizes, from one measuring sixty litres to one

de todos los tamaños, desde la que mide treinta azumbres[13] de vino, hasta la que cabe en el bolsillo del pantalón. Pacheco me propuso que, para adoptar el tono de la fiesta, comprásemos una botita muy cuca que colgaba sobre el escaparate y la llenásemos de Valdepeñas: proposición que rechacé horrorizada.

No sé quién fue el primero que llamó feas y áridas a las orillas del Manzanares, ni por qué los periódicos han de estar siempre soltándole pullitas al pobre río, ni cómo no prendieron a aquel farsante de escritor francés (Alejandro Dumas, si no me engaño) que le ofreció de limosna un vaso de agua. Convengo en que no es muy caudaloso, ni tan frescachón como nuestro Miño o nuestro Sil; pero vamos, que no falta en sus orillas algún rinconcito ameno, verde y simpático. Hay árboles que convidan a descansar a la sombra, y unos puentes rústicos por entre los lavaderos, que son bonitos en cualquier parte. La verdad es que acaso influía en esta opinión que formé entonces, el que se me iba quitando el susto y me rebosaba el contento por haber realizado la escapatoria. Varios motivos se reunían para completar mi satisfacción. Mi traje de céfiro gris sembrado de anclitas rojas, era de buen gusto en una excursión matinal como aquella; mi sombrero negro de paja me sentaba bien, según comprobé en el vidrio delantero de la berlina; el calor aún no molestaba mucho; mi acompañante me agradaba, y la calaverada, que antes me ponía miedo, iba pareciéndome lo más inofensivo del mundo, pues no se veía por allí ni rastro de persona regular que pudiese conocerme. Nada me aguaría tanto la fiesta como tropezarme con algún tertuliano de la Sahagún, o vecina de butacas en el Real, que fuese luego a permitirse comentarios absurdos. Sobran personas maldicientes y deslenguadas que interpretan y traducen siniestramente las cosas más sencillas, y de poco le sirve a una mujer pasarse la vida muy sobre aviso, si se descuida una hora … (Sí, y lo que es a mí, en la actualidad, me caen muy bien estas reflexiones. En fin, prosigamos.) El caso es que la pradera ofrecía aspecto tranquilizador. Pueblo aquí, pueblo allí, pueblo en todas direcciones; y si algún hombre vestía americana, en vez de chaquetón

---

13　Medida de capacidad que equivale a poco más de dos litros.

that would fit in a trouser pocket. Pacheco suggested that, in order to absorb the spirit of the fiesta, we buy a very pretty little wineskin hanging out of the window and fill it with Valdepeñas, a suggestion I rejected with horror.

I don't know who was the first to call the banks of the River Manzanares ugly and arid, nor why the newspapers must forever make cutting remarks about our poor river, nor how they didn't arrest that charlatan of a French writer (Alexandre Dumas, if I'm not mistaken) who offered it a glass of water in alms.[20] I agree that it isn't exactly flowing with water or as robust as our Miño or Sil; but, well, its banks are not without the odd green and pleasant little corner. There are trees which invite one to rest in the shade, and a few rustic bridges amongst the washing places which in some parts are pretty. The truth is that perhaps the opinion I formed at that moment was influenced by the fact that I was losing my fear and overflowing with happiness at having carried out the escapade. Various reasons came together to complete my satisfaction. My grey zephyr dress dotted with little red anchors was in good taste for a morning excursion like that; my black straw hat looked good on me from what I could see in the front window of the berlin; the heat didn't make me feel uncomfortable yet; my companion pleased me, and the crazy escapade, which at first scared me, was beginning to appear the most inoffensive thing in the world, since no trace of anyone who might know me could be seen round there. Nothing would ruin the fiesta for me as much as bumping into someone from Sahagún's circle of friends, or a neighbour at the Royal Theatre who might then take it upon herself to make ridiculous comments. There are more than enough foul-mouthed slanderers to interpret perversely and traduce the most innocent of things, and it is of little avail for a woman to spend her life very much on her guard, if she then drops it for an hour… (Yes, and as for me at present, these reflections are very pertinent. Oh well, let's continue.) The fact is that the Pradera had a reassuring look. People here, there and everywhere; and if some man was wearing a lightweight, instead of a long jacket

---

20   The Manzanares River has been the butt of many jokes throughout history. Alexandre Dumas, *père* (1802–70) is a French writer best known for his adventure novels *Les Trois Mousquetaires* (1844) and *Le Comte de Monte-Cristo* (1845–46).

o chaquetilla, debía de ser criado de servicio, escribiente temporero, hortera, estudiante pobre, lacayo sin colocación, que se tomaba un día de asueto y holgorio. Por eso cuando a la subida del cerro, donde ya no pueden pasar los carruajes, Pacheco y yo nos bajamos de la berlina, parecíamos, por el contraste, pareja de archiduques que tentados de la curiosidad se van a recorrer una fiesta populachera, deseosos de guardar el incógnito, y delatados por sus elegantes trazas.

En fuerza de su novedad me hacía gracia el espectáculo. Aquella romería no tiene nada que ver con las de mi país, que suelen celebrarse en sitios frescos, sombreados por castaños o nogales, con una fuente o riachuelo cerquita y el santuario en el monte próximo … El campo de San Isidro es una serie de cerros pelados, un desierto de polvo, invadido por un tropel de gente entre la cual no se ve un solo campesino, sino soldados, mujerzuelas, chisperos, ralea apicarada y soez; y en lugar de vegetación, miles de tinglados y puestos donde se venden cachivaches que, pasado el día del Santo, no vuelven a verse en parte alguna: pitos adornados con hojas de papel de plata y rosas estupendas; vírgenes pintorreadas de esmeralda, cobalto y bermellón; medallas y escapularios igualmente rabiosos; loza y cacharros; figuritas groseras de toreros y picadores; botijos de hechuras raras; monigotes y fantoches con la cabeza de Martos, Sagasta o Castelar: ministros a *dos reales*; esculturas de los *ratas* de *la Gran Vía*, y al lado de la efigie del bienaventurado San Isidro, unas figuras que … ¡Válgame Dios! Hagamos como si no las viésemos.

Aparte del sol que le derrite a uno la sesera y del polvo que se masca, bastan para marear tantos colorines vivos y metálicos. Si sigo mirando van a dolerme los ojos. Las naranjas apiñadas parecen de fuego; los dátiles relucen como granates obscuros; como pepitas de oro los garbanzos tostados y los cacahuetes: en los puestos de flores no se ven sino claveles amarillos, sangre de toro, o de un rosa tan encendido como las nubes a la puesta del sol: las emanaciones de toda esta clavelería no consiguen vencer el olor a aceite frito de

or a short jacket, he must be a servant on duty, a temporary clerk, a grocer's boy, a poor student or a lackey without a job who was taking a day of rest and merriment. That is why, on the way up the hill where carriages can no longer go, when Pacheco and I got out of the berlin, the contrast made us look like an archduke and archduchess who, tempted by curiosity, go round a popular festival, eager to remain incognito but betrayed by their elegant appearance.

Because of its novelty the spectacle amused me. That pilgrimage is nothing like those in my region, which are usually celebrated in cool spots shaded by chestnut or walnut trees, with a fountain or brook very close by and the sanctuary on the next hill... Saint Isidro's field is a series of bare hills, a dusty desert invaded by a crowd of people amongst whom not a single peasant can be seen; just soldiers, loose women, blacksmiths, a mischievous and vulgar crew. And, instead of vegetation, hundreds of sheds and stalls selling knick-knacks which, after the day of the fair, cannot be seen again anywhere: whistles adorned with silver paper and amazing roses; virgins daubed with emerald, cobalt and vermilion; equally gaudy medals and scapularies; crockery and earthenware; coarsely made figures of bullfighters and picadors; strangely shaped jugs with spouts and handles; rag dolls and puppets with the heads of Martos, Sagasta or Castelar;[21] two-a-penny ministers; sculptures of Gran Vía[22] thieves; and next to the effigy of the blessed Saint Isidro some figures that... Good Lord! Let's pretend we didn't see them!

Apart from the sun which melts your brains and the dust which gets in your mouth, so many bright, metallic colours are enough to make you dizzy. If I carry on looking my eyes will hurt. The pyramids of oranges look like fire; the dates shine like dark garnets, the roasted chickpeas and peanuts like gold nuggets. In the flower stalls all you can see are yellow, blood-red or rose carnations glowing like sunset clouds: the smell of all these carnations doesn't manage to overcome

---

21   Cristino Martos y Balbí (1830–93), Práxedes Mateo Sagasta (1825–1903) and Emilio Castelar (1832–99) were all famous politicians of the time.
22   The Gran Vía is one of Madrid's most famous streets. Starting at the Plaza de Alcalá and crossing the city to the Plaza de España, it has many shops, stores, hotels, banks, restaurants, bars, cinemas and theatres.

los buñuelos, que se pega a la garganta y produce un cosquilleo inaguantable. Lo dicho, aquí no hay color que no sea desesperado: el uniforme de los militares, los mantones de las chulas, el azul del cielo, el amarillento de la tierra, los tiovivos con listas coloradas y los columpios dados de almagre con rayas de añil ... Y luego la música, el rasgueo de las guitarras, el tecleo insufrible de los pianos mecánicos que nos aporrean los oídos con el paso doble de *Cádiz*, repitiendo desde treinta sitios de la romería: –¡*Vi-va España!*

Nadie imagine maliciosamente que se me había pasado lo de oír misa. Tratamos de romper por entre el gentío y de deslizarnos en la ermita, abierta de par en par a los devotos; pero estos eran tantos, y tan apiñados, y tan groseros, y tan mal olientes, que si porfío en llegar a la nave, me sacan de allí desmayada o difunta. Pacheco jugaba los brazos y los puños, según podía, para defenderme; sólo lograba que nos apretasen más y que oyésemos juramentos y blasfemias atroces. Le tiré de la manga.

–Vámonos, vámonos de aquí ... Renuncio ... No se puede.

Cuando ya salimos a atmósfera respirable, suspiré muy compungida:

–¡Ay, Dios mío! ... Sin misa hoy ...

–No se apure –me contestó mi acompañante–, que yo oiré por usted aunque sea todas las gregorianas ... Ya ajustaremos esa cuenta.

–A mí sí que me la ajustará el padre Urdax tan pronto me eche la vista encima –pensé para mis adentros, mientras me tentaba el hombro, donde había recibido un codazo feroz de uno de aquellos cafres.

the odour of fritters fried in oil, which sticks in your throat and produces an unbearable tickling sensation. As I've said, there is no colour here which isn't intense: the soldiers' uniforms, the lower-class women's shawls, the blue of the sky, the yellowish terrain, the roundabouts with brightly coloured strips, the red ochre swings with their bands of indigo... And then the music, the strumming of the guitars, the insufferable tapping of the player-pianos which bash our ears with the *paso doble de Cádiz*, repeating from thirty different stations of the pilgrimage: *Long live Spain!*

Let no one maliciously imagine that going to mass had slipped my mind. We tried to force a way through the crowd and slip into the Hermitage, wide open to the devout; but there were so many of them, so tightly packed and so vulgar and foul-smelling that if I'd insisted on reaching the nave they'd have brought me out either fainting or dead. Pacheco used his arms and fists to defend me as much as he could, but he only managed to get them to press against us more and for us to hear terrible cursing and swearing. I pulled him by the sleeve.

'Let's be off, let's be off from here ... I give up... It's impossible.'

When we were in a breathable atmosphere, I sighed with great remorse:

'My God! ... No mass today...'

'Don't worry,' my companion answered, 'I'll hear it on your behalf, even if that means all the Gregorian chants... We'll settle that score.'

'Yes, Father Urdax will settle it as soon as he sets eyes on me,' I thought to myself whilst I rubbed my shoulder where one of those brutes had elbowed me ferociously.

IV

Don Diego, que en el coche se me figuraba reservado y tristón, se volvió muy dicharachero desde que andábamos por San Isidro, justificando su fama de buena sombra. Sujetando bien mi brazo para que las mareas de gente no nos separasen, él no perdía ripio, y cada pormenor de los tinglados famosos le daba pretexto para un chiste, que muchas veces no era tal sino en virtud del tono y acento con que lo decía, porque es indudable que si se escribiesen las ocurrencias de los andaluces, no resultarían tan graciosas, ni la mitad, de lo que parecen en sus labios; al sonsonete, al ceceíllo y a la prontitud en responder, se debe la mayor parte del salero.

Lo peor fue que como allí no había más personas regulares que nosotros, y Pacheco se metía con todo el mundo y a todo el mundo daba cuerda, nos rodeó la canalla de mendigos, fenómenos, chiquillos harapientos, gitanas, buñoleras y vendedoras. El impulso de mi acompañante era comprar cuanto veía, desde los escapularios hasta los botijos, hasta que me cuadré.

4

Don Diego, who in the carriage had appeared reserved and downhearted to me, became very talkative as soon as we set foot in the Saint Isidro Fair, justifying his reputation for being nice and friendly. Holding my arm fast so the human tide wouldn't separate us, he didn't miss a trick, and every detail of the famous sheds provided him with a pretext for a joke, which often was only one by virtue of the tone and accent with which it was said, because it is undeniable that, written down, the witty remarks of Andalusians wouldn't be even half as funny as they sound, most of the wit being due to the mocking undertone, the little lisp and the speed of response.

The worst of it was that we were the only respectable people there, and as Pacheco teased and encouraged everyone, the mob of beggars, freaks, children dressed in rags, gypsies, fritter makers and vendors surrounded us. My companion's impulse was to buy everything he saw, from scapularies to earthenware drinking jugs, until I put my foot down.

–Si compra usted más, me enfado.

–¡Soniche! Sanacabao las compras. ¡Que sanacabao digo! Al que no me deje en paz, le doy en igual de dinero, cañaso. ¿Tiene usted más que mandar?

–Mire usted, pagaría por estar a la sombra un ratito.

–¿En la cárcel por comprometeora? Llamaremos a la pareja y verasté que pronto.

Ahora que reflexiono a sangre fría, caigo en la cuenta de que era bastante raro y muy inconveniente que a los tres cuartos de hora de pasearnos juntos por San Isidro nos hablásemos don Diego y yo con tanta broma y llaneza. Es posible, bien mirado, que mi paisano tenga razón; que aquel sol, aquel barullo y aquella atmósfera popular obren sobre el cuerpo y el alma como un licor o vino de los que más se suben a la cabeza, y rompan desde el primer momento la valla de reserva que trabajosamente levantamos las señoras un día y otro contra osadías peligrosas. De cualquier índole que fuese, yo sentía ya un principio de mareo cuando exclamé:

–En la cárcel estaría a gusto con tal que no hiciese sol … Me encuentro así … no sé cómo: parece que me desvanezco.

–Pero ¿se siente usted mala? ¿Mala? –preguntó Pacheco seriamente, con vivo interés.

–Lo que se dice mala, no: es una fatiga, una sofocación … Se me nubla la vista.

Echóse Pacheco a reír y me dijo casi al oído:

–Lo que usted tiene ya lo adivino yo, sin necesidad de ser sahorí … Usted tiene ni más ni menos que … gasusa.[14]

–¿Eh?

–Debilidad, hablando pronto … Y no es usted sola … yo hace rato que doy las boqueás de hambre. ¡Si debe de ser mediodía!

–Puede, puede que no se equivoque usted mucho. A estas horas suelen pasearse los ratoncitos por el estómago … Ya hemos visto el Santo; volvámonos a Madrid y podrá usted almorzar, si gusta acompañarme …

---

14 *Un zahorí*: una persona perspicaz que descubre o adivina lo que otras personas piensan o sienten. *La gazuza*: el hambre (ambas palabras pronunciadas con seseo andaluz).

'If you buy anything else, I'll get angry.'

'Silence! I've finished buyin'. Finished I say! The next one who doesn't leave me in peace, I'll pay the equivalent in fisticuffs. Have you any more orders?'

'Look, I'd pay to be in the shade for a while.'

'How about prison for a compromising situation? I'll call the pair o' Civil Guard officers on patrol and you'll soon see.'

Now that I think about it in the cold light of day, I realise that it was rather strange and very inappropriate that after strolling around Saint Isidro for three quarters of an hour Don Diego and I should be talking with such jocular familiarity. All things considered, it's possible that my compatriot is right: the sun and a tumultuous, lively atmosphere affect our body and soul like one of those spirits or wines that really go to the head, and immediately break down the barrier of reserve which we females painstakingly raise every day against dangerous audacity. Whatever the nature of it was, I was already feeling the beginning of that dizziness when I exclaimed:

'I'd be at home in prison as long as it wasn't sunny… I feel like … I don't know what. I feel like I'm fainting.'

'Do you feel bad? Really bad?' Pacheco asked seriously, with a lively interest.

'Bad, no. It's fatigue, a stifling sensation … I can't see clearly.'

Pacheco began to laugh and said in my ear:

'I can already guess what's wrong with you without havin' to be a mind reader… It's nothing more and nothing less than … famishment.'

'Eh?'

'Weakness, speaking plainly… And you're not the only one … I've been dyin' for food for a while. It must be midday!'

'Maybe, just maybe you're not far wrong. Hunger pangs are usual at this time of day… We've already seen the fair; let's go back to Madrid and you can have lunch, if you want to accompany me…'

–No señora ... Si eso que usted discurre es un pueblo. Si lo que vamos a haser es almorsá en una fondita de aquí. ¡Que las hay! ...

Se llevó los dedos apiñados a la boca y arrojó un beso al aire, para expresar la excelencia de las fondas de San Isidro.

Aturdida y todo como me encontraba, la idea me asustó: me pareció indecorosa, y vi de una ojeada sus dificultades y riesgos. Pero al mismo tiempo, allá en lo íntimo del alma, aquellos escollos me la hacían deliciosa, apetecible, como es siempre lo vedado y lo desconocido. ¿Era Pacheco algún atrevido, capaz de faltarme si yo no le daba pie? No, por cierto, y el no darle pie quedaba de mi cuenta. ¡Qué buen rato me perdía rehusando! ¿Qué diría Pardo de esta aventura si la supiese? Con no contársela ... Mientras discurría así, en voz alta me negaba terminantemente ... Nada, a Madrid de seguida.

Pacheco no cejó, y en vez de formalizarse, echó a broma mi negativa. Con mil zalamerías y agudezas, ceceando más que nunca, afirmó que espicharía de necesidad si tardase en almorzar arriba de veinte minutos.

–Que me pongo de rodillas aquí mismo ... –exclamaba el muy truhán–. Ea, un sí de esa boquita ... ¡Usted verá el gran armuerso del siglo! Fuera escrúpulos ... ¿Se ha pensao usted que mañana voy yo a contárselo a la señá duquesa de Sahagún? A este probetico ..., ¡una limosna de armuerso!

Acabó por entrarme risa y tuve la flaqueza de decir:

–Pero ... ¿y el coche, que está aguardando allá abajo?

–En un minuto se le avisa ... Que procure cochera aquí ... Y si no, que se vuelva a Madrid, hasta la puesta del sol ... Espere usted, buscaré alguno que lleve el recao ... No la he de dejar aquí solita pa que se la coma un lobo: eso sí que no.

Debió de oírlo un guindilla[15] que andaba por allí ejerciendo sus funciones, y en tono tan reverente y servicial como bronco lo usaba para intimar a la gentuza que se *desapartase*, nos dijo con afable sonrisa:

–Yo aviso si justan ... ¿Dónde está o coche?[16] ¿Cómo le llaman al cochero?

---

15   Agente de policía.

16   *Justan* (gustan): ejemplo del fenómeno fonológico de la *gheada* gallega; o coche (*el coche*): galleguismo en el empleo del artículo masculino.

'No, madam... This is a town you're wandering around. What we'll do is have lunch in a small restaurant here. There's enough of 'em!'

He pressed his fingers to his mouth and blew a kiss in the air to express the excellence of the Saint Isidro restaurants.

Totally bewildered as I was, the idea scared me: I thought it unseemly, and I could see in a glance the difficulties and risks. But at the same time, in the depths of my soul, those hidden dangers made it delightful and attractive to me, as what is forbidden and unknown always is. Was Pacheco some cheeky person capable of being rude to me if I didn't give him cause? Certainly not, and the business of not giving him cause was my responsibility. What a good time I should miss out on by refusing! What would Pardo say about this adventure if he knew? But if he's not told... Whilst I was thinking in this way, I refused out loud categorically... Nothing for it, back to Madrid immediately.

Pacheco didn't back down, and instead of becoming serious he joked about my refusal. With flattery and witticisms galore, lisping more than ever, he vowed he would die of hunger if lunch were delayed more than twenty minutes.

'I'll go down on my knees right here,' the big rogue exclaimed. 'Hey, a yes from that sweet mouth... You'll see the great lunch o' the century! Out with scruples... D'you think I'll tell the Duchess of Sahagún about it tomorrow? For this poor thing ... a late breakfast treat!'

I ended up laughing and I had the weakness to say:

'But ... what about the carriage that's waiting down there?'

'It'll only take a minute to notify him... For him to get a coach house here... And if not, for him to go back to Madrid until sunset ... Wait, I'll look for someone to take the message ... I can't leave you here on yer own to be eaten by a wolf. No way.'

A bobby who was carrying out his duties must have heard and, in a tone as reverent and obliging as it was gruff when ordering the riff-raff *to move out the way*, said to us with an affable smile:

'I'll take it if yous want... Where's de carriage? What's de coachman's name?'

–Éste no es de mi tierra, ni nada. ¿De qué parte de Galicia? – pregunté al agente.

–Desviado de Lujo tres légoas, a la banda de Sarria, para servir a vusté[17] –explicó él, y los ojos le brillaron de alegría al encontrarse con una paisana–. «¿Si éste me conocerá por conducto de la Diabla?» –pensé yo recelosa; pero mi temor sería infundado, pues el agente no añadió nada más. Para despacharle pronto, le expliqué:

–¿Ve aquella berlina con ruedas encarnadas ..., cochero mozo, con patillas, librea verde? Allá abajo ... Es la octava en la fila.

–Bien veo, bien.

–Pues va usted –ordenó Pachecho–, y le dice que se largue a Madrí con viento fresco, y que por la tardesita vuerva y se plantifique en el mismo lugar. ¿Estamos, compadre?

Noté que mi acompañante extendía la mano y estrechaba con gran efusión la del guindilla; pero no sería esta distinción lo que tanto le alegró la cara a mi conterráneo, pues le vi cerrar la diestra deslizándola en el bolsillo del pantalón, y entreoí la fórmula gallega clásica:

–De hoy en cien años.[18]

Libre ya del apéndice del carruaje, por instinto me apoyé más fuerte en el brazo de don Diego, y él a su vez estrechó el mío como ratificando un contrato.

–Vamos poquito a poco subiendo al cerro ... Ánimo y cogerse bien.

El sol campeaba en mitad del cielo, y vertía llamas y echaba chiribitas. El aire faltaba por completo: no se respiraba sino polvo arcilloso. Yo registraba el horizonte tratando de descubrir la prometida fonda, que siempre sería un techo, preservativo contra aquel calor del Senegal. Mas no se veía rastro de edificio grande en toda la extensión del cerro, ni antes ni después. Las únicas murallas blancas que distinguí a mi derecha eran las tapias de la Sacramental, a cuyo amparo descansaban los muertos sin enterarse de las locuras que del otro lado cometíamos los vivos. Amenacé a Pacheco con el palo de la sombrilla:

–¿Y esa fonda? ¿Se puede saber hasta qué hora vamos a andar buscándola?

---

17 *Lujo*: Lugo (otro ejemplo de la *gheada* gallega); *vusté*: castellanización del gallego *vostede* (usted).
18 Del gallego *De hoxe en cen anos*: que se repita otra vez dentro de cien años.

'Why, if he isn't from my region. Which part of Galicia?' I asked the policeman.

'Three leagues from Lugo in de area of Sarria, 'ere to serve yous,' he explained and his eyes sparkled with joy at finding himself with a fellow countrywoman. "What if he knows me through Diabla?" I thought with suspicion, but my fear would prove unfounded, because the policeman added nothing else. In order to get rid of him quickly, I said:

'You see that berlin with red wheels ... the young coachman with sideburns and green livery? Down there... It's the eighth in the line.'

'Yeah, I can see it clearly.'

'Well,' Pacheco ordered, 'go 'n' tell him to shoot off to Madrid, to come back towards evenin' and plant himself in the same place. Are we agreed?'

I noticed that my companion held out his hand and shook the policeman's hand effusively; but it couldn't have been this special consideration which cheered up my fellow countryman's face so much, for I saw him shut his right hand and slip it into his trouser pocket, and I half-heard the classic Galician formula:

'May it come about again widdin de next hundred years.'

Now we were free from the encumbrance of the carriage, I instinctively leaned more heavily on Don Diego's arm, and for his part he pressed mine, as if ratifying a contract.

'Let's make our way up the hill bit by bit... Come on, hold tight.'

The sun was encamped in the middle of the sky, pouring down flames and shooting forth rays of dazzling light. There was no breeze at all: the only thing to breathe in was clay-like dust. I scanned the horizon trying to find the promised inn, which would certainly be a roof, protection against that Senegalese heat. But no sign of a large building could be seen on the whole of the hill either behind or in front of us. The only white walls I could make out on my right were those of the Hermitage, in whose shelter the dead rested unaware of the follies committed by those of us living on the other side. I threatened Pacheco with the parasol handle:

'What about that inn? May I inquire how long we're going to wander round looking for it?'

–¿Fonda? –saltó Pacheco como si le sorprendiese mucho mi pregunta–. ¿Dijo usted fonda? El caso es ... Mardito si sé a qué lado cae.

–¡Hombre ..., pues de veras que tiene gracia! ¿No aseguraba usted que había fondas preciosas, magníficas? ¡Y me trae usted con tanta flema a asarme por estos vericuetos! Al menos entérese ... Pregunte a cualquiera, ¡al primero que pase!

–¡Oigasté[19] ... cristiano!

Volvióse un chulo de pelo alisado en peteneras, manos en los bolsillos de la chaquetilla, hocico puntiagudo, gorra alta de seda, estrecho pantalón y viciosa y pálida faz: el tipo perfecto del rata, de esos mocitos que se echa uno a temblar al verlos, recelando que hasta el modo de andar le timen.

–¿Hay por aquí alguna fonda, compañero? –interrogó Pacheco alargándole un buen puro.

–Se estima ... Como haber fondas, hay fondas: misté por ahí too alredor, que fondas son; pero tocante a fonda, vamos, según se ice, de comías finas, pa la gente e aquel, me pienso que no hallarán ustés conveniencia: digo, esto me lo pienso yo: ustés verán.

–No hay más que merenderos, está visto –pronunció Pacheco bajo y con acento pesaroso.

Al ver que él se mostraba disgustado, yo, por ese instinto de contradicción humorística que en situaciones tales se nos desarrolla a las mujeres, me manifesté satisfecha. Además, en el fondo, no me desagradaba comer en un merendero. Tenía más carácter. Era más nuevo e imprevisto, y hasta menos clandestino y peligroso. ¿Qué riesgo hay en comer en un barracón abierto por todos lados donde está entrando y saliendo la gente? Es tan inocente como tomar un vaso de cerveza en un café al aire libre.

---

19 Vulgarismo de *Oiga usted.*

'Inn?' said Pacheco suddenly as if my question greatly surprised him. 'Did you say inn? The fact is … I'll be damned if I know where it is.'

'Why … you certainly are a funny man! Didn't you assure me that there were lovely, magnificent inns? And you bring me so casually to roast round these rough tracks! At least find out… Ask someone, the first passer-by!'

''Scuse me, pal!'

A working-class Madrilenian with hair smoothed out into waves, hands in pockets, pointed mouth, high silk cap, tight trousers and a vicious, pallid face turned round: the perfect example of a thief, one of those youngsters who make you tremble when you see them, fearing that even their way of walking will swindle you.

'Are there any inns round here, mate?' Pacheco asked, handing him a good cigar.

'Much appreciated… As for inns, yeah there are inns: look all round 'ere, they're inns. But regarding the inn, let's see, according to what they say about gourmet food, for refined people, I don't think mesen you'll find aught suitable. That's what I think: you'll see.'

'There's only open-air cafés, that's clear,' stated Pacheco in a low voice and with a remorseful accent.

On seeing him upset, I showed myself, with that instinct of humorous contradiction which women develop in these situations, to be satisfied. Moreover, deep down, eating at an open-air café didn't displease me. It had more character. It was newer and more unexpected, and even less clandestine and dangerous. What risk is there eating in a tent that is open on every side and with people coming and going? It's as innocent as having a glass of beer outside at a café.

V

Convencidos ya de que no existía fonda ni sombra de ella, o de que nosotros no acertábamos a descubrirla, miramos a nuestro alrededor, eligiendo el merendero menos indecente y de mejor trapío. Casi en lo alto del cerro campeaba uno bastante grande y aseado; no ostentaba ningún rótulo extravagante, como los que se leían en otros merenderos próximos, verbigracia: –«Refrescos de los que usava el Santo» –«La mar en vevidas y comidas» –«La Brillantez: callos y caracoles». A la entrada (que puerta no la tenía) hallábase de pie una chica joven, de fisonomía afable, con un puñal de níquel atravesado en el moño: y no había otra alma viviente en el merendero, cuyas seis mesas vacías me parecieron muy limpias y fregoteadas. Pudiera compararse el barracón a una inmensa tienda de campaña: las paredes de lona: el techo de unas esteras tendidas sobre palos: dividíase en tres partes desiguales, la menor ocultando la hornilla y el fogón donde guisaban, la grande que formaba el comedor, la mediana que venía a ser una trastienda donde se lavaban platos y cubiertos; pero estos misterios convinimos en que sería mejor no profundizarlos mucho, si habíamos de almorzar. El piso del merendero era de greda amarilla, la misma greda de todo el árido cerro: y una vieja sucia y horrible que frotaba con un estropajo las mesas, no necesitaba sino bajarse para encontrar la materia primera de aquel aseo inverosímil.

Tomamos posesión de la mesa del fondo, sentándonos en un banco de madera que tenía por respaldo la pared de lona del barracón. La muchacha, con su perrera pegada a la frente por grandes churretazos de goma y su puñal de níquel en el moño, acudió solícita a ver qué mandábamos: olfateaba parroquianos gordos, y acaso adivinaba o presentía otra cosa, pues nos dirigió unas sonrisitas de inteligencia que me pusieron colorada. Decía a gritos la cara de la chica: –«Buen par están estos dos … ¿Qué manía les habrá dado de venir a arrullarse en el Santo? Para eso más les valía quedarse en su nido … que no les faltará de seguro»–. Yo, que leía semejantes pensamientos en los ojos de la muy entremetida, adopté una actitud reservada y digna, hablando a Pacheco como se habla a un amigo íntimo, pero *amigo* a

5

Now convinced that the inn didn't exist, nor anything that resembled it, or that we wouldn't manage to find it, we looked around and chose the least filthy and most salubrious open-air café. A fairly large, clean one was positioned almost at the top of the hill; it displayed none of the absurd signs that could be seen in other nearby open-air cafés, for example: "Our Saint's favouritest refreshments", "A sea of beveridges and food", "Speciality: tripe and snails". At the entrance (there was no door) a young, pleasant-faced girl was standing with a nickel stiletto through her bun: and there was no other living soul in the open-air café, whose six empty tables seemed very clean and scrubbed to me. The stall could be compared to a huge tent: the canvas walls, the roof formed of pieces of matting stretched over sticks. It was divided into three unequal parts, the smallest hiding the hob and stove where they cooked, the large one which was the dining room, the medium-sized one a backroom where plates and dishes were washed. But we agreed it would be best not to delve too deeply into these mysteries if we were to have lunch. The café floor was made of yellow sand, the same sand as on the whole arid hill: and a horrible, dirty old woman who was scrubbing the tables with a scouring pad only had to bend down to find the raw material for that unbelievable cleanliness.

We took the table at the far end, sitting down on a wooden bench which had the canvas wall of the tent as its back. The girl, with her fringe stuck to her forehead with globs of gel and the nickel stiletto in her bun, came over attentively to take our order. She sniffed out important customers, and maybe guessed or had a hunch of something else, for she gave us some little knowing smiles which made me blush. The girl's face cried out: "A nice pair these two make... What folly could have induced them to come billing and cooing at Saint Isidro? They'd have been better off staying in their nest for that ... they're bound to have one". Reading thoughts like these in the busybody's eyes, I adopted a reserved and dignified air, speaking to Pacheco as

secas; precaución que lejos de desorientar a la maliciosa muchacha, creo que sólo sirvió para abrirle más los ojos. Nos dirigió la consabida pregunta:

–¿Qué van a tomar?

–¿Qué nos puede usted dar? –contestó Pacheco–. Diga usted lo que hay, resalada …, y la señora irá escogiendo.

–Como haber …, hay de todo. ¿Quieren almorzar formalmente?

–Con toa formaliá.

–Pues de primer plato … una tortillita … o huevos revueltos.

–Vaya por los huevos revueltos. ¿Y hay magras?

–¿Unas magritas de jamón? Sí.

–¿Y chuletas?

–De ternera, muy ricas.

–¿Pescado?

–Pescado no … Si quieren latas … tenemos escabeche de besugo, sardinas …

–¿Ostras no?

–Como ostras …, no señora. Aquí pocas cosas finas se pueden despachar. Lo general que piden … callos y caracoles, Valdepeñas, chuletas.

–Usted resolverá –indiqué volviéndome a Pacheco.

–¿He de ser yo? Pues tráiganos de too eso que hemos dicho, niña bonita …, huevos, magras, ternera, lata de sardinas … ¡Ay!, y lo primero de too se va usted a traer por los aires una boteya e mansaniya y unas cañitas … Y aseitunas.

–Y después … ¿qué es lo que les he de servir? ¿Las chuletas antes de nada?

–No: misté,[20] azucena: nos sirve usted los huevos, luego el jamón, las sardinas, las chuletitas … De postre, si hay algún queso …

–¡Ya lo creo que sí! De Flandes y de Villalón … Y pasas, y almendras, y rosquillas y avellanas tostás …

–Pues vamos a armorsá mejor que el Nuncio.

Esto mismo que exclamó Pacheco frotándose las manos, lo pensaba yo. Aquellas ordinarieces, como diría mi paisano el filósofo, me abrían

---

20   De *mire usted* (madrileñismo).

you speak to a close friend, but solely a *friend*; a precaution, I believe, which, far from baffling the sly girl, only served to open her eyes wider. She asked us the usual question:

'What would you like?'

'What can you offer us?' Pacheco answered. 'Say what there is, sweetheart ... and the lady will choose.'

'What there is ... there's everything. Do you want a proper meal?'

'Yeah, good 'n' proper.'

'Right, for the first course ... a Spanish omelette ... or scrambled eggs.'

'Let's go with scrambled eggs. And have you got any rashers of bacon?'

'Sliced ham? Yes.'

'And chops?'

'Veal, very tasty.'

'Fish?'

'Not fresh fish... If you want canned ... we've got pickled sea bream, sardines...'

'No oysters?'

'As for oysters ... no, madam. We can't serve many good quality things here. People usually order ... tripe and snails, Valdepeñas wine, chops.'

'You can decide,' I instructed, turning to Pacheco.

'Does it have to be me? Well then, bring us everything we've said, my little charmer ... eggs, ham, veal, tin of sardines... Ay! and first of all you can quickly bring a bottle o' *manzanilla* 'n' some small glasses... And olives.'

'And now ... what shall I serve you? The chops first of all?'

'No. Look, me flower. Serve us the eggs, then the ham, the sardines, the chops... For dessert, if there's any cheese...'

'I should think so! From Flanders and Villalón...[23] And raisins and almonds and ring-shaped pastries and roasted hazelnuts...'

'Well our lunch'll be better than the pope's.'

I was thinking the very same thing that Pacheco exclaimed rubbing his hands. That common fare, as my compatriot the philosopher would

---

23   A municipality located in the province of Valladolid, Castile and León region.

el apetito de par en par. Y aumentaba mi buena disposición de ánimo el encontrarme a cubierto del terrible sol.

Verdad que estaba a cubierto lo mismo que el que sale al campo a las doce del día bajo un paraguas. El sol, si no podía ensañarse con nuestros cráneos, se filtraba por todas partes y nos envolvía en un baño abrasador. Por entre las esteras mal juntas del techo, al través de la lona, y sobre todo, por el abierto frente de la tienda, entraban a oleadas, a torrentes, no sólo la luz y el calor del astro, sino el ruido, el oleaje del humano mar, los gritos, las disputas, las canciones, las risotadas, los rasgueos y punteos de guitarra y vihuela, el infernal paso doble, el *¡Viva España!* de los duros pianos mecánicos.

Casi al mismo punto en que la chica del puñal de níquel depositaba en la mesa una botella rotulada *Manzanilla superior*, dos cañas del vidrio más basto y dos conchas con rajas de salchichón y aceitunas *aliñás*, se coló por la abertura una mujer desgreñada, cetrina, con ojos como carbones, saya de percal con almidonados faralaes y pañuelo de crespón de lana desteñido y viejo, que al cruzarse sobre el pecho dejaba asomar la cabeza de una criatura. La mujer se nos plantó delante, fija la mano izquierda en la cadera y accionando con la derecha: de qué modo se sostenía el chiquillo, es lo que no entiendo.

–En er nombre e Dios, Pare, Jijo y Epíritu Zanto, que donde va er nombre e Dios no va cosa mala. Una palabrita les voy a icir, que lase a ostés mucha farta saberla …

–¡Calle! –grité yo contentísima–. ¡Una gitana que nos va a decir la buenaventura!

–¿Le mando que se largue? ¿La incomoda a usted?

–¡Al contrario! Si me divierte lo que no es imaginable. Verá usted cuántos enredos va a echar por esa boca. Ea, la buenaventura pronto, que tengo una curiosidad inmensa de oírla.

–Pué diñe osté la mano erecha, jermosa, y una moneíta de plata pa jaser la crú.

Pacheco le alargó una peseta, y al mismo tiempo, habiendo descorchado la manzanilla y pedido otra caña, se la tendió llena de vino a la egipcia. Con este motivo armaron los dos un tiroteo de agudezas y bromas; bien se conocía que eran hijos de la misma tierra,

say, made me more and more hungry. And my good humour increased on finding myself sheltered from the terrible sun.

It's true that anyone going out into the country at midday under an umbrella was sheltered just as much. The sun, if it couldn't torment our skulls, filtered through on every side and covered us in a scorching bath. Coming in waves and torrents through the badly joined mats of the roof, the canvas and especially the open entrance, was not only the light and heat from the sun, but also the noise, the swell of the human sea, the shouts, disputes, songs, loud laughter, the strumming and plucking of guitar and viols, the infernal *paso doble*, the *Long live Spain!* of the harsh mechanical pianos.

At almost the same moment that the girl with the stiletto was placing on the table a bottle labelled *Manzanilla superior*, two cheap little glasses and two slices of salami-style sausage and *seasoned* olives, there slipped through the opening a dishevelled, sallow woman with eyes like pieces of coal, a percale skirt with starched ruffles and an old, faded wool crepe shawl with a child's head poking out where it crossed her breast. The woman planted herself in front of us, her left hand on her hip and gesturing with her right. How the child was supported I'll never know.

'In ve name o' ve Farver, Thon 'n' 'Oly Thpirit, that wherever ve name o' God goes nuffink evil can go. I'm gonna tell you thummat what you really need to know…'

'Listen,' I shouted full of joy. 'A gypsy who's going to tell our fortune!'

'Shall I tell her to clear off? Is she bothering you?'

'On the contrary! You can't imagine how much she amuses me. You'll see what mischief and nonsense come out of that mouth. Hey, a quick fortune telling, I'm dying to hear it.'

'Well give us yer right 'and, me pretty un, 'n' cross me palm wiv silver.'

Pacheco handed her a peseta, and at the same time, having uncorked the *manzanilla* and asked for another glass, he held it out full of wine to the Egyptian lady.[24] For this reason the two of them began an exchange of witticisms and jokes; it was easy to see that they

---

24 It was believed that the gypsies originated from Egypt.

y que ni a uno ni a otro se les atascaban las palabras en el gaznate, ni se les agotaba la labia aunque la derramasen a torrentes. Al fin la gitana se embocó el contenido de la cañita, y yo la imité, porque, con la sed, tentaba aquel vinillo claro. ¡Manzanilla superior! ¡A cualquier cosa llaman *superior* aquí! La manzanilla dichosa sabía a esparto, a piedra alumbre y a demonios coronados; pero como al fin era un líquido, y yo con el calor estaba para beberme el Manzanares entero, no resistí cuando Pacheco me escanció otra caña. Sólo que en vez de refrescarme, se me figuró que un rayo de sol, disuelto en polvo, se me introducía en las venas y me salía en chispas por los ojos y en arreboles por la faz. Miré a Pacheco muy risueña, y luego me volví confusa, porque él me pagó la mirada con otra más larga de lo debido.

–¡Qué bonitos ojos azules tiene este perdis! –pensaba yo para mí.

El gaditano estaba sin sombrero; vestía un traje ceniza, elegante, de paño rico y flexible; de vez en cuando se enjugaba la frente sudorosa con un pañuelo fino, y a cada movimiento se le descomponía el pelo, bastante crecido, negro y sedoso; al reír, le iluminaba la cara la blancura de sus dientes, que son de los mejor puestos y más sanos que he visto nunca, y aún parecía doblemente morena su tez, o mejor dicho, doblemente tostada, porque hacia la parte que ya cubre el cuello de la camisa se entreveía un cutis claro.

–La mano, jermosa –repitió la gitana.

Se la alargué y ella la agarró haciéndomela tener abierta. Pacheco contemplaba las dos manos unidas.

–¡Qué contraste! –murmuró en voz baja, no como el que dice una galantería a una señora, sino como el que hace una reflexión entre sí.

En efecto, sin vanidad, tengo que reconocer que la mano de la gitana, al lado de la mía, parecía un pedazo de cecina feísimo: la tumbaga de plata, donde resplandecía una esmeralda falsa espantosa, contribuía a que resaltase el color cobrizo de la garra aquella, y claro está que mi diestra, que es algo chica, pulida y blanca, con anillos de perlas, zafiros y brillantes, contrastaba extrañamente. La buena de la bohemia empezó a hacer sus rayas y ensalmos, endilgándonos una retahíla de esas que no comprometen, pues son de doble sentido y se aplican a cualquier circunstancia, como las respuestas de los oráculos. Todo muy recalcado con los ojos y el ademán.

were children of the same soil, that words didn't get stuck in either of their throats, nor did they run out of smooth talk even if it spilt out in torrents. Finally the gipsy swallowed the contents of her small glass, and I followed suit because that clear liquid was tempting my thirsty lips. Manzanilla Superior! They call anything *superior* here. The blessed *manzanilla* tasted of esparto grass, of alum, devilishly bad; but as, after all, it was a liquid, and with the heat I was ready to drink up the whole River Manzanares, I didn't resist when Pacheco poured me another glass. But instead of feeling refreshed, it seemed like a pulverised sunbeam had entered my veins and was coming out of my eyes in sparks and my cheeks in a red glow. I looked at Pacheco with a big smile, and then became confused, for he repaid my glance with one that was longer than necessary.

'What lovely blue eyes this rake has got,' I thought to myself.

He wasn't wearing a hat, just an elegant, ash-coloured suit of rich, soft cloth. From time to time he wiped his moist forehead with a fine handkerchief, and every movement he made disarranged his longish, silky black hair; when he laughed his white teeth, which are the amongst the most even, healthiest looking I've ever seen, lit up his face, and his complexion seemed twice as dark, or rather twice as sunburnt, because pale skin was visible near the part the shirt collar covers.

'Yer 'and, me pretty un,' repeated the gypsy.

I held it out to her and she grabbed it to make me hold it open. Pacheco looked at the two joined hands.

'What a contrast!' he murmured, not like a man complimenting a lady, but like one talking to himself.

Indeed, vanity apart, I must admit that next to mine the gypsy's hand looked like a very ugly lump of cured meat: her silver ring sparkling with a hideous false emerald helped make the coppery colour of her paw stand out, and with its pearl, sapphire and diamond rings my right hand, which is rather small, well cared for and white, certainly made a strange contrast. The good old Bohemian began with palm lines and incantations, making us listen to a series of those predictions that make no commitments, because they have double meanings and apply to all circumstances, like oracles. Everything well emphasised with the eyes and gestures.

–Una cosa diquelo[21] yo en esta manica, que hae suseder mu pronto, y nadie saspera que susea … Un viaje me vasté a jaser, y no ae ser para má, que ae ser pa sastisfasión e toos … Una carta me vasté a resibir, y lae alegrá lo que viene escribío en eya … Unas presonas me tiene usté que la quieren má, y están toas perdías por jaserle daño; pero der revé les ae salir la perra intensión … Una presoniya está chalaíta por usté (al llegar aquí la bruja clavó en Pacheco las ascuas encendidas de sus ojos) y un convite le ae dar quien bien la quiere … Amorosica de genio me es usté; pero cuando se atufa, una leona brava de los montes se me güerve … Que no la enriten a usté y que le yeven toiticas las cosas ar pelo de la suavidá, que por la buena, corasón tiene usté pa tirarse en metá e la bahía e Cadis … Con mieles y no con hieles me la han de engatusar a usté … Un cariñiyo me vasté a tener mu guardadico en su pechito y no lo ae sabé ni la tierra, que secretica me es usté como la piedra e la sepultura … También una cosa le igo y es que usté mesma no me sabe lo que en ese corasonsiyo está guardao … Un cachito e gloria le va a caer der sielo y pasmáa se quedará usté; que a la presente me está usté como los pajariyos, que no saben el árbol onde han de ponerse …

Si la dejamos creo que aún sigue ahora ensartando tonterías. A mí su parla me entretenía mucho, pues ya se sabe que en esta clase de vaticinios tan confusos y tan latos, siempre hay algo que responde a nuestras ideas, esperanzas y aspiraciones ocultas. Es lo mismo que cuando, al tiempo de jugar a los naipes, vamos corriéndolos para descubrir sólo la pinta, y adivinamos o presentimos de un modo vago la carta que va a salir. Pacheco me miraba atentamente, aguardando a que me cansase de gitanerías para despedir a la profetisa. Viendo que ya la chica del puñal en el moño acudía con la fuente de huevos revueltos, solté la mano, y mi acompañante despachó a la gitana, que antes de poner pies en polvorosa aún pidió no sé qué para *er churumbeliyo*.[22]

Empezábamos a servirnos del apetitoso comistrajo y a descorchar una botella de jerez, cuando otro cuerpo asomó en la abertura de la tienda, se adelantó hacia la mesa y recitó la consabida jaculatoria:

---

21 Veo, miro (gitanismo).
22 Niñito (gitanismo).

'One fing I can dik in vis teeny 'and, somefin'ut'll 'appen real soon, and nobody 'spects it'll 'appen… Yer gonna take a trip, and it'll turn out cushty, it's gonna be to ev'ryone's satisfaction… Yer gonna ge' a letter, and what's wrote in it'll make ya 'appy… Certain people wish ya ill and they're all misguided in veir wish to 'urt ya, but veir evil intentions'll come back to 'aunt 'em… Someone's 'ead over 'eels in love wiv ya' (when she got to this topic, the witch fixed the burning embers of her eyes on Pacheco) 'and someone who loves ya very much is gonna give ya an invitation… You've a gentle nature, but when ya ge' angry, ya turn into a wild mountain lioness… Ya mus' not be irritated and all fings mus' be carried out delicately since you've a temperament vat'd make ya frow yousen in ve middle o' ve Bay o' Cádiz… Ya mus' be coaxed wiv 'oney and not wiv bile… Yer 'idin' affectionate feelins in yer breast and nobody knows aught about it, a teeny secret, yer as silent as a tombstone … I'll tell ya anovver fing too, you yousen dunno what yer keepin' guarded in vat teeny 'eart o' yours… Summat spectacular from ve 'eavens'll fall upon ya and you'll be amazed; currently yer like ve teeny birds vat don't know which tree to settle on…'

I believe she'd still be reeling off her nonsense if we'd let her. Her chatter amused me greatly, because, as we all know, in these vague, lengthy predictions there is always something which responds to our own hidden feelings, hopes and aspirations. It's the same when, as we're about to play cards, we go through them in order to discover the suit, and we guess or foresee in a vague way which card will come up. Pacheco watched me attentively, ready to dismiss the prophetess the moment her talk wearied me. Seeing that the girl with the nickel stiletto was now bringing the scrambled eggs, I pulled my hand away and my companion sent the gypsy off, who before scarpering still asked for a certain something for *me li'le chava*.

We were beginning to serve ourselves the appetising medley of dishes and uncork a bottle of sherry when another figure appeared at the entrance, approached our table and recited the usual short prayer:

–En er nombre e Dió Pare, Jijo y Epíritu Zanto, que onde va er nombre e Dió ...

–¡Estamos frescos! –gritó Pacheco–. ¡Gitana nueva!

–Claro –murmuró con aristocrático desdén la chica del merendero–. Como a la otra le han dado cuartos y vino, se ha corrido la voz ... Y tendrán aquí a todas las de la romería.

Pacheco alargó a la recién venida unas monedas y un vaso de Jerez.

–Bébase usté eso a mi salú ..., y andar con Dios, y najensia.

–E que les igo yo la buenaventura e barde ... por el aqué de la sal der mundo que van ustés derramando.

–No, no ... –exclamé yo casi al oído de Pacheco–. Nos va a encajar lo mismo que la otra; con una vez basta. Espántela usted ... sin reñirla.

–Bébase usté el Jerés, prenda ... y najarse he dicho –ordenó el gaditano sin enojo alguno, con campechana franqueza. La gitana, convencida de que no sacaba más raja ya, después de echarse al coleto el jerez y limpiarse la boca en el dorso de la mano, se largó con su indispensable *churumbeliyo*, que lo traía también escondido en el mantón como gusano en queso.

–¿Tienen todas su chiquitín? –pregunté a la muchacha.

–Todas, pues ya se ve –explicó ella con tono de persona desengañada y experta–. Valientes maulas están. Los chiquillos son tan suyos como de una servidora de ustedes. Infelices, los alquilan por ahí a otras bribonas, y sabe Dios el trato que les dan. Y está la romería plagada de estas tunantas, embusteronas. Lástima de Abanico.[23]

–¿Ustedes duermen aquí? –la dije por tirarle de la lengua–. ¿No tienen miedo a que de noche les roben las ganancias del día o la comida del siguiente?

–Ya se ve que dormimos con un ojo cerrado y otro abierto ... Porque no se crea usted: nosotros tenemos un café a la salida de la Plaza Mayor y venimos aquí no más a poner el ambigú.[24]

Comprendí que la chica se daba importancia, deseando probarme que era, socialmente, muy superior a aquella gentecilla de poco

---

23 Se refiere a la cárcel Modelo de Madrid, construida sobre planta de abanica. Inaugurada en 1884, fue la principal prisión de Madrid durante el último cuarto del siglo XIX y primera mitad del XX.

24 Sitio en las fiestas donde se sirven cosas de comer y beber (galicismo).

'In ve name o' ve Farver, Thon 'n' 'Oly Thpirit, vat wherever ve name o' God goes…'

'We're in a fine pickle,' shouted Pacheco. 'Another gypsy!'

'Of course,' muttered the girl from the café with aristocratic disdain. 'You gave money and wine to the other, so the word's spread… You'll have the whole lot from the fair here.'

Pacheco passed the newcomer some coins and a glass of sherry.

'Drink that to my health … God be with you, and scarper.'

'I'll tell yer fortunes for free … 'cos yuv showed yousens to be ve salt o' ve earff.'

'No, no…', I almost cried out in Pacheco's ear. 'She'll come out with the same as the other one. Once is enough. Scare her away … without reprimanding her.'

'Drink the sherry, sweetheart … and scarper I said,' ordered the man from Cádiz, not in anger but with good-natured frankness. After drinking the sherry and wiping her mouth with the back of her hand, the gypsy, convinced that she wasn't going to get anything else, made off with the indispensable *li'le chava* she too was carrying hidden in her shawl like a worm in cheese.

'Have they all got their little one?' I asked the girl.

'All of them, as you can see,' she explained with the tone of one who knew it all. 'What cheats they are. The little ones are as much theirs as they are mine. The wretches, they hire them from other tramps, and God knows how they treat them. The fair is plagued with these crooks, these imposters. Shameful jailbirds.'

'Do you live here?' I said to get her talking. 'Aren't you afraid they'll rob today's earnings and tomorrow's food?'

'You can see that we sleep with one eye closed and the other open… Don't you believe it, we've got a café just off the Plaza Mayor and we come here just to lay the buffet.'

I realised that the girl was giving herself airs, wishing to prove that socially she was far superior to that contemptible rabble that

más o menos que andaba por los demás figones. A todo esto íbamos despachando la ración de huevos revueltos y nos disponíamos a emprenderla con las magras. Interceptó la claridad de la abertura otra sombra. Ésta era una chula de mantón terciado, peina de bolas, brazos desnudos, que traía en un jarro de loza un inmenso haz de rosas y claveles, murmurando con voz entre zalamera y dolorida: −«¡Señoritico! ¡Cómpreme usté flores pa osequiar a esa buena moza!»−. Al mismo tiempo que la florera, entraron en el merendero cuatro soldados, cuatro húsares jóvenes y muy bulliciosos, que tomaron posesión de una mesa pidiendo cerveza y gaseosa, metiendo ruido con los sables y regocijando la vista con su uniforme amarillo y azul. ¡Válgame Dios, y qué virtud tan rara tienen la manzanilla y el jerez, sobre todo cuando están encabezados y compuestos! Si en otra ocasión me veo yo almorzando así, entre soldados, creo que me da un soponcio; pero empezaba a tener subvertidas las nociones de la corrección y de la jerarquía social, y hasta me hizo gracia semejante compañía y la celebré con la risa más alegre del mundo. Pacheco, al observar mi buen humor, se levantó y fue a ofrecer a los húsares jerez y otros obsequios; de suerte que no sólo comíamos con ellos en el mismo bodegón, sino que fraternizábamos.

Cuando está uno de buen temple, ninguna cosa le disgusta. Alabé la comida; de la chula de los claveles dije que parecía un boceto de Sala; y entonces Pacheco sacó de la jarra las flores y me las echó en el regazo, diciendo: −«Póngaselas usted todas»−. Así lo ejecuté, y quedó mi pecho convertido en búcaro. Luego me hizo reír con toda mi alma una desvergonzada riña que se oyó por detrás de la pared de lona, y las ocurrencias de Pacheco que se lió con los húsares no recuerdo con qué motivo. Volvió a nublarse el sol que entraba por la abertura y apareció un pordiosero de lo más remendado y haraposo. No contento con aflojar buena limosna, Pacheco le dio palique largo, y el mendigo nos contó aventuras de su vida: una sarta de embustes, por supuesto. Oyóle el gaditano muy atentamente, y luego empezó a exigirle que trajese un guitarrillo y se cantase por lo más jondo. El pobre juraba y

wandered around the other cheap restaurants. Meanwhile we were disposing of the portion of scrambled eggs and about to attack the ham. Another shadow darkened the doorway. It was a bare-armed girl with a shawl across her chest and a decorative hairpin ball, carrying a huge bundle of roses and carnations in an earthenware jug, murmuring in a voice somewhere between flattering and pained: "Young sir! Buy some flowers to give this good lady!" At the same time as the flower vendor, four soldiers entered the café, four young, boisterous hussars grabbing a table and ordering beer and soda water, causing a stir with their sabres, their blue and yellow uniforms a joy to behold. Good heavens, what strange virtue dwells in *manzanilla* and sherry, especially when they are fortified and mixed! If I found myself at any other time breakfasting like this with soldiers I think I'd have a fit; but my notions of propriety and social hierarchy were beginning to be overturned, and company like this even gave me pleasure, and I rejoiced with the happiest laughter in the world. Observing my good humour, Pacheco got up and offered the hussars sherry and other gifts, in such a way that we were not only eating with them in the same tavern, but also fraternising with them.

When you're in a good mood nothing upsets you. I praised the food, said the girl with the carnations looked like a Sala sketch;[25] whereupon Pacheco took the flowers out of the jar and threw them in my lap, saying: "Put all of them on you!" I did this and my chest became a vase. After that I laughed with all my heart at a shameless quarrel which could be heard from behind the canvas wall, and at Pacheco's witty remarks as he got involved with the hussars for some reason I cannot recall. The sunlight coming through the doorway clouded over again and a beggar patched up in rags appeared. Not content with forking out generous alms, Pacheco chattered at length with him, and the beggar told us stories from his life: a pack of lies, of course. The man from Cádiz listened to him attentively, and then began to insist that he fetch a little four-stringed guitar and sing the deepest, most serious *jondo*. The poor thing swore over and over that

---

25 A reference to the Spanish painter Emilio Sala (1850–1910), author of *Gramática del color* (1906). Another example of the author's penchant for inserting artistic references into her novels.

perjuraba que no sabía sino unas coplillas, pero sin música, y al fin le soltamos, bajo palabra de que nos traería un buen cantaor y tocador de bandurria para que nos echase polos y peteneras hasta morir. Por fortuna hizo la del humo.

Yo, a todo esto, más divertida que en un sainete, y dispuesta a entenderme con las chuletas y el Champagne. Comprendía, sí, que mis pupilas destellaban lumbre y en mis mejillas se podía encender un fósforo; pero lejos de percibir el atolondramiento que suponía precursor de la embriaguez, sólo experimentaba una animación agradabilísima, con la lengua suelta, los sentidos excitados, el espíritu en volandas y gozoso el corazón. Lo que más me probaba que *aquello* no era cosa alarmante era que comprendía la necesidad de guardar en mis dichos y modales cierta reserva de buen gusto; y en efecto la guardaba, evitando toda palabra o movimiento que siendo inocente pudiese parecer equívoco, sin dejar por eso de reír, de elogiar los guisos, de mostrarme jovial, en armonía con la situación ... Porque allí, vamos, convengan ustedes en ello, también sería muy raro estar como si me hubiese tragado el molinillo.

he only knew a few little songs, but without music, and in the end we let him go with his word that he would fetch us a good singer and *bandurria* player so that he could give us popular Andalusian tunes to our heart's content. Fortunately, he vanished into thin air.

All this entertained me more than a one-act comedy, and disposed me to do full justice to the chops and champagne. I realised that my eyes were throwing out fire, and that you could light a match on my cheeks; but far from perceiving the bewilderment which I supposed preceded intoxication, I felt a highly agreeable animation, with my tongue loosened, my senses excited, my wit quickened and my heart full of joy. The biggest proof for me that it wasn't anything to be alarmed about was that I understood the necessity of maintaining a tasteful discretion in my speech and manners; and indeed I maintained it, avoiding every innocent word or movement which might appear equivocal, without stopping my laughter, praising the dishes, showing myself jovial, in keeping with the occasion... For, after all, you must agree, it would also be very odd to be too stiff in my demeanour and actions.

VI

Pacheco, por su parte, me llevaba la corriente; cuidaba de que nunca estuviesen vacíos mi vaso ni mi plato, y ajustaba su humor al mío con tal esmero, cual si fuese un director de escena encargado de entretener y hacer pasar el mejor rato posible a un príncipe. ¡Ay! Porque eso sí: tengo que rendirle justicia al grandísimo truhán, y una vez que me encuentro a solas con mi conciencia, reconocer que, animado, oportuno, bromista y (admitamos la terrible palabra) en *juerga* redonda conmigo, como se encontraba al fin y al cabo Pacheco, ni un dicho libre, ni una acción descompuesta o siquiera familiar llegó a permitirse. En ocasión tan singular y crítica, hubiera sido descortesía y atrevimiento lo que en otra mero galanteo o *flirtación* (como dicen los ingleses). Esto lo entendía yo muy bien, aun entonces, y a la verdad, temía cualquiera de esas insinuaciones impertinentes que dejan a una mujer volada y le estropean el mejor rato. Sin la caballerosa delicadeza de Pacheco, aquella situación en que impremeditadamente me había colocado pudo ser muy ridícula para mí. Pero la verdad por delante: su miramiento fue tal, que no me echó ni una flor, mientras hartaba de lindas, simpáticas y retrecheras a las gitanas, a la chica del puñal de níquel y hasta a la fregona del estropajo. Cierto que a veces sorprendí sus ojos azules que me devoraban a hurtadillas; sólo que apenas notaba que yo había caído en la cuenta, los desviaba a escape. Su acento era respetuoso, sus frases serias y sencillas al dirigirse sólo a mí. Ahora se me figura que tantas exquisiteces fueron calculadas, para inspirarme confianza e interés: ¡ah malvado! Y bien que me iba comprando con aquel porte fino.

Surgió de repente ante nosotros, sin que supiésemos por dónde había entrado, una figurilla color de yesca, una gitanuela de algunos trece años, típica, de encargo para modelo de un pintor: el pelo azulado de puro negro, muy aceitoso, recogido en castaña, con su peina de cuerno y su clavel sangre de toro; los dientes y los ojos, brillantes, por contraste con lo atezado de la cara; la frente, chata como la de una víbora, y los brazos desnudos, verdosos y flacos lo mismo que dos reptiles. Y con el propio tonillo desgarrado de las demás, empezó la retahíla consabida:

6

For his part, Pacheco humoured me, making sure that my glass and plate were never empty, adjusting his mood to mine with such care, as if he were a stage manager charged with entertaining a prince and making him have the best time possible. Oh dear! Because I've got to be fair to the great rogue and, sitting alone with my conscience, admit that although Pacheco was animated, witty, full of jokes and (let's accept the terrible word) completely *rumbustious* with me, never at the end of the day did he indulge in either a licentious word or an insolent or even familiar action. On such an odd and critical occasion, what elsewhere was mere gallantry or *flirtation* (as the English say) would have been discourteous and presumptuous. Even then I understood this very well and, to tell the truth, was afraid of any of those impertinent insinuations which leave a woman uneasy and destroy the best moments. Without Pacheco's gentlemanly tact, the situation in which I had unpremeditatedly placed myself could have been quite ridiculous for me. But to tell the truth, his circumspection was such that he didn't pay me a single compliment, whilst with his lovely, charming and flattering remarks he overwhelmed the gypsy women, the woman with the nickel poniard in her hair, and even the kitchen maid with the dishcloth. It's true that at times I caught his blue eyes devouring me on the sly; but as soon as he saw that I had caught on, he averted them at full speed. His tone was respectful, and his phrases serious and simple when he addressed just me. Now I imagine that this refinement was calculated to inspire me with confidence and interest. Oh the villain! And clearly he was winning me over with that refined demeanour.

Suddenly, without our knowing where she had come in, a little, dark figure appeared before us, a gypsy about thirteen years old, characteristic, tailor-made for an artist's model: her blue-black hair, very oily, tied back in a bun, with its horn comb and a blood-red carnation; her shining eyes and teeth in contrast with her tanned face; her forehead, as flat as a viper's, and her bare arms, greenish and thin like two reptiles. And with the same impudent tone as the others, she began the usual short prayer:

–En er nombre de Dió Pare, Jijo ...

De esta vez, la chica del merendero montó en cólera, y dando al diablo sus pujos de señorita, se convirtió en chula de las más boquifrescas.

–¿Hase visto hato de pindongas? ¿No dejarán comer en paz a las personas decentes? ¿Conque las barre uno por un lado y se cuelan por otro? ¿Y cómo habrá entrado aquí semejante calamidá, digo yo? Pues si no te largas más pronto que la luz, bofetá como la que te arrimo no la has visto tú en tu vía. Te doy un recorrío al cuerpo, que no te queda lengua pa contarlo.

La chiquilla huyó más lista que un cohete; pero no habrían transcurrido dos segundos, cuando vimos entreabrirse la lona que nos protegía las espaldas, y por la rendija del lienzo asomó una jeta que parecía la del mismo enemigo, unos dientes que rechinaban, un puño cerrado, negro como una bola de bronce, y la gitanilla berreó:

–Arrastrá, condená, tía cochina, que malos retortijones te arranquen las tripas, y malos mengues te jagan picaíllo e los jígados, y malas culebras te piquen, y remardita tiña te pegue con er moño pa que te quedes pelá como tu ifunta agüela ...

Llegaba aquí de su rosario de maldiciones, cuando la del puñal, que así se vio tratada, empuñó el rabo de una cacerola y se arrojó como una fiera a descalabrar a la egipcia: al hacerlo, dio con el codo a una botella de jerez, que se derramó entera por el mantel. Este incidente hizo que la chica, olvidando el enojo, se echase a reír exclamando: –¡Alegría, alegría! Vino en el mantel ... ¡boda segura!– y, por supuesto, la gitana tuvo tiempo de afufarse más pronta que un pájaro.

No ocurrió durante el almuerzo ninguna otra cosa que recordarse merezca, y lo bien que hago memoria de todo cuanto pasó en él, me prueba que estaba muy despejada y muy sobre mí. Apuramos el último sorbo de Champagne y un empecatado café; saldó Pacheco la cuenta, gratificando como Dios manda, y nos levantamos con ánimo de recorrer la romería. Notaba yo cierta ligereza insólita en piernas y pies; me figuraba que se había suprimido el peso de mi cuerpo, y, en vez de andar, creía deslizarme sobre la tierra.

Al salir, me deslumbró el sol: ya no estaba en el cenit ni mucho menos; pero era la hora en que sus rayos, aunque oblicuos, queman

'In ve name o' ve Farver, Thon…'

This time the café girl flew into a rage, and dropping her pretensions to being a young lady, she turned into one of the most shamelessly outspoken lower-class women.

'Have you seen such a herd of loiterers? Won't they let decent people eat in peace? You sweep them to one side and they sneak in through the other. And how can such a nuisance have got in here I ask? Well, if you don't clear off faster than the speed of light, you'll gerra slap the likes o' which you've never felt in yer life. I'll give you a thrashin' such that you'll have no tongue left to recount it.'

The little girl shot off faster than a rocket; but before two seconds were out, we saw the tarpaulin protecting our shoulders half-open and through the crack in the canvas a face like that of the devil himself poked out, teeth gnashing and a clenched fist like a bronze ball, and the little gypsy bellowed:

'Slut, wretch, filffy pig, may terrible stomach cramps tear out yer guts and wickid devils make minced meat from yer liver. May evil snakes bite ya. May a cursed ringworm strike yer bun and leave ya bald like yer deceased grandmuvver…'

She had got this far with her rosary of curses when the one with the poniard, being treated in this way, grasped the handle of a saucepan and rushed forward like a wild animal to split the Egyptian's head open. As she did so her elbow knocked over a bottle of sherry which spilt all over the tablecloth. This incident made the girl forget her anger and burst into laughter, exclaiming: 'Joy, o joy! Wine on the tablecloth … a wedding for sure!' and, of course, the gypsy girl had time to fly off quicker than a bird.

Nothing else worthy of mention occurred during the meal, and my clear recollection of everything that happened is proof that I had all my wits about me. We finished off the last drop of champagne and a bad coffee; Pacheco settled the bill, giving a generous tip, and we got up with the intention of walking around the fair. I noticed an unusual lightness in my legs and feet, imagining my body had lost its weight, and instead of walking I felt like I was gliding over the earth.

When we stepped outside, the sun dazzled me. It was no longer at its zenith but it was the time when its rays, although oblique, are the most

más: debían de ser las tres y media o cuatro de la tarde, y el suelo se rajaba de calor. Gente, triple que por la mañana, y veinte veces más bullanguera y estrepitosa. Al punto que nos metimos entre aquel bureo, se me puso en la cabeza que me había caído en el mar: mar caliente, que hervía a borbotones, y en el cual flotaba yo dentro de un botecillo chico como una cáscara de nuez: golpe va y golpe viene, ola arriba y ola abajo. ¡Sí, era el mar; no cabía duda! ¡El mar, con toda la angustia y desconsuelo del mareo que empieza!

Lejos de disiparse esta aprensión, se aumentaba mientras iba internándome en la romería apoyada en el brazo del gaditano. Nada, señores, que estaba en mitad del golfo. Los innumerables ruidos de voces, disputas, coplas, pregones, juramentos, vihuelas, organillos, pianos, se confundían en un rumor nada más: el mugido sordo con que el Océano se estrella en los arrecifes: y allá a lo lejos, los columpios, lanzados al aire con vuelo vertiginoso, me representaban lanchas y falúas balanceadas por el oleaje. ¡Ay Dios mío, y qué desvanecimiento me entró al convencerme de que, en efecto, me encontraba en alta mar! Me agarré al brazo de Pacheco como me agarro en la temporada de baños al cuello del bañero robusto, para que no me lleve el agua … Sentía un pánico atroz y no me atrevía a confesarlo, porque tal vez mi acompañante se reiría de mí, por fuera o por dentro, si le dijese que me mareaba, que me mareaba a toda prisa.

Una peripecia nos detuvo breves instantes. Fue una pelea de mujerotas. Pelea muy rara: por lo regular, estas riñas van acompañadas de vociferaciones, de chillidos, de injurias, y aquí no hubo nada de eso. Eran dos mozas: una que tostaba garbanzos en una sartén puesta sobre una hornilla: otra que pasó y con las sayas derribó el artilugio. Jamás he visto en rostro humano expresión de ferocidad como adquirió el de la tostadora. Más pronta que el rayo, recogió del suelo la sartén, y echándose a manera de irritada tigre sobre la autora del desaguisado, le dio con el filo en mitad de la cara. La agredida se volvió sin exhalar un ay, corriéndole de la ceja a la mejilla un hilo de sangre: y trincando a su enemiga por el moño, del primer arrechucho le arrancó un buen mechón, mientras le clavaba en el pescuezo las uñas de la mano izquierda: cayeron a tierra las dos amazonas, rodando entre trébedes, hornillas y cazos; se formó alrededor corro de mirones,

intense; it must have been half past three or four in the afternoon, and the ground was cracking with heat. Three times more people than in the morning, and twenty times rowdier and noisier. As soon as we got involved with the amusement it came into my head that I had fallen in the sea: the boiling hot sea where I was floating inside a little boat like a nutshell, to and fro, up and down. Yes, it was the sea, no doubt about it! The sea, with all the anguish and distress of incipient seasickness!

This fear, far from dissipating, grew stronger as I went into the fair on the Gaditano's arm. That was it, ladies and gentlemen, I was in the deep sea. The innumerable sounds of voices, quarrels, popular songs, oaths, guitars, barrel organs, pianos mingled into just one noise: the dull roar with which the ocean crashes on the reefs. And there in the distance, the swings thrown into the air with a vertiginous flight represented for me launches and feluccas rocked by the waves. My God, the dizziness that overwhelmed me when I came to the conclusion that I was indeed on the high seas! I held onto Pacheco's arm as I hold onto the strong attendant's neck in the bathing season so the sea won't sweep me away … I felt a terrible panic and didn't dare confess to it, because my companion might laugh at me, openly or secretly, if I told him I was getting seasick, quickly getting seasick.

An incident detained us a few minutes. It was a fight between big, coarse women. A very strange fight: these brawls are normally accompanied by shouting and screaming and insults, but there was none of that here. They were two girls, one roasting chickpeas in a frying pan on a small stove, the other who went by and knocked the contraption over with her skirt. Never have I seen on a human face such an expression of ferocity like that of the toaster. As quick as a flash, she picked the frying pan up from the floor, and throwing herself like an angry tigress at the author of the crime, smacked her with the edge in the middle of her face. The victim of the attack turned round without even an 'ouch', a trickle of blood running from her eyebrow to her cheek; and grabbing her enemy's bun pulled out a good lock of hair in a fit of rage whilst digging the nails of her left hand in her neck. The two Amazons fell to the ground, rolling amongst cooking tripods, stoves and saucepans; a circle of onlookers formed round them without anyone

sin que nadie pensase en separarlas, y ellas seguían luchando, calladas y pálidas como muertas, una con la oreja rasgada ya, otra con la sien toda ensangrentada y un ojo medio saltado de un puñetazo. Los soldados se reían a carcajadas y les decían requiebros indecentes, en tanto que se despedazaban las infelices. Advertí por un instante que se me quitaba el mareo, a fuerza de repugnancia y lástima: me acordé de mi paisano Pardo, y de aquello del salvajismo y la barbarie española. Pero duró poco esta idea, porque en seguidita se me ocurrió otra muy singular: que las dos combatientes eran dos pescados grandes, así como golfines[25] o tiburones, y que a coletazos y mordiscos, sin chistar, estaban haciéndose trizas. Y este pensamiento me renovó la fatiga del mareo de tal modo, que arrastré a Pacheco.

–Vámonos de aquí … No me gusta ver esto … Se matan.

Preguntóme don Diego si me sentía mal, en cuyo caso no visitaríamos los barracones donde enseñan panoramas y fenómenos. Respondí muy picada que me encontraba perfectamente y capaz de examinar todas las curiosidades de la romería. Entramos en varias barracas, y vimos un enano, un ternero de dos cabezas, y por último

25 Delfines.

thinking of separating them, and they carried on fighting, silent and pale as death, one with her ear torn and the other with her temple covered in blood and an eye half out from a punch. The soldiers were roaring with laughter and paying the poor wretches indecent compliments as they were tearing each other apart. I noticed for an instant that my dizziness was abating on account of the repugnance and pity I felt. I remembered my compatriot Pardo and the thing about savagery and Spanish barbarism. But this idea didn't last long, because straightaway another very strange one crossed my mind: that the two combatants were two big fish, like dolphins or sharks, and without saying a word they were tearing each other to shreds with bites and swipes of their tail. And this thought renewed the sickness fatigue so much that I dragged Pacheco away.

'Let's get away from here... I don't like seeing this... They're killing each other.'

Pacheco asked me if I felt ill, in which case we wouldn't visit the booths where they had panoramas and freak shows. I replied in a fit of pique that I was perfectly well and capable of examining all the curiosities of the fair. We went into various booths, and saw a dwarf, a

la mujer de cuatro piernas, muy pizpireta, muy escotada, muy vestida de seda azul con puntillas de algodón, y que enseñaba sonriendo –la risa del conejo– sus dobles muñones al extremo de cada rodilla. En esta pícara barraca se apoderó de mí, con más fuerza que nunca, la convicción de que me hallaba en alta mar, entregada a los vaivenes del Océano. En el lado izquierdo del barracón había una serie de agujeritos redondos por donde se veía un cosmorama: y yo empeñada en que eran las portas del buque, sin que me sacase de mi error el que al través de las susodichas portas se divisase, en vez del mar, la plaza del Carrousel ... el Arco de la Estrella ... el Coliseo de Roma ... y otros monumentos análogos. Las perspectivas arquitectónicas me parecían desdibujadas y confusas, con gran templequeteo y vaguedad de contornos, lo mismo que si las cubriese el trémulo velo de las olas. Al volverme y fijarme en el costado opuesto de la barraca, los grandes espejos de *rigolada*,[26] de lunas cóncavas o convexas, que reflejaban mi figura con líneas grotescamente deformes, me parecieron también charcos de agua de mar ... ¡Ay, ay, ay, qué malo se pone esto! Un terror espantoso cruzó por mi mente: ¿apostemos a que todas estas chifladuras marítimas y náuticas son pura y simplemente una ... vamos, una *filoxerita*,[27] como ahora dicen? ¡Pero si he bebido poco! ¡Si en la mesa me encontraba tan bien!

–Hay que disimular –pensé–. Que Pacheco no se entere ... ¡Virgen, y qué vergüenza, si lo nota! ... Volver a Madrid corriendo ... ¡Quia! El movimiento del coche me pierde, me acaba, de seguro ... Aire, aire ... ¡Si hubiese un rincón donde librarse de este gentío!

O Pacheco leyó en mis pensamientos, o coincidió conmigo en sensaciones, pues se inclinó y con el más cariñoso y deferente tono murmuró a mi oído:

–Hace aquí un calor intolerable ... ¿Verdad que sí? ¿Quiere usted que salgamos? Daremos una vueltecita por la pradera y la alameda; estará más despejado y más fresco.

–Vamos –respondí fingiendo indiferencia, aunque veía el cielo abierto con la proposición.

---

26   Otro galicismo, de *rigolade*: diversión, risa, broma.
27   Borracherita.

two-headed calf and lastly a very lively four-legged woman with a really low neckline, dressed in blue silk with cotton lace and showing with a smile – a fake laugh – the two stumps at the end of each knee. In that despicable booth the conviction that I was at high sea, at the mercy of the swaying ocean, took hold of me with more force than ever. On the left side of the tent there was a series of little round peepholes through which a cosmorama could be seen.[26] And I, adamant that they were the portholes of a ship, was not disabused of my erroneous belief by the fact that through the above-mentioned portholes you could make out the Place du Carrousel ... the Arc de Triomphe de l'Etoile ... the Colosseum in Rome ... and other similar monuments. The architectural perspectives looked blurred and indistinct to me, with vague, trembling outlines, just as if they were covered by the flickering veil of the waves. When I turned round and looked at the opposite side of the booth, the large distorting mirrors, with concave or convex sections which reflected my face with grotesquely deformed lines, also looked like puddles of seawater to me... Dear oh dear oh dear, how bad this is getting! A frightening thought crossed my mind: let's bet that all this maritime, nautical madness is purely and simply ... well, *tostication* as they say now. But I didn't drink much! I felt so good at the table!

'I'll have to cover up,' I thought. 'Don't let Pacheco find out...! Holy Virgin, how embarrassing if he notices! ... Run back to Madrid... Not on your life! The motion of the carriage would be my ruin, finish me off for sure... Air, air...! If there were just a corner to escape from this crowd!'

Either Pacheco read my thoughts or he was experiencing the same sensations, because he leant over and in the most affectionate, deferential tone whispered in my ear:

'It's unbearably hot here, isn't it? ... Do you want us to leave? We'll go for a little walk through the Pradera and the Alameda; it'll be more open and cooler.'

'Let's go,' I replied with feigned indifference, although the proposal came as a great relief.

---

26   An exhibition of perspective images of different places in the world, usually famous landmarks. The use of various optical effects, including mirrors, lenses and illumination, gives the images greater realism.

VII

Salimos de la barraca y bajamos del cerro a la alameda, siempre empujados y azotados por la ola del gentío, cuyas aguas eran más densas según iba acercándose la noche. Llegó un momento en que nos encontramos presos en remolino tal, que Pacheco me apretó fuertemente el brazo y tiró de mí para sacarme a flote. Me latían las sienes, se me encogía el corazón y se me nublaban los ojos: no sabía lo que me pasaba: un sudor frío bañaba mi frente. Forcejeábamos deseando romper por entre el grupo, cuando nos paró en firme una cosa tremenda que se apareció allí, enteramente a nuestro lado: un par de navajas desnudas, de esas *lenguas de vaca*[28] con su letrero de *Si esta bíbora te pica no hay remedio en la botica*, volando por los aires en busca de las tripas de algún prójimo. También relucían machetes de soldados, y se enarbolaban garrotes, y se oían palabras soeces, blasfemias de las más horribles … Me arrimé despavorida al gaditano, el cual me dijo a media voz:

–Por aquí … No pase usted cuidado … Vengo prevenido.

---

28   Una navaja, llamada así por las dimensiones de su hoja.

7

We left the booth and went down the hill to the Alameda, constantly pushed and lashed by the human wave whose waters grew denser as night approached. A moment came when we found ourselves trapped in such a crowd that Pacheco squeezed my arm tightly and pulled me to keep me afloat. My temples throbbed, my heart stood still and my eyes clouded over. I didn't know what was happening to me: a cold sweat beaded my forehead. We struggled our way through the group when right by our side a terrible thing stopped us in our tracks: a pair of bare knives, of the *cow tongue* kind with the inscription *If this viper bites thee, there's no cure in the pharmacy*, flying through the air in search of a nearby human being's intestines. The soldiers' machetes were glistening too, and clubs were brandished, vulgar words could be heard, the most horrible blasphemies... Terrified, I moved closer to Pacheco, who said to me in a low voice:

'This way... Don't be afraid ... I've come prepared.'

Le vi meter la mano en el bolsillo derecho del chaleco y asomar en él la culata de un revólver: vista que redobló mi susto y mis esfuerzos para desviarme. No nos fue difícil, porque todo el mundo se arremolinaba en sentido contrario, hacia el lugar de la pendencia. Pronto retrocedimos hasta la alameda, sitio relativamente despejado. Allí y todo, continuaban mis ilusiones marítimas dándome guerra. Los carruajes, los carros de violín, los ómnibus, las galeras, cuanto vehículo estaba en espera de sus dueños, me parecían a mí embarcaciones fondeadas en alguna bahía o varadas en la playa, paquetes de vapor con sus ruedas, quechemarines con su arboladura. Hasta olor a carbón de piedra y a brea notaba yo. Que sí, que me había dado por la náutica.

–¿Vámonos a la orilla … allí, donde haya silencio? –supliqué a Pacheco–. ¿Donde corra fresquito y no se vea un alma? Porque la gente me mar …

Un resto de cautela me contuvo a tiempo, y rectifiqué:

–Me fatiga.

–¿Sin gente? Dificilillo va a ser hoy … Mire usted. –Y Pacheco señaló extendiendo la mano.

Por la praderita verde; por las alturas peladas del cerro; por cuanta extensión de tierra registrábamos desde allí, bullía el mismo hormiguero de personas, igual confusión de colorines, balanceo de columpios, girar de tiovivos y corros de baile.

–Hacia allá –indiqué–, parece que hay un espacio libre …

Para llegar a donde yo indicaba, era preciso saltar un vallado, bastante alto por más señas. Pacheco lo salvó y desde el lado opuesto me tendió los brazos. ¡Cosa más particular! Pegué el brinco con agilidad sorprendente. Ni notaba el peso de mi cuerpo; se había derogado para mí la ley de gravedad: creo que podría hacer volatines. Eso sí, la firmeza no estaba en proporción con la agilidad, porque si me empujan con un dedo, me caigo y boto como una pelota.

Atravesamos un barbecho, que fue una serie de saltos de surco a surco, y por senderos realmente solitarios fuimos a parar a la puerta de una casaca que se bañaba los pies en el Manzanares. ¡Ay, qué descanso! Verse uno allí casi solo, sin oír apenas el estrépito de la romería, con un fresquito delicioso venido de la superficie del agua, y con la media

I saw him put his hand in the right pocket of his waistcoat and the butt of a revolver poke out of it, a sight which redoubled my fright and my efforts to turn away. It wasn't difficult for us because everybody was milling around in the opposite direction towards the scene of the fight. We retreated quickly to the Alameda, a relatively clear place. There my maritime illusions continued to upset me. The carriages, carts, omnibuses, covered wagons, any vehicle waiting for its owners, appeared to me as boats anchored in some bay or run aground on the beach, steamboats with their wheels, ketches with their rigging. I could even smell the coal and tar. Yes indeed, I'd really been overwhelmed by all things nautical.

'Shall we go to the riverbank ... there, where it's quiet?' I begged Pacheco. 'Where it will be cool and there won't be a soul to be seen? Because all these people make me si–'

A remnant of caution held me back just in time, and I corrected myself:

'They tire me.'

'Away from people? That'll be a little tricky today... Look.' And Pacheco pointed with his arm stretched out.

Over the green field, on the bare hilltops, whichever area of land we looked at from there, the same bustle of people formicating, the same confusion of bright colours, the same flight of swings, swirling roundabouts and dancing circles.

'Over there,' I indicated, 'there seems to be a quiet place...'

To get to where I was pointing we had to climb over a fence, a rather high one to be precise. Pacheco jumped over it and held his arms out to me from the other side. The strangest thing! I made the jump with surprising agility. I didn't even notice the weight of my body; the law of gravity had been rescinded for me. I believe I could have performed acrobatics. Yes, stability wasn't in proportion to agility, because if I'd been pushed with a finger, I'd have fallen and bounced like a ball.

We crossed a fallow field with a series of jumps from furrow to furrow, and by really solitary paths came to stop at the door of a shack right on the edge of the Manzanares River. Oh, what a relief! To find oneself there almost alone, scarcely hearing the noise of the fair, with a delicious freshness coming from the surface of the water, and with

obscuridad o al menos la luz tibia del sol que iba poniéndose … ¡Alabado sea Dios! Allá queda el tempestuoso Océano con sus olas bramadoras, sus espumarajos y sus arrecifes, y héteme al borde de una pacífica ensenada, donde el agua sólo tiene un rizado de onditas muy mansas que vienen a morir en la arena sin meterse con nadie …

¡Dale con el mar! ¡Mire usted que es fuerte cosa! ¿Si continuará aquello? ¿Si …?

A la puerta de la casaca asomó una mujer pobremente vestida y dos chiquillos harapientos, que muy obsequiosos me sacaron una silla. Sentóse Pacheco a mi lado sobre unos troncos. Noté bienestar inexplicable y me puse a mirar cómo se acostaba el sol, todo ardoroso y sofocado, destellando sus últimos resplandores en el Manzanares. Es decir, en el Manzanares no: aquello se parecía extraordinariamente a la bahía viguesa. La casa también se había vuelto una lancha muy airosa que se mecía con movimiento insensible; Pacheco, sentado en la popa, oprimía contra el pecho la caña del timón, y yo, muellemente reclinada a su lado, apoyaba un codo en su rodilla, recostaba la cabeza en su hombro, cerraba los ojos para mejor gozar del soplo de la brisa marina que me abanicaba el semblante … ¡Ay madre mía, qué bien se va así! … De aquí al cielo …

Abrí los párpados … ¡Jesús, qué atrocidad! Estaba en la misma postura que he descrito, y Pacheco me sostenía en silencio y con exquisito cuidado, como a una criatura enferma, mientras me hacía aire, muy despacio, con mi propio pericón.

No tuve tiempo a reflexionar en situación tan rara. No me lo permitió el afán, la fatiga inexplicable que me entró de súbito. Era como si me tirasen del estómago y de las entrañas hacia fuera con un garfio para arrancármelas por la boca. Llevé las manos a la garganta y al pecho, y gemí:

−¡A tierra, a tierra! ¡Que se pare el vapor … me mareo, me mareo! ¡Que me muero… Por la Virgen, a tierra!

Cesé de ver la bahía, el mar verde y espumoso, las crespas olitas; cesé de sentir el soplo del nordeste y el olor del alquitrán … Percibí, como entre sueños, que me levantaban en vilo y me trasladaban … ¿Estaríamos desembarcando? Entreoí frases que para mí entonces carecían de sentido. «−Probetica, sa puesto mala. −Por aquí, señorito

semi-darkness or at least the tepid glow of the setting sun. Praise the Lord! Leaving the tempestuous ocean there with its roaring waves, its foam and its reefs, and here I am on the shore of a peaceful cove, where the water just ripples up in gentle little waves that die on the sand without disturbing anybody…

Back with the sea again. This is too much! If this continues? If…?

Appearing at the door of the shack were a poorly dressed woman and two children in rags who very obligingly brought out a chair for me. Pacheco sat down next to me on some logs. I felt an inexplicable well-being and I began to watch the setting sun twinkling its last gleams in the Manzanares. That is to say, not in the Manzanares; it was just like the Bay of Vigo. The house too had turned into a very draughty boat which was rocking with an imperceptible motion. Pacheco, sitting in the stern, was pressing against the tiller, and I, gently reclined beside him, rested my elbow on his knee, leant my head on his shoulder and shut my eyes better to enjoy the sea breeze which fanned my face… Good heavens, how nice this is! From here to Heaven…

I opened my eyes… Good lord, how awful! I was in the very position I have described, and Pacheco was holding me quietly and with exquisite care, like a sick child, whilst fanning me very slowly with my own very large fan.

In such a strange situation I had no time to reflect. The urge, the inexplicable fatigue which suddenly came upon me didn't allow it. It was as if my stomach and insides were being pulled outwards by a hook in order to drag them out through my mouth. I put my hands to my throat and breast, and gasped:

'Let me ashore! Stop the boat … I'm seasick, I'm seasick! I'm dying! In the Virgin's name, let me ashore.'

I lost sight of the bay, the green, foaming sea, the crinkly little waves; I stopped hearing the gust of the north-east wind and smelling the tar… I sensed, as if between dreams, that they were lifting me into the air and carrying me away… Could we be disembarking? I half-heard sentences which lacked meaning for me at that moment. "Poor fing, she's 'ad a turn! This way, sir. There's certainly a bed

… –Sí que hay cama y lo que se necesite … –Mandar …» –Sin duda ya me habían depositado en tierra firme, pues noté un consuelo grandísimo y luego una sensación inexplicable de desahogo, como si alguna manaza gigantesca rompiese un aro de hierro que me estaba comprimiendo las costillas y dificultando la respiración. Di un suspiro y abrí los ojos …

Fue un intervalo lúcido, de esos que se tienen aún en medio del síncope o del acceso de locura, y en que comprendí claramente todo cuanto me sucedía. No había mar, ni barco, ni tales carneros, sino turca de padre y muy señor mío; la tierra firme era el camastro de la tabernera, el aro de hierro el corsé que acababan de aflojarme; y no me quedé muerta de sonrojo allí mismo, porque no vi en el cuarto a Pacheco. Sólo la mujer, morena y alta, muy afable, se deshacía en cuidados, me ofrecía toda clase de socorros …

–No, gracias … Silencio y estar a obscuras … Es lo único … Bien, sí, llamaré si ocurre. Ya, ya me siento mejor … Silencio y dormir; no necesito más.

La mujer entornó el ventanuco por donde entraba en el chiribitil[29] la luz del sol poniente y se marchó en puntillas. Me quedé sola: me dominaba una modorra invencible: no podía mover brazo ni pierna; sin embargo, la cabeza y el corazón se me iban sosegando por efecto de la penumbra y la soledad. Cierto que andaba otra vez a vueltas con la manía náutica, pues pensaba para mis adentros: –¡Qué bien me encuentro así …, en este camarote …, en esta litera …, y qué serena debe de estar la mar! … ¡Ni chispa de balance! ¡El barco no se mueve!

Yo había oído asegurar muchas veces que si tenemos los ojos cerrados y alguna persona se pone a mirarnos fijamente, una fuerza inexplicable nos obliga a abrirlos. Digo que es verdad y lo digo por experiencia. En medio de mi sopor empecé a sentir cierta comezón de alzar los párpados, y una inquietud especial, que me indicaba la presencia de *alguien* en el tugurio … Entreabrí los ojos y con gran sorpresa vi el agua del mar, pero no la verde y plomiza del Cantábrico, sino la del Mediterráneo, azul y tranquila … Las pupilas de Pacheco, como ustedes se habrán imaginado. Estaba de pie, y cuando clavé en él la mirada, se inclinó y me arregló delicadamente la falda del vestido para que me cubriese los pies.

---

29 Cuarto muy pequeño.

'n' whatever else... Just say the word..." Without doubt they had already put me on solid ground, for I felt tremendous solace and then an inexplicable sensation of relief, as if some giant hand had broken an iron ring squeezing my ribs and making it difficult to breathe. I sighed and opened my eyes...

It was a lucid interval such as occurs in the middle of a fainting fit or a bout of madness, and in which I understood clearly everything that was happening to me. There was no sea, boat or any such thing, just a case of being royally drunk; dry land was the tavern keeper's makeshift bed; the iron ring, my corset which they had just loosened for me. And if I didn't die of embarrassment on the spot, it was because I couldn't see Pacheco in the room. Only the tall, dark and very affable woman, lavishing care and offering all kinds of help...

'No thanks... Some quiet and a darkened room ... that's all. Yes, I'll call if I need anything. I feel better already... Quiet and sleep, I don't need anything else.'

The woman half-closed the small, narrow window through which a faint gleam of light from the setting sun entered the cubbyhole, and tiptoed out. I was on my own. An invincible drowsiness overcame me, and I could move neither arms nor legs. My head and heart, however, began to calm down with the dark and quiet. It is true that once again I was trying to come to terms with the nautical madness, for deep down I was thinking: 'How comfortable I am like this ... in this cabin ... in this bunk ... and how calm the sea must be... Not even a tiny amount of rocking! The boat isn't moving!'

I had heard it said many times that if our eyes are closed, and somebody begins to stare at us, an inexplicable force will compel us to open them. I say this is true and I say it from experience. In the midst of my drowsiness I began to feel a certain urge to look up, and a peculiar uneasiness intimated to me the presence of *someone* in the hut... I half-opened my eyes and to my great astonishment saw the sea water, not the green-and-lead-coloured Cantabrian, but the blue and quiet Mediterranean ... Pacheco's eyes, as you may have imagined. He was standing and when I fixed my eyes on him he stopped and delicately arranged the folds of my skirt so as to cover my feet.

–¿Cómo vamos? ¿Hay ánimos para levantarse? –murmuró: es decir, sería algo por el estilo, pues no me atrevo a jurar que dijese esto. Lo que afirmo es que le tendí las dos manos, con un cariñazo repentino y descomunal, porque se me había puesto en el moño que me encontraba allí abandonadita en medio de un golfo profundo y que iba a ahogarme si no acierta a venir en mi auxilio Pacheco. Él tomó las manos que yo ofrecía; las apretó muy afectuoso; me tentó los pulsos y apoyó su derecha en mis sienes y frente. ¡Cuánto bien me hacía aquella presioncita cuidadosa y firme! Como si me volviese a encajar los goznes del cerebro en su verdadero sitio, dándoles aceite para que girasen mejor. Le estreché la mano izquierda … ¡Qué pegajoso, qué majadero se vuelve uno en estas situaciones … anormales! Yo me estaba muriendo por mimos, igual que una niña pequeña … ¡Quería que me tuviesen lástima! … Es sabido que a mucha gente le dan las turcas por el lado tierno. Ganas me venían de echarme a llorar, por el gusto de que me consolasen.

Había a la cabecera de la cama una mugrienta silla de Vitoria,[30] y el gaditano tomó asiento en ella acercando su cara a la dura almohada donde reclinaba la mía. No sé qué me fue diciendo por lo bajo: sí que eran cositas muy dulces y zalameras, y que yo seguía estrujándole la mano izquierda con fuerza convulsiva, sonriendo y entornando los párpados, porque me parecía que de nuevo bogábamos en el esquife, y las olas hacían un *¡clap! ¡clap!* armonioso contra el costado. Sentí en la mejilla un soplo caliente, y luego un contacto parecido al revoloteo de una mariposa. Sonaron pasos fuertes, abrí los ojos, y vi a la mujer alta y morena, figonera, tabernera o lo que fuese.

–¿Le traigo una tacita de té, señorita? Lo tengo mu bueno, no se piensen ustés que no … Se le pué echar unas gotas de ron, si les parece …

–¡No, ron no! –articulé muy quejumbrosa, como si pidiese que no me mataran.

–¡Sin ron … y calentito! –mandó Pacheco.

La mujer salió. Cerré otra vez los ojos. Me zumbaban los sesos: ni que tuviese en ellos un enjambre de abejas. Pacheco seguía apretándome las sienes, lo cual me aliviaba mucho. También noté

30　Un tipo de silla muy corriente y nada elegante.

'How are we? Well enough to get up?' he murmured, or at least something of the sort, for I wouldn't dare to swear that this is what he said. What I will state is that I stretched out both hands to him with sudden and extraordinary affection, because I had had the feeling that I was abandoned there in the midst of a deep gulf and that I was going to drown if Pacheco didn't manage to come to my aid. He took my outstretched hands, pressed them warmly, felt my pulse and put his right hand on my temples and brow. How good that careful, firm pressure felt to me! As if it pushed the hinges of my brain back into their correct place, oiling them so that they would move more smoothly. I squeezed his left hand... How clingy and foolish one becomes in these ... abnormal situations! I was desperate for shows of affection, just like a little girl ... I wanted to be felt sorry for! ... It's well known that intoxication makes many people sentimental. I was ready to burst out crying for the pleasure of being consoled.

At the head of the bed was a dirty simple chair, and Pacheco sat down on it and brought his face close to the hard pillow where mine was reclining. I don't know what he whispered to me, but it was something soothing and flattering and I continued to squeeze his left hand with convulsive force, smiling and half-closing my eyes because again it seemed like we were sailing in a boat with the waves making a harmonious *slap slap* against the side. I felt a warm breath on my cheek and then a contact like the fluttering of a butterfly. Loud steps resounded, I opened my eyes and saw the tall, dark woman, the restaurant keeper, innkeeper or whatever she was.

'Shall I bring you a cup of tea, madam? I have very good tea, don't be thinkin' otherwise ... I can pour a few drops o' rum in it, if you think ...'

'No, no rum!' I uttered very plaintively, as if asking not to be killed.

'Without rum ... nice and hot!' ordered Pacheco.

The woman went out. I closed my eyes again. My head was buzzing, as if I had a swarm of bees in it. Pacheco carried on stroking my forehead, which was a great relief. I also noticed that he fluffed

que me esponjaba la almohada, que me alisaba el pelo. Todo de una manera tan insensible, como si una brisa marina muy mansa me jugase con los rizos. Volvieron a oírse los pasos y el duro taconeo.

–El té, señorito ... ¿Se lo quié usté dar o se lo doy yo?

–Venga –exclamó el meridional.

Le sentí revolver con la cucharilla y que me la introducía entre los labios. Al primer sorbo me fatigó el esfuerzo y dije *que no* con la cabeza; al segundo me incorporé de golpe, tropecé con la taza, y ¡zas!, el contenido se derramó por el chaleco y pantalón de mi enfermero. El cual, con la insolencia más grande que cabe en persona humana, me preguntó:

–¿No lo quieres ya? ¿O te pido otra tacita?

Y yo ... ¡Dios de bondad! ¡De esto sí que estoy segura!, le contesté empleando el mismo tuteo y muy mansa y babosa:

–No, no pidas más ... Se hace noche ... Hay que salir de aquí ... Veremos si puedo levantarme. ¡Qué mareo, Señor, qué mareo!

Tendí los brazos confiadamente: el malvado me recibió en los suyos, y agarrada a su cuello, probé a saltar del camastro. Con el mayor recato y comedimiento, Pacheco me ayudó a abrocharme, me estiró las guarniciones de mi saya de surá, me presentó el imperdible, el sombrero, el velito, el agujón, el abanico y los guantes. No se veía casi nada, y yo lo atribuía a la mezquindad del cuchitril; pero así que, sostenida por Pacheco y andando muy despacio, salí a la puerta del figón, pude convencerme de que la noche había cerrado del todo. Allá a lo lejos, detrás del muro que cercaba el campo, hormigueaba confusamente la romería, salpicada de lucecillas bailadoras, innumerables ...

La calma de la noche y el aire exterior me produjeron el efecto de una ducha de agua fría. Sentí que la cabeza se me despejaba y que así como se va la espuma por el cuello de la botella de Champagne, se escapaban de mi mollera en burbujas el sol abrasador y los espíritus alcohólicos del endiablado vino compuesto. Eso sí: en lugar de meollo me parecía que me quedaba un sitio hueco, vacío, barrido con escoba ... Encontrábame aniquilada, en el más completo idiotismo.

Pacheco me guiaba, sin decir oste ni moste. Derechos como una flecha fuimos adonde mi coche aguardaba ya. Sus dos faroles lucían

up my pillow and smoothed down my hair. Everything in such an imperceptible way, as if a very gentle sea breeze were playing with my curls. The steps and hard tapping of heels could be heard again.

'The tea, sir... Do you wanna give it 'er, or shall I?'

'Bring it here,' exclaimed the southerner.

I heard him stir it with the teaspoon, which he then put between my lips. The effort of the first sip tired me and I shook my head; after the second I sat up suddenly, knocked the cup over and, bang, the contents spilled onto the waistcoat and trousers of my nurse, who, with the greatest insolence known to man, asked me:

'Don't you want it now? Or shall I ask for another cup?'

And I... Merciful heavens! Of this I'm sure, I answered using the same 'tú' form, very gentle and sentimental.

'No, don't ask for any more... It's getting dark... We have to leave here... Let's see if I can get up. What nausea. Lord, what nausea!'

I reached out trustingly; the villain took me in his arms and, clinging to his neck, I tried to jump out of the makeshift bed. With the greatest modesty and restraint, Pacheco helped me to button myself up, straightened the flounce of my *sura* silk skirt, and gave me my safety pin, hat, veil, hairpin, fan and gloves. I could hardly see anything, and I attributed this to the wretchedness of the hovel; but, supported by Pacheco and walking very slowly, I went to the door of the eating house and managed to deduce that night had closed in. In the distance, behind the wall that surrounded the field, the fair was a blurred swarm dotted with innumerable dancing lights...

The calm of night and the air outside had the effect of a cold shower on me. I felt my head clear and, like the foam in the neck of a bottle of champagne, the burning sun and alcoholic spirits of the diabolical wine escaped from my brain in bubbles. That's it: instead of brains I seemed to be left with a hollow, empty, broom-swept space ... I was wiped out, in complete ignorance.

Pacheco guided me without saying a single word. We went straight to where my carriage was already waiting. Its two lamps were shining

a la entrada de la alameda, en el mismo sitio en que por la mañana le mandáramos esperar. Entré y me dejé caer en el asiento medio exánime. Pacheco me siguió; dio una orden, y la berlina empezó a rodar poco a poco.

¡Ay Dios de mi vida! ¿Quién soñó que se habían acabado ya los barcos, el oleaje, mis fantasías marítimas todas? ¡Pues si ahora es cuando navegábamos de veras, encerrados en el camarote de un trasatlántico, y a cada tres segundos cuchareaba el buque o cabeceaba bajando a los abismos del mar y arrastrándome consigo! La voz de Pacheco no era tal voz, sino el ruido del viento en las jarcias ... ¡Nada, nada, que hoy naufrago!

–¿Vas disgustá conmigo? –gemía a mi oído el sudoeste–. No vayas. Mira, bien callé y bien prudente fui ... Hasta que me apretaste la mano ... Perdón, sielo, me da una pena verte afligía ... Es una rareza en mí, pero estoy así como aturdido de pensar si te enfadarás por lo que te dije ... Pobrecita, no sabes lo guapa que estabas mareá ... Los ojos tuyos echaban lumbre ... ¡Vaya unos ojos que tienes tú! Anda ... descansa así, en el hombro mío. Duerme, niñita, duerme ...

Tal vez equivoque yo las palabras, porque resultaban un murmullo y no más ... Lo que sí recuerdo con absoluta exactitud es esta frase, que sin duda cayó en el intervalo de una ola a otra:

–¿Sabes qué decían en aquel figón? Pues que debíamos de ser recién casados ... «porque él la trata con mucho cariño y no sabe qué hacer para cuidarla».

Y puedo jurar que no me acuerdo de ninguna cosa más; de ninguna. Sí ..., pero muy vagamente: que el coche se detuvo a mi puerta, y que por las escaleras me ayudó a subir Pacheco, y que desfallecida y atónita como me encontraba, le rogué que no entrase, sin duda obedeciendo a un instinto de precaución. No sé lo que me dijo al despedirse; sé que la despedida fue rápida y sosa. A la Diabla, que al abrir me incrustó en la cara su curioso mirar, le expliqué tartamudeando que me había hecho daño el sol, que deseaba acostarme. Claro que se habrá comido la partida ... Sí, que se mama ella el dedo ... ¡Buenas cosas pensará a estas horas de mí!

at the entrance to the Alameda, in the same place where in the morning we had ordered it to wait. I got in and dropped lifelessly onto the seat. Pacheco followed me, gave an order and the berlin began to roll forward gradually.

Good God! Who was it imagining that the boats, the swell of the sea, all my maritime fantasies had come to an end? Well now we really were sailing, enclosed in the cabin of an ocean liner, and every three seconds the boat pitched or plunged head first into the deep sea, dragging me down with it. Pacheco's voice wasn't a voice as such, but the noise of the wind on the rigging… No, no, I'm sinking!

'Are you cross with me?' the south-west wind howled in my ear. 'Don't be cross. Listen, I was very quiet and prudent … until you squeezed my hand… Forgive me, sweetheart, I'm sorry to see you suffer… It's a peculiarity in me, but I'm stunned to think of you being angry about what I said… Poor thing, you don't know how pretty you looked when you were feelin' seasick… There was fire in your eyes… What eyes you've got! Come … rest like this, on my shoulder. Sleep, little girl, sleep…'

Perhaps I'm getting the words mixed up for it was a murmur and nothing more… What I do remember with absolute accuracy is this sentence, which without any doubt came in the interval between one wave and another:

'Do you know what they said in that eatery? That we must be newly-weds … "because he treats her with lots of affection and can't do enough for her".'

And I can swear that I remember nothing more, nothing at all. Yes … but very vaguely, that the carriage stopped at my door, and that Pacheco helped me up the stairs, and that weak and dumbfounded as I was, I begged him not to come in, undoubtedly obeying an instinct of caution. I don't know what he said when he took his leave, but I know that our farewell was quick and perfunctory. I stammered an explanation to Diabla, who fixed her curious gaze on my face as she opened the door, that the sun had caused me a problem, that I wanted to go to bed. Of course she'll have understood my hidden intention and pretended not to understand… Yes, because she still sucks her thumb… She'll think really nice things of me now!

Me precipité a mi cuarto, me eché en la cama, me puse de cara a la pared, y aunque al pronto volví a amodorrarme, hacia las tres de la madrugada empezó la función y se renovó mi padecimiento. No quise llamar a Ángela … ¡Para que se escamase tres veces más! ¡Ay qué noche … noche de perros! ¡Qué bascas, qué calentura, qué pesadillas, qué aturdimiento, qué jaqueca al despertar!

Y sobre todo, ¡qué compromiso, qué lance, qué parchazo! ¡Qué lío tan espantoso! … ¡Qué resbalón! (ya es preciso convenir en ello).

I rushed into my room, threw myself on the bed, put my face to the wall, and although at first I fell into a slumber again, at about three o'clock in the morning the show started and my suffering resumed. I refused to call Ángela... Just for her to become three times more suspicious! What a night ... a terrible night! What nausea, what a fever, what nightmares, what bewilderment, what a headache when I woke up!

And above all, what an awkward position, what an incident, what deception! What a frightful mess! ... What a slip up! (we can all agree on that).

VIII

Convengamos: pero también en que Pacheco, habiéndose portado tan correctamente al principio, no debió luego echarla a perder. Si yo, por culpa de las circunstancias –eso es, de las circunstancias inesperadísimas en que me he visto– pude darle algún pie, a la verdad, ningún caballero se aprovecha de ocasiones semejantes; al contrario, en ellas debe manifestar su educación, si la tiene. Yo me trastorné completamente, por lo mismo que nunca anduve en pasos como estos; yo no estaba en mi cabal juicio; no señor; yo no tenía responsabilidad, y él, el grandísimo pillo, tan sereno como si le acabasen de enfriar en el pozo … Lo dicho: ¡fue una osadía, una serranada incalificable!

Cuanto más lo pienso … ¡Un hombre que hace veinticuatro horas no había cruzado conmigo media docena de palabras; un hombre que ni siquiera es visita mía! Cierta heroína de novela, de las que yo leía siendo muchacha, en un caso así recuerdo que empezó a devanarse los sesos preguntándose a sí propia: «¿Le amo?» ¡Valiente tontería la de aquella simple! ¡Qué amor ni qué …! Caso de preguntar, yo me preguntaría: «¿Le conozco a este caballero?» Porque maldito si sé hasta ni cómo se llama de segundo apellido … Lo que sé es que le detesto y le juzgo un pillastre. Motivos tengo sobrados: ¡que se ponga en mi caso cualquiera!

Y ahora … Supongamos que, naturalmente, cuando él aporte por aquí, me cierro a la banda y doy orden terminante a los criados: que he salido. Se pondrá furioso, y lo menos que hará, con el despecho, irse alabando en casa de Sahagún … Porque de fijo es uno de esos tipos que pegan carteles en las esquinas … ¡Como si lo viera! … Y resistir que se me presente tan fresco … vamos, es de lo que no pasa. Una, que me daría un sofoco de primera; otra, que en estas cosas, si no se empieza cortando por lo sano … Me parece lo más natural. Me niego … y se acabó. Escribirá … Bien, no contesto. Y dentro de unos días, como ya salgo de Madrid … Sí, todo se arregla.

Y … a sangre fría, Asís … ¿Es ese descarado quien tiene la culpa toda? Vamos, hija, que tú … ¿Quién te mandaba satisfacer el caprichito

8

Agreed; but let's also agree that Pacheco, having behaved so correctly at first, shouldn't have gone on to ruin it. If I, because of circumstances – that is to say the unexpected circumstances in which I found myself – had given him cause, surely no gentleman takes advantage of such occasions; on the contrary, that's where he should show his manners (if he has any). I was completely deranged, for the very reason that I never get entangled in affairs like these. I wasn't in my right mind; no sir, I wasn't responsible, and he, the big scoundrel, as calm as if he had just been cooling in a well... As I said: it was an audacity, an unspeakably dirty trick!

The more I think of it... A man who hadn't exchanged half a dozen words with me twenty-four hours ago, a man who isn't even my guest! I remember that in this sort of position a certain heroine of a novel, of the kind I read as a girl, began to rack her brains and ask herself: "Do I love him?" What nonsense from that simpleton! Love ... what are you talking about? If it comes to asking a question I'd ask myself: "Do I know this gentleman?" Because I'll be damned if I even know his second family name... What I do know is that I hate him and deem him a scoundrel. I've got more than enough reason: let any woman put herself in my place!

And now... Let's suppose, naturally, that when he comes here, I stick to my guns and give a categorical order to the servants to say I've gone out. He'll be furious, and the least he will do in his indignation is to go bragging at Sahagún's house... Because he is definitely one of those guys who shout everything from the rooftops ... I can just imagine! ... And put up with his coming here as cool as you like ... well, that won't happen. Firstly, it would cause me a major embarrassment; secondly, because if you don't start by taking drastic action in these matters ... It seems the most natural thing to me. I'll refuse ... and that's it! He'll write... Fine, I won't answer. And within a few days, as I'm leaving Madrid... Yes, everything will be sorted out.

And ... keep calm, Asís... Is this cheeky devil the sole culprit? Come on, you... Who ordered you to satisfy the little whim of going

de ir al Santo, y de acompañarte con una persona casi desconocida, y de almorzar allí en un merendero churri,[31] como si fueses una salchichera de los barrios bajos? ¿Por qué probaste del vino aquel, que está encabezado con el *amílico* más venenoso? ¿No sabías que, aun sin vino, a ti el sol te marea?

Te dejaste embarcar por la Sahagún ... Pero la Sahagún ... Para ciertas personas no rigen las ordenanzas sociales. La Sahagún no sólo es muy experta, y muy despabilada, y discretísima, y una de esas mujeres a quienes nadie se les atreve no queriendo ellas, sino que con su alta posición convierte en excentricidad graciosa e inofensiva lo que en las demás se toma por desvergüenza y liviandad. Hay gentes que tienen permiso para todo, y se imponen, y les caen bien hasta las barrabasadas. Pero yo que soy una señora como todas, una de tantas, debo respetar el orden establecido y no meterme en honduras. Era visto que Pacheco se había de figurar desde el primer instante ... No, no es justo acusarle a él solo.

Bien dice mi paisano. Somos ordinarios y populacheros; nos pule la educación treinta años seguidos y renace la corteza ... Una persona decente, en ciertos sitios, obra lo mismo que obraría un mayoral. Aquí estoy yo que me he portado como una chula.

Es decir ... más bien obré como una tonta. Caí de inocente. No supe precaver, pero no hubo en mí mala intención. Ello ocurrió ... porque sí. Me pesa, Señor. En toda mi vida me ha sucedido ni ha de volver a sucederme cosa semejante ... De eso respondo, y ahora, a remediar el daño. Puerta cerrada, esquinazo, mutis. No me vuelve a ver el pelo el señorito ese. En tomando el tren de Galicia ... Y sin tanto. Declaro la casa en estado de sitio ... Aquí no entra una mosca. Ya verá si es tan fácil marear a una mujer cuando ella sabe lo que se hace.

---

31 Andalucismo: desagradable, ruidoso.

to the Saint Isidro with a person you barely knew, and having lunch there in a grotty open-air café as if you were a sausage seller from the poorer areas of town? Why did you try that wine fortified with the most poisonous amyl alcohol? Didn't you know that, even with no wine, the sun makes you light-headed?

You let yourself get involved on account of Sahagún... But Sahagún... For certain people social laws don't prevail. Not only is Sahagún a real expert, very sharp and discreet, and one of those women who, if they weren't willing, nobody would dare try it on with, but also whose high position turns her into a charming, harmless eccentric which in others is taken for impudence and frivolity. Some people agree to everything, do as they please and even wicked things suit them. As for me, just a woman like all the others, I must respect the established order and not get into deep water. It was clear that from the first instant Pacheco must have imagined... No, it's not fair to lay the blame on him alone.

My compatriot is right. We are vulgar, common people; education polishes us for thirty years and the rough edges show up again... In certain situations, a respectable person acts the same as a drover would act. Look at me, I've behaved like a common, lower-class woman.

That is to say ... I acted like a fool. I refused to take precautions, but I had no evil intentions. It happened ... because it happened. It weighs down on me, Lord. In all my life a thing like this has never happened nor shall it again... I'm responsible for this, and now to remedy the damage. Door shut, cold shoulder, silence. That young man will see no sign of me again. I'll take the train to Galicia... And just like that. I declare the house in a state of siege... Not even a fly shall enter here. He'll soon see if it's that easy to befuddle a woman when she knows what's happening.

IX

Así, punto más, punto menos, hubiera redactado su declaración la dama, si confiase al papel lo que le bullía en el magín. No afirmamos que, aun dialogando con su conciencia propia, fuese la marquesa, viuda de Andrade, perfectamente sincera, y no omitiese algún detalle, que agravara su tanto de culpa en el terreno de la imprevisión, la ligereza o la coquetería. Todo es posible y no conviene salir fiador de nadie en este género de confesiones, que nunca se hacen sin pelos en la lengua y restricciones en la mente.

Sin embargo, no puede negarse que la señora había referido con bastante franqueza el terrible episodio, tanto más terrible para ella, cuanto que hasta dar este mal paso, caminara con pie firme y alegre espíritu por la senda de la honestidad. Mérito suyo, más que fruto de la educación paterna, no muy rígida, ni excesivamente vigilante. A Asís se le habían cumplido cuantos caprichos puede tener en un pueblo como Vigo una niña rica, huérfana de madre, y única. A los veinte años de edad, asistiendo a todos los bailes del Casino, a todos los paseos en la Alameda, a todas las verbenas y romerías de Cristos y Pastoras, visitando todos los buques de todas las escuadras que fondeaban en el puerto, Asís no había hecho cosa esencialmente mala, pues no hay severidad que baste a condenar de un modo rigoroso el carteo con un teniente de navío, a quien veía de higos a brevas –cuando la *Villa de Bilbao* andaba en aquellas aguas–. Por entonces le entró al papá de Asís, acaudalado negociante, la ventolera de las contratas acompañada naturalmente de la necesidad de meterse en política: tuvo distrito, y contrata va y legislatura viene, comenzó a llevarse a su hija a Madrid todos los inviernos, a dar una vueltecita –la frase sacramental–. Hospedábanse en casa de un primo de la difunta mamá de Asís, el marqués de Andrade, consejero de Estado, porque Asís era fruto de una de esas alianzas entre blasones y talegas que en Galicia y en todas partes se ven tan a menudo, sin que tuerza el gesto ningún venerable retrato de familia, ni ningún abuelo se estremezca en su tumba. El consejero de Estado se encontraba viudo y sin descendencia; conservaba un cerquillo de pelo alrededor de una

9

The lady would have drawn up her confession more or less like this if she had confided to paper what was bubbling in her mind. We cannot guarantee that, even in this dialogue with her own conscience, the widowed Marchioness of Andrade was completely sincere and didn't omit some detail that might exacerbate her level of guilt in the matter of lack of foresight, levity or coquetry. Everything is possible and it's not advisable to vouch for anyone in this kind of confession, which is never made bluntly or without mental reservations.

However, it cannot be denied that she was quite frank in her account of the terrible episode, all the more terrible for her because before this faux pas she had walked with a firm step and a happy spirit along the path of decency. Credit to her rather than parental upbringing, which had been neither very rigid nor overly vigilant. Asís had been indulged in all the whims a rich and motherless only child can have in a town like Vigo. By the age of twenty, going to all the Casino balls, strolling along the Alameda, participating in all the street festivals and celebrations of the Christ of Victory and the Divine Shepherdess, visiting every ship from every squadron anchored in the port, Asís hadn't done anything essentially bad, for nobody would be so strict as to condemn outright the exchange of letters with a navy lieutenant whom she saw once in a while when the *Villa de Bilbao* was in nearby waters. At this time, Asís's father, a wealthy businessman, got an itch for government contracts, along with the obvious need to get involved in politics: he was elected to office, government contracts and legislature sessions came and went, he began to take his daughter to Madrid every winter for a short excursion – the usual thing. They lodged with the Marquis of Andrade, a state adviser who was a cousin of Asís's late mother, because Asís was the fruit of one of those alliances between aristocracy and bourgeoisie that can be seen so often in Galicia and everywhere else, without any venerable family portrait showing displeasure or any grandfather turning in his grave. The state adviser, a widower without children, retained a fringe of hair around a

lucia calva; poseía buenos modales, carácter ameno (en la Corte no existen viejos avinagrados) y la suficiente mundología para saber cómo ha de insinuarse un cincuentón con una muchacha. Asís empezó por enseñarle a su tío, bromeando, las cartas del marino, y acabó por escribir a éste una significándole que sus relaciones «quedaban cortadas para siempre». Y así fue, y la esbelta sombra con gorrilla blanca y levita azul y anclas de oro, no se apareció jamás al pie del tálamo de los marqueses de Andrade.

El marqués tuvo el talento de no ser celoso y hacerle grata a su mujer la vida conyugal. Hasta se separó de otra hermana suya −con la cual vivía desde su primer matrimonio−, porque era devota, maniática, opuesta a la sociedad y a las distracciones, y no podía congeniar con la joven esposa; y no se mostró remiso en aflojar dinero para modistas, ni en gastar tiempo en teatros, saraos y tertulias. También supo evitar el delirio de los extremos amorosos, impropios de su edad y la de Asís combinadas; dejó dormir lo que no era para despertado, y así logró siete años de tranquila ventura y una chiquilla algo enclenque, que únicamente revivía con los aires marinos y agrestes de la tierra galaica. Un derrame seroso cortó el curso de los días del buen consejero de Estado, y Asís quedó libre, rica, moza, bien mirada y con el alma serena.

Pasaba en Madrid los inviernos, teniendo a su niña de medio interna en un atildado colegio francés; los veranos se iba a Vigo, al lado de su papá; a veces (como sucedía ahora), el viaje de la chiquilla se adelantaba un poco, porque el abuelo, al cerrarse las Cortes, se la llevaba consigo a desencanijarse en la aldea … Asís la dejaba marchar de buen grado. El amor maternal era en ella lo que había sido el cariño conyugal: sentimiento apacible, exento de esas divinas locuras que abrasan el alma y dan a la existencia sentido nuevo. La marquesa de Andrade vivía contenta, algo envanecida de haber soltado la cáscara provinciana, y satisfecha también de conservar su honradez como la conservan allá en Vigo las señoras muy visibles, que no dan un paso sin que el vecindario sepa si fue con el pie izquierdo o el derecho. Entretenía sus ocios pensando, por ejemplo, que el último vestido que le había mandado su modista era tan gracioso y menos caro que el de

shining bald patch; he possessed good manners, a pleasant personality (in Madrid there are no sour characters) and enough worldly wisdom to know how a man in his fifties has to ingratiate himself with a girl. Asís began to show her uncle the lieutenant's letters in fun, and ended up writing one to him making it clear that all contact "would be broken off forever". And so it was, and the graceful silhouette with the white cap and blue frock coat and gold anchors never appeared at the foot of the Marquis and Marchioness of Andrade's marriage bed.

The marquis had a talent for not being jealous and making conjugal life pleasant for his wife. He even separated from a sister, with whom he had lived since his first marriage, because she was devout, fanatical, opposed to society and entertainment, and couldn't get on with his young wife; he wasn't reluctant to fork out money for dressmakers or spend time at the theatre, evening parties and social gatherings. He also knew how to avoid the delirium of amorous extremes inappropriate to his and Asís's combined age; he let sleeping dogs lie, thereby achieving seven years of tranquil happiness and a rather sickly little daughter who only revived with the sea breeze and country air of Galicia. A haemorrhage of the serous membranes cut short the days of the good councillor of state, and Asís was left a free and rich girl, well thought of and with a clear conscience.

She spent her winters in Madrid, sending her daughter as a day pupil to an elegant French boarding school, and in summers went to Vigo with her father. Sometimes (as was happening now), the little girl's journey was moved forward a bit, because when parliament closed her grandfather took her with him to get stronger in their village … Asís let her go willingly. Her maternal love was what her conjugal affection had been: a calm feeling, free from that divine madness which sets the soul on fire and gives a new meaning to existence. The Marchioness of Andrade lived happily, rather proud of having cast off her provincial mask, and also pleased to keep her honour intact like the prominent ladies there in Vigo, who don't take a step without the whole neighbourhood knowing whether it was with the right or left foot. She spent her leisure time thinking, for example, that the last dress her dressmaker had sent her was just as elegant, but also

Worth de la Sahagún; que estaba a bien con el padre Urdax, merced a haber entrado en una asociación benéfica muy recomendada por los jesuitas; que ella era una dama formal, intachable, y que, sin embargo, no dejaban de citarla con elogio en las revistas de salones alguna que otra vez; que podía vivirse en el mundo sin dar entrada al demonio, y que ni el mundo ni Dios tenían por qué volverle la espalda.

Y ahora …

cheaper, than Sahagún's house of Worth dress;[27] that she was on good terms with Father Urdax, thanks to having joined a charitable society highly recommended by the Jesuits; that she was a responsible, irreproachable lady and that, nevertheless, the society columns didn't stop praising her now and again; that she could live in the world without allowing the devil access, and that neither the world nor God had reason to give her the cold shoulder.

And now…

---

27   Charles Frederick Worth was an English fashion designer who founded the house of Worth, one of the foremost fashion houses of the nineteenth and early twentieth centuries. Relocating to Paris in 1845, his fashion salon soon attracted European royalty. He is credited with revolutionising the business of fashion, and is often considered to be the father of *haute couture*.

X

Oyendo un nuevo repiqueteo de campanilla, acudió Ángela despavorida, a ver *qué era*. Su ama estaba medio incorporada sobre un codo.

–Venga quien venga, ¿entiendes?, venga quien venga …, que he salido.

–A todo el mundo, vamos; que ha salido la señorita.

–A todo el mundo: sin excepción. Cuidadito como me dejas entrar a nadie.

–¡Jesús, señorita! Ni el aire entrará.

–Y prepárame el baño.

–¿El baño? ¿No le sentará mal a la señorita?

–No –contestó Asís secamente–. (¡Manía de meterse en todo tienen estas doncellas!)

–¿Y la orden del coche, señorita? Ya dos veces ha venido Roque a preguntarla.

Al nombre del cochero, sintió Asís que le *subía un pavo* atroz, como si el cochero representase para ella la sociedad, el deber, todas las conveniencias pisoteadas y atropelladas la víspera. ¡El cochero sí que debía maliciarse …!

–Dile …, dile que … venga dentro de un par de horas …, a las cuatro y media … No, a las cinco y cuarto. Para paseo … Las cinco y media más bien.

Saltó de la cama, se puso la bata, y se calzó las chinelas. ¡Sentía un abatimiento grande, agujetas, cansancio, y al mismo tiempo una excitación, unas ganas de echar a andar, de huir de sí misma, de no verse ni oírse! No se podía sufrir.

–¡Qué vida tan incómoda la de las señoras que anden siempre en estos enredos! No les arriendo la ganancia … ¡Ay! aborrezco los tapujos y las ilegalidades … He nacido para vivir con orden y con decoro, está visto. ¿Le dará a ese tunante por venir?

Mientras no estaba dispuesto el baño, practicó Asís las operaciones de aseo que deben precederle: limpiarse y limarse las uñas, lavar y cepillar esmeradamente la dentadura, desenredar el pelo y pasarse

10

Hearing the bell ring again, a terrified Ángela came in to see *what it was*. Her mistress was half-sitting up, leaning on one elbow.

'Whoever comes, do you understand? Whoever comes ... I've gone out.'

'No matter who, that's it. Madam has gone out.'

'Everybody, without exception. Be careful not to let anyone in.'

'Upon my soul! Not even the air shall enter.'

'And run a bath for me.'

'A bath? Is madam ill?'

'No,' Asís answered curtly. (What a mania these maids have for meddling in everything!)

'And the order for the carriage, madam? Roque has already been twice to inquire.'

At the coachman's name, Asís felt herself *turn beet red*, as if the coachman represented society, duty, all the conventions trampled on and swept aside the day before. The coachman must surely suspect...!

'Tell him ... tell him to ... come in a couple of hours ... at half past four... No, at a quarter past five. For a drive... Better say half past five.'

She jumped out of bed and put on her dressing gown and slippers. She felt great dejection, stiffness, fatigue and at the same time excitement, an urge to start walking, to escape from herself, not see or hear herself! She couldn't bear herself.

'What an uncomfortable life it is for women who are always in these complicated situations! I wouldn't like to be in their shoes... Oh, I loathe deceit and misconduct... Clearly I was born to live with order and decorum. Will that rogue take it upon himself to come over?'

While waiting for the bath, Asís carried out the ablutions which should precede it: clean and file her nails, carefully clean and brush her teeth, untangle her hair and pass her small comb through it repeatedly,

repetidas veces el peine menudo, registrarse cuidadosamente las orejas con la esponjita y la cucharita de marfil, frotarse el pescuezo con el guante de crin suavizado con pasta de almendra y miel. A cada higiénica operación y a cada parte de su cuerpo que quedaba como una patena, Asís creía ver desaparecer la marca de las irregularidades del día anterior, y confundiendo involuntariamente lo físico y lo moral, al asearse, juzgaba regenerarse.

Avisó la Diabla que estaba listo el baño. Asís pasó a un cuartuco obscuro, que alumbraba un quinqué de petróleo (las habitaciones de baño fantásticas que se describen en las novelas no suelen existir sino en algún palacio, nunca en las casas de alquiler), y se metió en una bañadera de cinc con capa de porcelana –idéntica a las cacerolas–. ¡Qué placer! En el agua clara iban a quedarse la vergüenza, la sofoquina y las inconveniencias de la aventura … ¡Allí estaban escritas con letras de polvo! ¡Polvo doblemente vil, el polvo de la innoble feria! ¡Y cuidado que era pegajoso y espeso! ¡Si había penetrado al través de las medias, de la ropa interior, y en toda su piel lo veía depositado la dama! Agua clara y tibia –pensaba Asís– lava, lava tanta grosería, tanto flamenquismo, tanta barbaridad: lava la osadía, lava el desacato, lava el aturdimiento, lava el … Jabón y más jabón. Ahora agua de Colonia … Así.

Esta manía de que con agua de Colonia y jabón fino se le quitaban las manchas a la honra, se apoderó de la señora en grado tal, que a poco se arranca el cutis, de la rabia y el encarnizamiento con que lo frotaba. Cuando su doncella le dio la bata de tela turca para enjugarse, Asís continuó con sus fricciones mitad morales, mitad higiénicas, hasta que ya rendida se dejó envolver en la ropa limpia, suspirando como el que echa de sí un enorme peso de cuidados.

Llegó el coche algún tiempo después de terminada la faena, no sólo del baño, sino del tocado y vestido: Asís llevaba un traje serio, de señora que aspira a no llamar la atención. Ya tenía la Diabla la mano en el pestillo para abrir la puerta a su ama, cuando se le ocurrió preguntar:

–¿Vendrá a comer, señorita?

–No –y añadió como el que da explicaciones para que no se piense mal de él–. Estoy convidada a comer en casa de las tías de Cardeñosa.

go over her ears carefully with a small sponge and a little ivory spoon, rub her neck with a horsehair glove softened with almond and honey paste. With each hygienic operation and each part of her body cleansed like a paten, Asís believed she could see the marks of the previous day's aberrations disappear and, unintentionally confounding the physical and the moral, considered herself to be regenerating as she became clean.

Diabla announced that the bath was ready. Asís went into a small, dark room lit by an oil lamp (the fantastic bathrooms described in novels don't usually exist except in some palace, never in rented houses), and got into a zinc bathtub lined with porcelain, just like a saucepan. Such pleasure! The shame, stifling heat and inappropriateness of the adventure would be left behind in the clear water... They were written there in letters of dust! Doubly vile dust, the dust of that ignoble fair! And watch out, it was sticky and thick! It had worked its way through her stockings, her underwear, and the lady could see it deposited all over her skin! Clean, warm water, thought Asís, wash, wash away so much coarseness, so much flamenco culture, so much impropriety; wash away the audacity, wash away the disrespect, wash away the recklessness, wash away the... Soap and more soap. Now *eau de cologne*... That's it.

This obsession that the stains on her reputation would be removed with *eau de cologne* and fine soap took such a hold of Asís that she nearly ripped off her skin scrubbing at it with rage and fury. When the maid gave her the Turkish dressing gown to wipe herself, Asís continued with this half moral, half hygienic chafing until she was worn out and allowed herself to be wrapped in the clean linen, sighing like one who casts off an enormous burden of care.

The carriage arrived some time after the task was finished, not just the bath but also her hair and clothes. Asís put on a serious dress, that of a lady who doesn't wish to attract attention. Diabla already had her hand on the bolt to open the door for her mistress when she thought to ask:

'Will you be coming back to eat, madam?'

'No,' and added like someone giving explanations so as not to be thought badly of, 'I've been invited to eat at my Cardeñosa aunts' house.'

Al sentarse en su berlinita, respiró anchamente. Ya no había que temer la aparición del pillo. ¡Bah! Ni era probable que él se acordase de ella; estos troneras, así que pueden jactarse …, si te he visto no me acuerdo. Mejor que mejor. Qué ganga, si la historia se resolviese de una manera tan sencilla … Y la voz de Asís adquirió cierta sonoridad al decir al cochero:

–Castellana … Y luego a casa de las tías …

Aquella vibración orgullosa de su acento parece que quería significar:

–Ya lo ves, Roque … No se va uno todos los días de picos pardos … De hoy más vuelvo a mi inflexible línea de conducta …

Rodó el coche al trote hasta la Castellana y allí se metió en fila. Era tal el número y la apretura de carruajes, que a veces tenían que pararse todos por imposibilidad de avanzar ni retroceder. En estos momentos de forzosa quietud sucedían cosas chuscas: dos señoras que se conocían y se saludaban, pero no teniendo la intimidad suficiente para emprender conversación, permanecían con la sonrisa estereotipada, observándose con el rabillo del ojo, desmenuzándose el atavío y deseando que un leve sacudimiento del mare mágnum de carruajes pusiese fin a una situación tan pesadita. Otras veces le acontecía a Asís quedarse parada tocando con una *manuela*, en cuyo asiento trasero, dejando la bigotera libre, se apiñaban tres mozos de buen humor, horteras o empleadillos de ministerio, que le soltaban una andanada de dicharachos y majaderías: y nada: aguantarlos a quema ropa, sin saber qué era menos desairado, sonreírse o ponerse muy seria o hacerse la sorda. También era fastidioso encontrarse en contacto íntimo con el fogoso tronco de un *milord*,[32] que sacudía la espuma del hocico dentro de la ventanilla, salpicando el haz de lilas blancas sujeto en el tarjetero, que perfumaba el interior del coche. Incidentes que distraían por un instante a la marquesa de Andrade de la dulce quietud y del bienhechor reposo producido por la frescura del aire impregnado de aroma de lilas y flor de acacia, por la animación distinguida y silenciosa del paseo, por el grato reclinatorio que hacía a su cabeza y espalda el rehenchido del coche, forrado de paño gris.

---

32 Carruaje descubierto con capota (anglicismo, de *my lord*).

When she sat down in her little carriage she breathed freely. There was no longer any need to fear the rogue suddenly appearing. Bah! He probably didn't even remember her; these libertines, as soon as they can boast ... I don't remember seeing you before. All the better. What a boon if the whole affair could be resolved so easily... And Asís's voice took on a certain sonority when she said to the coachman:

'Along the Castellana... And then to my aunts' house...'

That proud intonation seemed to mean:

'You see, Roque ... one doesn't go out on the town all the time... From now on I'm going back to my strict line of conduct...'

The carriage rolled along to the Castellana, where it took its place in line. Such was the number of carriages and so tightly were they squeezed together that at times they all had to come to a halt because it was impossible to advance or recede. Funny things would happen during these moments of enforced standstill: two women who were acquainted would greet each other, but not being familiar enough to initiate conversation, would remain with a stereotyped smile, observing each other out of the corner of their eyes, examining closely each other's attire and hoping that a slight shaking up of the great sea of carriages would put an end to such an uncomfortable situation. On other occasions Asís would find herself stationary, right next to an open carriage in which, leaving the folding front seat free, were crammed together on the back seat three young men in high spirits, shop assistants or low-level government employees, unleashing a shower of vulgar expressions and stupid remarks. There was nothing for it except to put up with them point-blank, unsure as to whether it was less rude to smile, be very serious or turn a deaf ear. It was also annoying when she found herself in close proximity to a lively pair of Mylord coach horses shaking the foam off their muzzles into the window, splattering the bundle of white lilacs which, fastened to the card case, perfumed the interior of the carriage. Incidents which momentarily took the Marchioness of Andrade's mind off the sweet calm and beneficial rest produced by the cool air impregnated with the aroma of lilacs and acacia flower, the distinguished, quiet animation of the drive and the pleasant support which the cushioning of the carriage, lined with grey cloth, made for her head and back.

–¡Calle! Allí va Casilda Sahagún empingorotada en el campanario de su *break*. ¿De dónde vendrá, señor? ¡Toma! Ya caigo; de la novillada que armaron los muchachos finos, Juanito Albares, Perico Gonzalvo, Paco Gironellas, Fernandín Hurtado … –En un minuto recordó Asís la organización de la fiesta taurina: se habían repartido programas impresos en raso lacre, redactados con muy buena sombra; no había nada más salado que leer, por ejemplo: –Banderilleros: Fernando Alfonso Hurtado de Mendoza (a) *Pajarillas*.[33] –José María Aguilar y Austria (a) el *Chaval*. ¡Pues poca broma hubo en casa de Sahagún la noche que se arregló el plan de la corrida! Y Asís estaba convidada también. Se le había pasado: ¡qué lástima! La duquesa, tan sandunguera como de costumbre, hecha un cartón de Goya con su mantilla negra y su grupo de claveles; los muchachos, ufanísimos, en carretela descubierta, envueltos en sus capotes morados y carmesíes con galón de oro. Lo que es torear habrían toreado de echarles patatas; pero ahora, nadie les ganaba a darse pisto luciendo los trajes. Revolvían el paseo de la Castellana: eran el acontecimiento de la tarde. Asís sintió un descanso mayor aún después de ver pasar la comitiva taurómaca: comprendió, guiada por el buen sentido, que a nadie, en aquel conjunto de personas siempre entretenidas por algún suceso gordo del orden político, o del orden divertido, o del orden escandaloso con platillos y timbales, se le ocurriría sospechar su aventurilla del *Santo*. A buen seguro que por un par de días nadie pensase más que en la becerrada aristocrática.

Este convencimiento de que su escapatoria no estaba llamada a trascender al público, se robusteció en casa de las tías de Cardeñosa. Las Cardeñosas eran dos buenas señoritas, solteronas, de muy afable condición, rasas de pecho, tristes de mirar, sumamente anticuadas en el vestir, tímidas y dulces, no emancipadas, a pesar de sus cincuenta

---

33   (a): abreviatura de *alias*.

'Never! There goes Casilda Sahagún perched up high and mighty on her *break*. Where can she have been? Hey! Of course: to a second-rate bullfight organised by those well-bred fellows Juanito Albares, Perico Gonzalvo, Paco Gironellas, Fernandín Hurtado...' Asís soon remembered the organisation of the bullfighting festival: programmes printed in red satin had been distributed, written with very good humour. There was nothing more amusing, for example, than reading: 'Banderilleros: Fernando Alfonso Hurtado de Mendoza alias *Pajarillas*; José María Aguilar y Austria alias el *Chaval*'. What fun at Sahagún's house the night they arranged the programme for the bullfight! And Asís was invited too. What a shame she had forgotten it! The duchess, as charming as ever, was like a Goya tapestry cartoon[28] with her black *mantilla* and bunch of red carnations; the young fellows, very proud in their open carriage, wrapped in purple and crimson capes with gold stripes. As for fighting bulls, they might have fought very badly, but right now there was nobody who could beat them at showing off with their costumes. They stirred up the Paseo de la Castellana: they were the event of the afternoon. Asís felt even greater relief after seeing the bullfighting retinue; guided by her own common sense, she realised that nobody in that group of people, continually occupied by some important political or social event, or some scandal accompanied by the sound of cymbals and timpani, would dream of suspecting her little adventure at the Saint Isidro Fair. Certainly for a couple of days nobody would think of anything other than the aristocratic bullfight.

This conviction that her escapade wasn't destined to become public grew stronger at the Cardeñosa aunts' house. The Cardeñosas were two good spinsters, very affable, flat-chested, sad-eyed, extremely old-fashioned in the way they dressed, timid and gentle, and unemancipated from the eternal infancy of womanhood, despite their

---

28 A reference to the sixty-three large tapestry cartoons painted by Francisco de Goya on commission for Charles III and later Charles IV of Spain between 1775 and 1791 to hang in the San Lorenzo de El Escorial and El Prado palaces. The word 'cartoon' is derived from the Italian *cartone*, which describes a large sheet of paper used in preparation for a later painting or tapestry. Goya's were executed on canvas and then woven into wool tapestry to a large mural scale.

y pico, de la eterna infancia femenina; hablaban mucho de novenas, y comentaban detenidamente los acontecimientos culminantes, pero exteriores, ocurridos en la familia de Andrade y en las demás que componían su círculo de relaciones; para las bodas tenían aparejada una sonrisa golosa y tierna, como si paladeasen el licor que no habían probado nunca; para las enfermedades, calaveradas de chicos y fallecimientos de viejos, un melancólico arqueo de cejas, unos ademanes de resignación con los hombros y unas frases de compasión, que por ser siempre las mismas, sonaban a indiferencia. Religiosas de verdad, nunca murmuraban de nadie ni juzgaban duramente la ajena conducta, y para ellas la vida humana no tenía más que un lado, el anverso, el que cada uno quiere presentar a las gentes. Gozaban con todo esto las Cardeñosas fama de trato distinguidísimo, y su tarjeta *hacía bien* en cualquier bandeja de porcelana de esas donde se amontona, en forma de pedazos de cartulina, la consideración social.

Para Asís, la insulsa comida de las tías de Cardeñosa y la anodina velada que la siguió, fueron al principio un bálsamo. Se le disiparon las últimas vibraciones de la jaqueca y las postreras angustias del estómago, y el espíritu se le aquietó, viendo que aquellas señoras respetadísimas y excelentes la trataban con el acostumbrado afecto y comprendiendo que ni por las mientes se les pasaba imaginar de ella nada censurable.

El cuerpo y el alma se le sosegaban a la par, y gracias a tan saludable reacción, *aquello* se le figuraba una especie de pesadilla, un cuento fantástico …

Pero obtenido este estado de calma tan necesario a sus nervios, empezó la dama a notar, hacia eso de las diez, que se aburría ferozmente, por todo lo alto, y que le entraban ya unas ganas de dormir, ya unos impulsos de tomar el aire, que se revelaban en prolongados bostezos y en revolverse en la butaca como si estuviese tapizada de alfileres punta arriba. Tanto, que las Cardeñosas lo percibieron, y con su inalterable bondad comenzaron a ofrecerle otro sillón de distinta forma, el rincón del sofá, una silla de rejilla, un taburetito para los pies, un cojín para la espalda.

—No os incomodéis … Mil gracias … Pero si estoy perfectamente.

Y no atreviéndose a mirar el suyo, echaba un ojo al reloj de

fifty-odd years. They spoke a lot about *novenas* and discussed at great length notable but peripheral events that had happened in the Andrade family and in the others that made up their circle of acquaintances. For weddings they had an inviting, affectionate smile at the ready, as if they were savouring a liqueur they had never tried; for illness, the foolish actions of children and the death of old people, a melancholy arching of the eyebrows, resigned shrugs of the shoulders and phrases of compassion which, because they were always the same, smacked of indifference. Truly religious women, they never gossiped about anyone or judged other people's behaviour harshly, and for them human life only had one side, the obverse, the one we all want to show the world. With all this the Cardeñosas enjoyed a reputation for having a very distinguished manner, and their calling card *made a good show* on any of those porcelain trays where social importance is piled up in the shape of pieces of card.

For Asís, the Cardeñosa aunts' bland food and the dull evening gathering that followed were a comfort at first. The last of her throbbing headache and stomach pangs disappeared and her mind calmed down when, seeing those highly respected, excellent ladies treat her with their customary affection, she realised that nothing reprehensible about her had even crossed their mind.

Her body and soul calmed down at the same time, and thanks to such a beneficial reaction, she imagined *that thing* as a kind of nightmare, a fanciful story…

But as soon as the state of calm so necessary to her nerves had been attained, the lady began to notice at around ten o'clock that she was wildly and majorly bored, at first feeling sleepy, and then the urge to get some fresh air, revealed in prolonged yawns and shifting about in her armchair as if it were upholstered with pins, point upward. So much so that the Cardeñosas noticed, and with their unswayable kindness began to offer her a chair of a different shape, the edge of the sofa, a chair with a wicker seat, a foot stool, a cushion for her back.

'Don't trouble yourselves… Many thanks… I'm perfectly comfortable.'

And not daring to look at her own watch, she glanced at the

sobremesa, un Apolo de bronce dorado, de cuya clásica desnudez ni se habían enterado siquiera las Cardeñosas, en cuarenta años que llevaba el dios de estarse sobre la consola del salón en postura académica, con la lira muy empuñada. El reloj ... por supuesto, se había parado desde el primer día, como todos los de su especie. Asís quería disimular, pero se le abría la boca y se le llenaban de lágrimas los ojos; abanicándose estrepitosamente, contestando por máquina a las interrogaciones de las tías acerca de la salud de su niña y los proyectos de veraneo, inminentes ya. Las horas corrían, sin embargo, derramando en el espíritu de Asís el opio del fastidio ... Cada rodar de coches por la retirada calle en que habitaban las Cardeñosas, le producía una sacudida eléctrica. Al fin hubo uno que paró delante de la casa misma ... ¡Bendito sea Dios! Por encanto recobró la dama su alegría y amabilidad de costumbre, y cuando la criada vino a decir: –«Está el coche de la señora marquesa»– tuvo el heroísmo de responder con indiferencia fingida:

–Gracias, que se aguarde.

A los dos minutos, alegando que había madrugado un poco, arrimaba las mejillas al pálido pergamino de las de sus tías, daba un glacial beso al aire y bajaba la escalera repitiendo:

–Sí ..., cualquier día de estos ... ¡Qué! Si he pasado un rato buenísimo ... ¿Mañana sin falta ... eh? las papeletas de los Asilos. Mil cosas al padre Urdax.

Al tirar de la campanilla en su casa, tuvo una corazonada rarísima. Las hay, las hay, y el que lo niegue es un miope del corazón, que rehúsa a los demás la acuidad del sentido porque a él le falta. Asís, mientras sonaba el campanillazo, sintió un hormigueo y un temblor en el pulso, como si semejante tirón fuese algún acto muy importante y decisivo en su existencia. Y no experimentó ninguna sorpresa, aunque sí una violenta emoción que por poco la hace caerse redonda al suelo, cuando en vez de la Diabla o del criado, vio que le abría la puerta aquel pillo, aquel grandiosísimo truhán.

mantel clock, an Apollo of gilded bronze whose classical nudity the Cardeñosas hadn't even noticed in the forty years of having the god, with his lyre firmly grasped, in an academic posture on the console table in the living room. The clock ... of course, it had stopped on the first day like all of its kind. Asís tried to cover up, but her mouth opened and her eyes filled with tears, fanning herself noisily, mechanically answering the aunts' questions about her daughter's health and her own plans for the already imminent summer holidays. The hours ran by, however, pouring the opium of boredom over Asís's mind... Every carriage wheel in the remote street where the Cardeñosas lived produced an electric shock in her. At last there was one that stopped in front of the very house... Thank goodness! As if by magic the lady recaptured her customary joy and kindness, and when the maid came to say, "The marchioness's carriage is here," she had the courage to respond with feigned indifference:

'Thanks, tell him to wait.'

A couple of minutes later, alleging that she had got up rather early, she was bringing her cheeks to the pale parchment of those of her aunts, giving a glacial kiss in the air and going downstairs repeating:

'Yes ... any of those days... What! I've had such a good time... Tomorrow without fail, eh? The slips of paper about the Asylum. Regards to Father Urdax.'

When she tugged the bell pull at her own house, she had a very strange hunch. They exist, they exist, and anyone who denies it is a myopic of the heart who refuses other people the insight they themselves are lacking. While the bell was ringing, Asís felt a tingling and trembling in her pulse, as if a tug like this were some very important and decisive action in her life. And she felt no surprise, although indeed a violent emotion that nearly made her collapse in a heap on the ground, when she saw that, instead of Diabla or the servant, it was that scoundrel, that grandiose rogue who opened the door.

XI

Lo bueno fue que la dama, lejos de sorprenderse, saludó a Pacheco como si el encontrarle allí a tales horas le pareciese la cosa más natural del mundo, y, recíprocamente, Pacheco empleó también con ella todas las fórmulas de cortesía acostumbradas cuando un caballero se encuentra a una señora de cumplido, respetable, ya que no por sus años, por su carácter y condición. Se hizo atrás para dejarla pasar, y al seguirla al saloncito de confianza, donde ardía sobre la mesa de tijera la gran lámpara con pantalla rosa velada de encaje, se quedó próximo a la puerta y en pie, como el que espera una orden de despedida.

–Siéntese usted, Pacheco ... –tartamudeó la señora, bastante aturrullada aún.

El gaditano no se sentó, pero adelantó despacio, como receloso; parecía, por su continente, algún hombre poco avezado a sociedad: pero este aspecto, que Asís atribuyó a hipocresía refinada, contrastaba de un modo encantador con la soltura de su cuerpo y modales, la elegancia no estudiada de su vestir, la finura de su chaleco blanquísimo, su tipo de persona principal. Viéndole tan contrito, Asís se rehízo y cobró ánimos. –«Gran ocasión de leerle la cartilla al señorito este: ¿conque muy manso y fingiéndose arrepentido, eh? Ahora lo verás ...»– Porque la dama, en su inexperiencia, se había figurado que su compañero de romería iba a entrar hecho un sargento, y a las primeras de cambio le iba a soltar un abrazo furibundo o cualquier gansada semejante ... Pero ya que gracias a Dios se manifestaba tan comedido, bien podía la señora acusarle las cuarenta. Y Asís abrió la boca y exclamó:

–Conque usted aquí ... Yo quisiera ... yo ...

El gaditano se acercó todavía más, hasta ponerse al lado de la dama, que seguía en pie junto a la mesa. La miró fijamente y luego pronunció como el que dice la cosa más patética del mundo:

–A mí va usted a regañarme too lo que guste ... A los criados ni chispa ... La culpa es mía toa. Un cuarto de hora de conversasión con la chica me ha costao el entrar. Hasta requiebros le he soltao. Y na, ni por esas. Al fin le dije ... que vamos, que ya sabía usted que yo vendría

11

The good thing about it was that, far from being surprised, she greeted Pacheco as if finding him there at such a time seemed the most natural thing in the world to her; and, simultaneously, Pacheco employed all the usual formulas of courtesy when a gentleman meets a lady who is refined and respectable because of her character and social background rather than her age. He stepped back to let her go past, and when he followed her to the little boudoir where the big lamp with its rose-coloured, lace-covered shade was glowing on the folding table, he remained standing next to the door like someone waiting to be dismissed.

'Sit down, Pacheco…' stammered the lady, still rather bewildered.

The man from Cádiz didn't sit down, but moved forward slowly, as if apprehensive. From his bearing he looked like a man unaccustomed to society, but this countenance, which Asís attributed to refined hypocrisy, contrasted charmingly with the gracefulness of his body and manners, the unaffected elegance of his attire, the excellence of his clear white waistcoat, and his appearance of an illustrious person. Seeing him so contrite, Asís recovered and gained strength. "A great opportunity to give this gentleman a lecture. So here he is, very meek and pretending to be sorry, eh? You'll soon see…" Because the lady, with her lack of experience, had imagined that her companion at the fair was going to be overpowering and at the first opportunity would hug her frenziedly or something equally silly … But now, thank God, that he was proving so restrained, the lady could really give him a piece of her mind. Asís opened her mouth and exclaimed:

'So you're here … I'd like … I…'

Pacheco moved even closer, until he was next to the lady, who was still standing by the table. He stared at her and then, like someone expressing the most poignant thing in the world, said:

'You can scold me all you want… Not the servants… It's all my fault. It took a quarter of an hour talkin' to the girl to get in. I even heaped compliments on her. But nothing'd do. In the end I told her

y que para recibirme a mí se quería usted negar a los demás. Ríñame usted, que lo meresco too.

Estas enormidades las murmuró con tono lánguido y quejumbroso, con los ojos mortecinos y un aire de melancolía que daba compasión. Asís se quedó de una pieza, así al pronto; que después se le deshizo el nudo de la garganta y las palabras le salieron a borbotones. Ea ..., ahí va ... Ahora sí que me desato ...

–Sí señor, que merece usted ... Pues hombre ... me pone usted en berlina con mis criados ... ¡Por eso se escondieron cuando yo entraba ... y le dejan a usted que abra la puerta! ¡Gandules de profesión! A la Angelita yo le diré cuántas son cinco ... Y lo que es a Perfecto ... Alguno podrá ser que no duerma en casa esta noche ... Los enemigos domésticos ... Aguarde usted, aguarde usted ... Estas jugadas no me las hacen ellos a mí ... ¡Habráse visto! ¡Para esto los trata uno del modo que los trata! ¡Para que le vendan a las primeras de cambio!

Comprendía la misma señora que se ponía algo ordinaria chillando y manoteando así, y lo peor de todo, que era predicar en desierto, pues ni siquiera podían oírla desde la cocina; además, Pacheco, en vez de asustarse con tan caliente reprimenda, pareció que recobraba los espíritus, se llegó más, y bajando la cabeza, acarició las sienes de la enojada. Esta se echó atrás, no tan pronto que ya no la sujetase blandamente por la cintura un brazo del gaditano y que éste no balbuciese a su oído:

–¿A qué te enfadas con los criados, chiquilla? ¿No te he dicho que no tienen culpa? Mira, esa chica que te sirve, vale un Perú. Te quiere bien. Le daba dinero y no lo admitió ni hecha peazos. Dijo que con tal que tú no la riñeses ... Ahora si gritas se armará un escándalo ... Pero me iré cuanto tú lo mandes. Que sí me iré, mujer ...

Al anunciar que se iba, se sentó en el sofá diván, obligando a la señora a sentarse también. Ésta notaba una turbación que ya no se parecía a la pseudo-cólera de antes, y, por lo bajo, murmuraba:

–Pues váyase usted ... Hágame el favor de irse. Por Dios ...

–¿Ni un minuto hay para mí? Estoy enfermo ... ¡Si vieses! En toda la noche no he dormido, no he pegado los ojos.

Asís iba a preguntar: «¿por qué?» pero calló, pareciéndole inconveniente y necia la pregunta.

… that, well, you already knew I'd come and in order to see me you wished to deny everyone else. Tell me off, I deserve everything.'

He muttered these crass remarks in a languid, plaintive tone, with dull eyes and a melancholy air that aroused compassion. Asís was left speechless at first; then the knot in her throat came undone and the words gushed out of her. Come on … well, well … now I can talk…

'Yes indeed, you do deserve… Well … you make me look ridiculous to my servants… That's why when I came in they hid … and let you open the door! Professional good-for-nothings! I'll be telling Angelita a thing or two… And as for Perfecto… He for one might not be sleeping in this house tonight… Domestic enemies… Hold on, hold on… They're not going to play these tricks on me… Unbelievable! You treat them like you do, only for them to betray you at the first opportunity!'

The lady herself realised that she had become rather coarse shrieking and gesticulating in this way, and, worst of all, that it was preaching in the wilderness since they couldn't even hear her from the kitchen. Moreover, instead of being frightened by such a heated reprimand, Pacheco's spirits seemed to be raised. He came closer and, lowering his head, stroked the angry lady's temples. She drew back, but not quickly enough to prevent the man from Cádiz tenderly stealing an arm round her waist and spluttering in her ear:

'Why are you angry with the servants, pet? Haven't I told you they're not to blame? Look, that girl who waits on you is worth her weight in gold. She loves you dearly. I offered her money, but she'd rather be cut into pieces than accept it. She said as long as you don't tell her off… If you shout now it'll cause a scene… But I'll leave as soon as you tell me to. Of course I'll leave…'

As he announced that he'd leave, he sat down on the sofa, forcing the lady to sit down too. She felt upset in a way that no longer resembled the mock anger of before, and murmured under her breath:

'Well go then… Do me the favour of leaving. For God's sake…'

'Not even a minute for me? I'm ill… If only you could see! I haven't slept all night. I didn't shut me eyes.'

Asís was going to ask why, but she remained silent, the question seeming inappropriate and foolish.

–Necesitaba saber de ti … Si estabas ya buena, si habías descansado … Si me querías mal, o si me mirabas con alguna indulgencia. ¿Dura el mal humor? ¿Y esa cabecita? ¿A ver?

Se la recostó sobre el hombro, sujetándola con la palma de la mano derecha. Asís, esforzándose en romper el lazo, notaba disminuidas sus fuerzas por dos sentimientos: el primero, que viendo tan sumiso y moderado al gran pillo, le habían entrado unas miajas de lástima; el segundo …, el sentimiento eterno, la maldita curiosidad, la que perdió en el Paraíso a la primera mujer, la que pierde a todas, y tal vez no sólo a ellas sino al género humano … ¿A ver? ¿Cómo sería? ¿Qué diría Pacheco ahora?

Pacheco, en un rato, no dijo nada; ni chistó. Su palma fina, sus dedos enjutos y nerviosos oprimían suavemente la cabeza y sienes de Asís, lo mismo que si a ésta le durase aún el mareo de la víspera y necesitase la medicina de tan sencillo halago. En la sala parecía que la varita de algún mágico invisible derramaba silencio apacible y amoroso, y la luz de la lámpara, al través de su celosía de encaje, alumbraba con poética suavidad el recinto. La sala estaba amueblada con esas pretensiones artísticas que hoy ostenta todo bicho viviente, sepa o no sepa lo que es arte, y con ese aspecto de prendería que resulta de aglomerar el mayor número posible de cosas inconexas. Sitiales, butacas bajas y coquetonas, mesillas forradas de felpa imitando un corazón o una hoja de trébol, columnas que sostienen quinqués, divancitos cambiados donde la gente puede gozar del placer de darse la espalda y coger un tortícolis, alguna drácena en jardineras de cinc, un perro de porcelana haciendo centinela junto a la chimenea, y dos hermosos vargueños patrimoniales restaurados y dorados de nuevo … Todo revuelto, colocado de la manera que más dificultase el paso a la gente, haciendo un archipiélago donde no se podía navegar sin práctico. ¿Y las paredes? Si el suelo estaba intransitable, en las paredes no quedaba sitio libre para un clavo, pues el buen marqués de Andrade, incapaz de distinguir un Ticiano de un Ribera, le había

'I needed to know how you were... If you were well again, if you'd rested... If you wished me ill, or if you looked on me with some indulgence. Are you still in a mood? And that little head? Let's see.'

He pressed it against his shoulder, holding it with the palm of his right hand. Asís, trying to break the tie, felt her strength diminished on account of two feelings: the first, seeing the great rogue so submissive and moderate, made her feel a smidgen of pity; the second ... the eternal feeling, that accursed curiosity which ruined the first woman in Paradise, which ruins all women and perhaps not just them but the whole human race... Shall we see? How would it be? What would Pacheco say now?

For a while Pacheco said nothing, not a word. His delicate palm and thin, nervous fingers pressed gently on Asís's head and temples, just as if she were still feeling the sickness of the day before and required the medicine of such a simple pleasure. It seemed like the wand of some invisible magician was shedding calm, loving silence in the room, and through its lace lattice the light from the lamp illuminated the space with poetic softness. The room was furnished with those artistic pretensions which every living soul flaunts nowadays, whether or not he knows anything about art, and with that pawn-shop aspect which comes from the conglomeration of the greatest possible number of disparate things. Stools, low, neat armchairs, little tables resembling a heart or trefoil leaf, covered with plush, columns supporting lamps, little couches where people can enjoy the pleasure of turning their back and getting a stiff neck, dracaenas in zinc *jardinières*, a porcelain dog keeping watch by the hearth and two beautiful, inherited *vargueño* cabinets, restored and regilded ... everything in disorder, placed in a way to maximise difficulty of movement, making an archipelago where it was impossible to navigate without practice. And the walls? If the floor was impassable, there wasn't a free space for a nail on the walls because the good Marquis of Andrade, incapable of distinguishing a Titian from a Ribera,[29] had for some time been a

---

29   Titian, born Tiziano Vecellio or Vecelli (1488/90–1576), was the greatest Italian Renaissance painter of the Venetian school. He gained recognition as a supremely gifted painter early in his own lifetime, and in 1590 the art theorist Giovanni Lomazzo declared him 'the sun amidst small stars not only among

dado algún tiempo de protector de jóvenes artistas, llenando la casa de acuarelas con chulas, matones del Renacimiento o damas Luis XV; de *manchas*, apuntes y bocetos hechos a punta de cuchillo, o a yema de dedo, tan *libres* y tan *francos*, que ni el mismo demonio adivinaría lo que representaban; de tablitas lamidas y microscópicas, encerradas en marcos cinco veces mayores; de fotografías con retumbantes dedicatorias; migajas de arte, en suma, que al menos cubren la vulgaridad del empapelado y distraen gratamente la vista. Y en hora semejante, en medio de la amable paz que flotaba en la atmósfera y con la luz discreta transparentada por el encaje, los cachivaches se armonizaban, se fundían en una dulce intimidad, en una complicidad silenciosa; la misma horrible carátula japonesa colgada encima de un vargueño y de uno de cuyos ojos se descolgaba una procesión de monitos de felpa, tenía un gesto menos infernal; el pañolón de Manila que cubría el piano, abría alegremente todas sus flores; las begonias, próximas a la entreabierta ventana, se estremecían como si las acariciase el vientecillo nocturno … Sólo el *bull-dog* de porcelana, sentado como una esfinge, miraba con alarmante persistencia al grupo del sofá, guardando una actitud digna y enérgica, como si fuese celoso guardián puesto allí por el espíritu del respetable marqués difunto … Casi parecería natural que abriese las fauces, soltase un ladrido de alarma, y se abalanzase dispuesto a morder …

Pacheco decía bajito, con el ceceo[34] mimoso y triste de su pronunciación:

–¿Te sospechabas tú lo de ayer, chiquilla? ¿A que sí? Mira, no me digas no, que las mujeres estáis siempre de vuelta en esas cosas … ¡A ver si se calla usted y no me replica! Tú veías muy bien, picarona, que yo estaba muerto, lo que se dice muerto … Sólo que creíste poder dejarme en blanco … Pero sospechar … ¡Quia! ¡Si lo calaste desde el mismo momento que tiré el puro en los jardines! ¿Y tú te gosabas en verme a mí sufrir, no es eso? ¡Somos más malos! Toma en castigo … ¡Y qué bonita estabas, gitana salá! ¿Te ha dicho

---

34   Parece que Emilia Pardo Bazán confunde *ceceo* (pronunciación de la *s* como *z*) con *seseo* (pronunciación de la *z*, y de la *c* ante *e* o *i*, como *s*).

patron of young artists, filling the house with watercolours of back-street women, Renaissance thugs or Louis XV ladies; rough paintings, sketches and outlines done with the point of a knife or fingertip, so *free* and *open* that not even the devil himself would guess what they represented; thin, microscopic paintings on wood, mounted in frames five times bigger; photographs with pompous dedications. In a word, scraps of art which at least cover the tasteless wallpaper and provide pleasant distraction to the eyes. And at such a time, in the midst of the sweet peace pervading the atmosphere and with the sober light showing through the lace, these knick-knacks harmonised, melted into a tender intimacy, into a silent complicity. Even the horrible Japanese mask hanging from a *vargueño* cabinet, and from one of whose eyes a string of plush little monkeys was climbing down, had a less infernal grimace; the Manila shawl covering the piano opened joyously all its flowers; the begonias next to the half-open window were trembling as if the night breeze were caressing them... Only the porcelain bulldog, sitting like a sphinx, was watching the couple on the sofa with alarming persistence, maintaining a dignified and energetic attitude as if he were a jealous guardian put there by the ghost of the late, respectable marquis... It would almost not have been surprising if he had opened his jaws, barked out a warning, and pounced ready to bite...

Pacheco was talking very quietly with the affectionate, sad lisp of his pronunciation:

'Did you have a feeling about yesterday, my dear? I bet you did! Look, don't tell me no, for you women are always ahead in these things... Let's see if you remain silent and don't reply! You could see very well, you little minx, that I was dead, what's called dead ... only you thought you could ignore me... But have a feeling... Never! You grasped it all from the very moment I threw my cigar in the gardens! And you enjoyed seeing me suffer, didn't you? We're so bad! Take that for punishment... How pretty you looked, you charmin' gypsy!

---

the Italians but all the painters of the world'. José de Ribera (1591–1652) was a leading painter of the Spanish school, noted for his Baroque dramatic realism and his depictions of religious and mythological subjects. He was also called 'Lo Spagnoletto' (the Little Spaniard) by his contemporaries and early writers.

a ti algún hombre bonita? ¿No? ¡Pues ahora te lo digo yo, vamos!, y valgo más que toos … Oye, en el coche te hubiese yo requebrado seis dosenas de veses …, te hubiese llamao mona, serrana, matadora de hombres … Sólo que no me atrevía, ¿sabes tú? Que si me atrevo, te suelto toas las flores de la primavera en un ramiyetico.

Aquí Asís, sin saber por qué, recobró el uso de la palabra, y fue para gritar:

–Sí …, como a la chica del merendero …, y a mi criada …, y a todas cuantas se ofrece … Lo que es por palabrería no queda.

La interrumpió un enérgico tapabocas.

–No compares, chiquiya, no compares … Tonterías que se disen por pasá el rato, pa que se encandilen las mujeres … Contigo …, ¡Virgen Santa!, tengo yo una ilusión …, ¡una ilusionasa de volverme loco! Has de saber que yo mismo estoy pasmao de lo que me sucede. Nunca me quedé triste después de una cosa así sino contigo. Hasta me falta resolución pa hablarte. Estoy así … medio orgulloso y medio pesaroso. Más quisiera que nos hubiésemos vuelto ayer antes de almorsá. ¿No lo crees? ¿Ah, no lo crees? Por estas …

Y el meridional puso los dedos en cruz y los besó con ademán popular. Asís se echó a reír mal de su grado. Ya no había posibilidad de enfadarse: la risa desarma al más furioso. Y ahora, ¿qué hacer?, pensaba la dama, llamando en su auxilio toda su presencia de ánimo, toda su habilidad femenil. Nada, muy sencillo … No negarle la cita que pedía para el día siguiente por la tarde; porque si se le negaba, era capaz de hacer cualquier desatino. No, no …, contemporizar …, otorgar la cita, y a la hora señalada …, ¡busca!, estar en cualquier sitio menos donde Pacheco esperase … Y ahora, procurar *por bien* que se largase cuanto más pronto … ¡Qué diría el servicio! ¡En esa cocina estaría la Diabla haciendo unos calendarios!

Has any man called you pretty? No? Well, I'm telling you now and I'm worth more than all of 'em... Listen, in the carriage I could have complimented you half a dozen times ... I could have called you pretty, temptress, man-killer... Only I didn't dare, you know? If I'd dared I'd have showered you with all the flowers of spring in a bouquet.'

Here, without knowing why, Asís recovered the power of speech to shout:

'Yes ... like with the waitress ... and my maid ... and all that come along... As far as hot air goes, you've used it all.'

An energetic interruption cut her short.

'There's no comparison, my little dear, no comparison... Silly things said to pass the time, to please the women... With you ... Holy Virgin! I have a feeling ... a great big feeling of goin' mad! You should know that I myself am amazed at what's happ'ning to me. I've never been sad after somethin' like this except with you. I don't even have the courage to talk to you. This is what I'm like ... half proud and half remorseful. I'd have preferred us to come back before lunch yesterday. D'you believe me? Ah, d'you believe me? By all that...'

And the southerner made a cross with his fingers and kissed them with a popular gesture. Asís began to laugh in spite of herself. There was no longer any chance of being angry: laughter disarms the most furious. And now what shall I do, thought the lady, summoning all her presence of mind and feminine skill to her aid. Nothing, very simple... Don't deny him the meeting he requested for the next afternoon; because if he were refused it he'd be capable of committing some foolish act. No, no ... be compliant ... agree to the meeting, and at the appointed time ... be any place other than where Pacheco is waiting... And now, *for your own good*, get him to leave as soon as possible... What would the servants say! Diabla will be in the kitchen making predictions!

XII

Doloroso es tener que reconocer y consignar ciertas cosas; sin embargo, la sinceridad obliga a no eliminarlas de la narración. Queda, eso sí, el recurso de presentarlas de forma indirecta, procurando con maña que no lastimen tanto como si apareciesen de frente, insolentonas y descaradas, metiéndose por los ojos. Así la implícita desaprobación del novelista se disfraza de habilidad.

Tocante a la cita que la marquesa viuda de Andrade pensaba conceder en falso, con resolución firmísima de hacer la del humo, la novela puede guardar un discreto mutismo; y no faltará a su elevada misión, con tal que refiera lo que ocurría a la puerta de la dama: indicación sobria y a la vez sumamente expresiva.

La berlina de la señora, enganchada desde las cinco, esperaba allí. El cochero, inmóvil, bien afianzado en su cuña, había permanecido algún tiempo en la actitud reglamentaria, enarbolada la fusta, recogidas las riendas, ladeado graciosamente el sombrero y muy juntas las punteras de las botas; pero transcurrido un cuarto de hora, el

12

It is painful to have to recognise and record certain things; nevertheless, honesty forbids their exclusion from the account. There does remain the recourse of presenting them in an indirect way, craftily ensuring that they don't offend as much as if they appeared head-on, haughty and shameless, right before your eyes. In this way the novelist skilfully disguises her implicit disapprobation.

Regarding the false meeting the dowager Marchioness of Andrade was intending to allow, with the resolute decision of disappearing in a puff of smoke, the novel may keep a discreet silence; and it won't fail in its high mission, as long as it relates what took place at the lady's door: a sober and at the same time extremely expressive gesture.

The lady's carriage, hitched up since five o'clock, was waiting there. The coachman, motionless, firmly secured in the driver's seat, had remained some time with the proper posture, his riding whip raised, the reins held together, his hat tilted graciously and the toecaps of his boots joined together; but after a quarter of an hour, the lull of

recalmón de la tardecita y el aburrimiento de la espera le derramaron en los párpados grato beleño y fue dejando caer la cabeza sobre el pecho, aflojando las manos, exhalando una especie de silbido y a veces un ronquido súbito, que le asustaba a él mismo despertándole … También el caballo, durante los primeros momentos de quietud, se mantuvo engallado, airoso, dispuesto a beberse la distancia; pero al convencerse de que teníamos plantón, desplomó el cuerpo sobre las patas, sacudió el freno regándolo con espuma, entornó los ojos y se dispuso a la siesta. Hasta la misma berlina pareció afianzarse en las ruedas con ánimo de descansar.

Y fue poniéndose el sol, subiendo de piso en piso a despedirse de los cristales, refugiándose en la copa de las acacias de Recoletos cuando ya las envolvía la azul y vaporosa bruma del anochecer; y el calor disminuyó un tantico, y el farolero corrió encendiendo hilos de luz a lo largo de las calles … Berlina, caballo y cochero dormían, resignados con su suerte, sin que se les ocurriese que para semejante viaje no se necesitaban alforjas y que mejor se encontrarían la una metida en su funda, el otro despachando su ración de pienso, el último en su taberna favorita o viendo la novillada de aquella tarde …

Cerca de las siete serían cuando salió de la casa un hombre. Era apuesto y andaba aprisa, recatándose de la portera. Atravesó la calle y en la acera de enfrente se detuvo, mirando hacia las ventanas del cuarto de Asís. Ni rastro de persona asomada en ellas. El hombre siguió su camino hacia Recoletos.

the late afternoon and the tedium of waiting spilled sweet henbane on his eyelids and his head dropped onto his chest, his hands relaxed, he breathed out a kind of whistling noise and an occasional sudden snore which would startle him awake… The horse, too, during the first moments of calm, remained erect, graceful, ready to soak up the distance; but coming to the conclusion there was a long wait ahead, its body collapsed on its legs, it shook the bit splattering it with foam, half-closed its eyes and got ready for a siesta. Even the carriage itself seemed to settle down on its wheels with the intention of resting.

The sun was gradually setting, going up from storey to storey to kiss goodbye to the window panes, taking refuge in the top of the acacias on the Recoletos Boulevard, already shrouded in the blue mist of dusk; and the heat diminished a bit, and the lamplighter ran and illuminated threads of light along the streets… Carriage, horse and driver were sleeping, resigned to their fate, without it occurring to them that there was no need to go to such trouble for a journey like this, and that the first would be better inside its cover, the second disposing of its ration of fodder, the last in his favourite tavern or watching that afternoon's bullfight…

It must have been close to seven o'clock when a man left the house. He was handsome and walked quickly, hiding himself from the porter. He crossed the street and stopped on the pavement on the other side, looking towards the windows of Asís's bedroom. No sign of anyone there. The man continued on his way towards Recoletos.

XIII

Solía el comandante Pardo ir alguna que otra noche a casa de su paisana y amiga la marquesa de Andrade. Charlaban de mil cosas, disputando, acalorándose, y en suma, pasando la velada solos, contentos y entretenidos. De galanteo propiamente dicho, ni sombra, aun cuando la gente murmuraba (de la tertulia de la Sahagún saldría el chisme) que don Gabriel hacía tiro al decente caudal y a la agradable persona de Asís; si bien otros opinaban, con trazas y tono de mejor informados, que ni a Pardo le importaba el dinero, por ser desinteresadísimo, ni las mujeres, por hallarse mal curada todavía la herida de un gran desengaño amoroso que en Galicia sufriera: una historia romántica y algo obscura con una sobrina, que por huir de él se había metido monja en un convento de Santiago.

Ello es que Pardo resolvió consagrar a la dama la noche del día en que la berlina echó la siesta famosa. Serían las nueve cuando llamó a la puerta. Generalmente, los criados le hacían entrar con un apresuramiento que delataba el gusto de la señora en recibir semejantes visitas. Pero aquella noche, así Perfecto (el mozo de comedor, a quien Asís llamaba *Imperfecto* por sus *gedeonadas*)[35] como la Diabla, se miraron y respondieron a la pregunta usual del comandante, titubeando e indecisos.

–¿Qué pasa? ¿Ha salido la señorita? Los martes no acostumbra.

–Salir …, como salir … –balbució Imperfecto.

–No, salir no –acudió la Diabla, viéndole en apuro–. Pero está un poco …

–Un poco *dilicada* –declaró el criado con tono diplomático.

–¿Cómo delicada? –exclamó el comandante alzando la voz–. ¿Desde cuándo se encuentra enferma? ¿Y qué tiene? ¿Guarda cama?

---

35   Neologismo: simplezas, derivado de Gedeón (personaje cómico que aparece en muchas obras dramáticas del siglo XIX).

13

Major Pardo was in the habit of going to the house of his friend and fellow countrywoman the Marchioness of Andrade at night now and then. They chatted about a thousand things, arguing, getting worked up and, in short, spending the evening on their own, happy and entertained. Of courtship, properly speaking, no trace at all, even when people whispered (the rumour must have come from the Sahagún circle) that Don Gabriel was attracted by the honest wealth and the agreeable person of Asís; but others, looking and sounding better informed, thought that Pardo wasn't bothered either about money, because he was so unselfish, or women, because he still wasn't cured from the wound of a great disappointment in love he had suffered in Galicia: a romantic and rather shady story about a niece who, in order to escape from him, had become a nun in a convent in Santiago.[30]

The fact is that Pardo decided to dedicate the evening of the very day on which her carriage had its memorable siesta to the lady in question. It would have been about nine o'clock when he rang the doorbell. Ordinarily the servants showed him in with a haste which disclosed the lady's pleasure at receiving such visits. But that night both Perfecto (the dining waiter whom Asís called "Imperfecto" on account of his ineptitude) and Diabla looked at each other and answered the major's usual question with hesitation and indecision.

'What's the matter? Has she gone out? She doesn't usually on Tuesdays.'

'Go out ... as in out...,' stammered Imperfecto.

'No, not out,' helped Diabla, seeing him in difficulty. 'But she's a bit...'

'A bit *dilicate*,' declared the servant in a diplomatic tone.

'Delicate in what way?' exclaimed the major, raising his voice. 'How long has she been ill? What's she got? Is she in bed?'

---

30 A reference to Pardo Bazán's novel *La madre naturaleza* (1887), in which Gabriel Pardo proposes marriage to his niece Manuela Moscoso Pardo. She rejects him because she prefers to enter a convent in order to repent for having unknowingly committed incest with her half-brother.

–No señor, guardar cama no … Unas *miagas*[36] de jaqueca …

–¡Ah!, bien: díganle ustedes que volveré mañana a saber … y que le deseo alivio. ¿Eh? ¡No se olviden!

Acabar de decir esto el comandante y aparecer en la antesala Asís en bata y arrastrando chinelas finas, fue todo uno.

–Pero que siempre han de entender al revés cuanto se les manda … Estoy, Pardo, estoy visible … Entre usted … Qué tienen que ver las órdenes que se dan así, en general, para la gente de cumplido …! Haga usted el favor de pasar aquí …

Gabriel entró. La sala estaba tan simpática, tan tentadora, tan fresca como la víspera; la pantalla de encaje filtraba la misma luz rosada y ensoñadora; en un talavera *de botica* se marchitaba un ramo de lilas y rosas blancas. Tropezó el pie del comandante, al ir a sentarse en su butaca de costumbre, con un objeto medio oculto en las arrugas del tapiz turco arrojado ante el diván. Se bajó y recogió del suelo el estorbo, maquinalmente. Asís extendió la mano, y a pesar de lo muy distraído y sonámbulo que era Gabriel, no pudo menos de observar la agitación de la dama al recobrar la prenda, que era uno de esos tarjeteros sin cierre, de cuero inglés, con dos iniciales de plata enlazadas, prenda evidentemente masculina. Por un instinto de discreción y respeto, Gabriel se hizo el tonto y entregó su hallazgo sin intentar ver la cifra.

–Pues me habían dado un susto ese Imperfecto y esa Diabla … – murmuró, tratando de disimular mejor la sorpresa–. Están en Belén … ¿Se había usted negado, sí o no?

–Le diré a usted … Di una orden … Claro que con usted no rezaba; bien ha visto usted que le llamé … –alegó la señora con acento contrito, cual si se disculpase de alguna falta gorda, y muy inmutada, aunque esforzándose también en no descubrirlo.

–¿Y qué es ello? ¿Jaqueca?

–Sí …, bastante incómoda. (Asís se llevó la mano a la sien.)

–Entonces le voy a dar a usted la noche si me quedo. La dejaré a usted descansar … En durmiendo se pasa.

–No, no, qué disparate … No se va usted. Al contrario …

---

36 Perfecto y Diabla suelen sustituir la fricativa palatal por la velar oclusiva en palabras como *miajas*, lo cual es un vulgarismo frecuente en el hablante gallego al expresarse en castellano.

'No, sir, not in bed... A *lickle* bit of a headache...'

'Ah, okay. Tell her that I'll come back tomorrow to find out ... and that I hope she's better soon, eh? Don't forget!'

The major finished saying this at the very same moment Asís shuffled into the ante-chamber in her dressing gown and fine slippers.

'They just always have to get the wrong end of the stick when they're given orders... Of course I'm in for you, Pardo... Come in... How could general orders like that apply to formal acquaintances! Please come this way...'

Gabriel went in. The room was as pleasant, inviting and fresh as on the previous night; the lace shade filtered the same pink, dreamy light; a bouquet of lilacs and white roses was withering in a ceramic Talavera medicinal jar. As the major went to sit down in his usual armchair, his foot struck something half hidden in the folds of the Turkish rug in front of the divan. He instinctively bent down and picked up the obstacle. Asís held out her hand and, despite his being very absent-minded and somnolent, Gabriel couldn't help noticing the lady's agitation when she got her accessory back, one of those English leather card cases without a fastener, with two linked-up silver initials, evidently a male accessory. By an instinct of discretion and respect, Gabriel acted dumb and handed over his discovery without trying to see the monogram.

'Well, your Imperfecto and Diabla gave me a fright,' he murmured, trying to hide his surprise better. 'They have their head in the clouds... Did you refuse, yes or no?'

'I'll tell you ... I gave an order... It wasn't for you, of course, and you can see quite clearly that I called you back...,' the lady pleaded with a penitent tone, as if she were excusing some grave fault and very upset, although also struggling not to show it.

'And what is it? A migraine?'

'Yes ... quite annoying.' (Asís raised her hand to her temple.)

'Then I'll cause you to have a bad night if I stay. I'll leave you to have a rest... It'll go away with sleep.'

'No, no, what rubbish ... don't go. On the contrary...'

–¿Cómo que *al contrario*? Ruego que se expliquen esas palabras –exclamó el comandante, aprovechando la ocasión de bromear para que se le quitase a Asís el sobresalto.

–Se explicarán … Significan que va usted a acompañarme por ahí fuera un ratito … A dar una vuelta a pie. Me conviene esparcirme, tomar el aire …

–Iremos a un teatrillo … ¿Quiere usted? Dicen que es muy gracioso *El Padrón Municipal*, en Lara.

–Teatrillo …, ¿calor, luces, gente? Usted pretende asesinarme. No: si lo que me pide el cuerpo es ejercicio. Así, conforme estoy, sin vestirme … Me planto un abrigo y un velo … Me calzo … y jala.

–A sus órdenes.

Cuando salieron a la calle, Asís suspiró, aliviada, y con el impulso de su andar señaló la dirección del paseo.

El barrio de Salamanca, a trechos, causa la ilusión gratísima de estar en el campo: masas de árboles, ambiente oxigenado y oloroso, espacio libre, y una bóveda de firmamento que parece más elevada que en el resto de Madrid.

La noche era espléndida, y al levantar Asís la cabeza para contemplar el centelleo de los astros, se le ocurrió, por decir alguna cosa, compararlos a las joyas que solía admirar en los bailes.

–Aquellas cuatro estrellitas seguidas parecen el imperdible de la marquesa de Riachuelo … cuatro brillantazos que le dejan a uno bizco. Esa constelación … ¡allí, hombre, allí!, hace el mismo efecto que la joya que le trajo de París su marido a la Torres-Nobles … Hasta tiene en medio una estrellita amarillenta, que será el brillante brasileño del centro. Aquel lucero tan bonito, que está solo …

–Es Venus … Tiene algo de emblemático eso de que Venus sea tan guapa.

–Usted siempre confundiendo lo humano y lo divino …

–No, si la mezcolanza fue usted quien la armó comparando los

'What do you mean *on the contrary*? I beg you to explain those words,' exclaimed the major, making the most of the opportunity to make a joke so that Asís would stop being startled.

'I'll explain them... They mean that you are going to accompany me outside for a while... For a little walk. I need to unwind, get some fresh air...'

'We'll go to the theatre... Do you want to? They say *El Padrón Municipal*[31] at the Lara is very amusing.'

'The theatre ... heat, lights, people? You're trying to kill me. No. What my body needs is exercise. I'm fine like this, without dressing up ... I'll get a coat and veil ... I'll put my shoes on ... and off we go.'

'Yes, madam.'

When they went out into the street, Asís sighed with relief and with the momentum of her walking set the direction of their stroll.

Here and there the Salamanca quarter creates the very pleasant illusion of being in the country: masses of trees, fresh, sweet-smelling air, open space and an arch of heaven which seems higher than in the rest of Madrid.

It was a splendid night and when Asís lifted her head to contemplate the twinkling stars, it occurred to her, for the sake of saying something, to compare them to the jewels she used to admire at dances.

'Those four little stars in a row look like the Marchioness of Riachuelo's pin ... four huge diamonds which leave you dumbfounded. That constellation ... look, over there ... has the same effect as the jewel which Torres-Nobles's husband brought her from Paris... It's even got a little yellowish star in the middle, akin to the Brazilian diamond in the centre. That beautiful bright star, on its own...'

'It's Venus... There's something symbolic about Venus being so pretty.'[32]

'You're always muddling human and divine...'

'No, you're the one who started the mishmash by comparing the

---

31 *El Padrón Municipal* is a two-act *zarzuela* (librettist unknown, music by Guillermo Cereceda). Lara is the name of a theatre in Madrid, built by Cándido Lara.

32 The second planet from the Sun, named after the Roman goddess of love and beauty.

astros a las joyas de sus amiguitas. ¡Qué hermoso es el cielo de Madrid! –añadió después de breve silencio–. En esto tenemos que rendir el pabellón, paisana. Nuestro suelo es más fresco, más bonito: pero la limpieza de esta atmósfera ... Allá hay que mirar hacia abajo, aquí hacia arriba.

Callaron un ratito.

En aquel dosel azul sembrado de flores de pedrería, Asís y el comandante veían la misma cosa, un tarjetero de piel inglesa; y como por magnética virtud, sentían al través de sus brazos, que se tocaban, el mutuo pensamiento.

Hallábanse al final del Prado, enteramente desierto a tales horas, con sus sillas recogidas y vueltas. Se escuchaba el murmurio monótono de la Cibeles, y allá en el fondo del jardincillo, tras las irregulares masas de las coníferas, destacaba el Museo su elegante silueta de palacio italiano. No pasaba un alma, y la plazuela de las Cortes, a la luz de sus faroles de gas, parecía tan solitaria como el Prado mismo.

–¿Subimos hacia la Carrera? –interrogó Pardo.

–No, paisano ... ¡Ay Jesús! A los dos pasos nos encontrábamos algún conocido, y mañana ..., chi, chi, chi ..., cuentecito en casa de Sahagún o donde se les antojase. Bajemos hacia Atocha.

–Y usted, ¿por qué da a eso tanta importancia? ¿Qué tiene de particular que salga usted a tomar el fresco en compañía de un amigo formal? Cuidado que son majaderas las fórmulas sociales. Yo puedo ir a su casa de usted y estarme allí las horas muertas sin que nadie se entere ni se ocupe, y luego, si salimos reunidos a la calle media hora ... cataplum.

–Qué manía tiene usted de ir contra la corriente ... Nosotros no

stars to your friends' jewels. How beautiful the sky in Madrid is!' he added after a brief silence. 'On that score we have to concede, my dear compatriot. Our soil is fresher, prettier, but this clean air... Over there you have to look down, but here upwards.'

They were quiet for a moment.

In that blue canopy studded with precious stones, Asís and the major could see the same thing, a card case made of English leather; and is if by magnetic force they could feel through their arms, which were touching, the shared thought.

They were at the end of the Prado,[33] entirely deserted at that hour, with its chairs collected and piled up. They listened to the monotonous murmur of the Cibeles Fountain, and there at the bottom of the little garden, behind the irregular mass of conifers, the museum showed off its elegant silhouette of an Italian palace.[34] Not a soul went by and the light from the gas streetlamps made the Plaza de las Cortes look as solitary as the Prado.

'Shall we go up towards the Carrera?'[35] asked Pardo.

'No, dear... Good heavens! Every other step we'd bump into some acquaintance, and tomorrow ... sh-sh-sh ... gossip at Sahagún's or wherever they want. Let's go down towards Atocha.'[36]

'And why do you attach so much importance to that? What's so unusual about you getting some fresh air in the company of a serious-minded friend? How stupid social conventions are! I can go to your house and stay there hour after hour without anyone either knowing or caring, but then if we go out in the street together for half an hour ... bang.'

'You're obsessed with going against the tide. ...We're not going to

---

33   The Paseo del Prado, one of the main boulevards in Madrid, is a wide, tree-lined avenue running between the Plaza de Cibeles and the Plaza del Emperador Carlos V (also known as Plaza de Atocha).

34   A reference to the Museo del Prado, the main national art museum of Spain. It has a very impressive collection of European art dating from the twelfth century to the early twentieth, and the single best collection of Spanish art.

35   A street in the centre of Madrid that runs from the Puerta del Sol to the Plaza de las Cortes.

36   The name apparently comes from the fact that, before the street was built, the area was *un atochar*, or field of esparto grass.

vamos a volver el mundo patas arriba. Dejarlo que ruede. Todo tiene sus porqués, y en algo se fundan esas precauciones o fórmulas, como usted les llama. ¡Ay! ¡Qué fresquito tan hermoso corre!

–¿Está usted mejor?

–Un poco. Me da la vida este aire.

–Quiere usted sentarse un rato? El sitio convida.

Sí que convidaba el sitio, a la vez acompañado y solo: unos anchos asientos de piedra que hay delante del Museo, a la entrada de la calle de Trajineros, la cual si por su gran proximidad a la plazuela de las Cortes resulta céntrica y decorosa, a semejante hora compite en lo desierta con el despoblado más formidable de Castilla. Las acacias prodigaban su rica esencia, y si el comandante tuviese propósito de declarar a la señora algún atrevido pensamiento, nunca mejor. No sería así, porque después de tomar asiento se quedaron mudos ella y él; Asís, además de muda, estaba cabizbaja y absorta.

No es posible que esta clase de pausas se establezcan en una entrevista a solas de hombre y mujer, en tales sitios y horas, sin producirles a los dos un estado de ánimo singular, a la vez atractivo y embarazoso. El comandante limpió sus quevedos, operación que verificaba muy a menudo, volvió a calárselos y salió por la puerta o por la ventana, juzgando que la señora desearía explayarse.

–A mí no me la pega usted con jaquecas, Paquita … usted tiene algo … alguna cosa que la preocupa en gordo … No se me alarme usted: ya sabe que somos amigos viejos.

–Pero si no tengo nada … ¡Qué ocurrencia!

–Mejor, señora, mejor, celebro que sea así –dijo don Gabriel retrocediendo discretamente–. Yo, en cambio, le podría confiar a usted penas muy grandes …, cosas raras.

–¿Lo de la sobrina? –preguntó Asís con curiosidad, pues ya dos o tres veces en conversación familiar habían aludido de rechazo a ese misterio de la vida de don Gabriel.

–Sí: al menos la parte mía …, lo que me toca …, eso puedo contárselo a usted. Sabe Dios cómo lo glosa la gente. –(Pardo se alzó el sombrero porque tenía las sienes húmedas de sudor.) –Creo que se dice que la pobrecilla me detestaba y que por librarse de mí entró

turn the world upside down. Let it roll on. Everything's got its whys and wherefores, and those precautions or conventions, as you call them, are based on something. Oh, what a delightful breeze!'

'Are you better?'

'A bit. This air is reviving me.'

'Do you want to sit down a while? This spot is inviting.'

In truth this was an inviting place, offering company and solitude at the same time: wide stone seats in front of the museum, at the entrance of the Calle de Trajineros, which whilst being central and decorous because of its proximity to the Plaza de las Cortes, is on a par in terms of bleakness at this time of day with the most formidable of deserted spots in Castile. The acacias lavished their rich perfume, and never would the time be better if the major's intention was to declare some daring thought to the lady. It wouldn't, because after sitting down they remained silent. Asís, as well as being silent, was downcast and absorbed in thought.

It isn't possible for this kind of pause to establish itself in a conversation between a man and woman alone together, at such a time and place, without it producing an odd state of mind in both of them, at the same time appealing and embarrassing. The major cleaned his pince-nez, a procedure he carried out very often, put it on again and went off on a tangent, judging that the lady would like to open her heart.

'You don't deceive me with talk of migraines, Paquita … there's something … something bothering you a lot… Don't be afraid: you know full well we're old friends.'

'But there's nothing wrong… What an idea!'

'All the better, I'm delighted,' said Don Gabriel, retreating discreetly. 'I, on the other hand, could confide my greatest worries to you … strange things.'

'The thing about your niece?' asked Asís with curiosity, for already two or three times in intimate conversation that mystery from Don Gabriel's life had been alluded to incidentally.

'Yes, at least my part … what concerns me … I can tell you that. God knows how people comment on it.' (Pardo raised his hat, for his temples were moist with sweat.) 'I believe they say that the poor thing hated me and entered a convent as a novice to escape from me…

en un convento de novicia ... Falso. No me detestaba, y es más: me hubiera querido con toda su alma a la vuelta de poco tiempo ... Sólo que ella misma no acertó a descifrarlo. Cuando me conoció, estaba comprometida con otro hombre ... cuya clase ... no ... En fin, que no podía aspirar a ser su marido. Y al convencerse de esto, la infeliz muchacha pensó que se acababa el mundo para ella y que no tenía más refugio que el convento. ¡Ay, Paquita! ¡Si supiese usted qué ratos ... qué tragedia! Es asombroso que después de ciertos acontecimientos pueda uno volver a vivir como antes ..., y vaya a tertulias y se chancee, y mire otra vez a las mujeres, y le agraden, sí ..., como me agrada usted, por ejemplo ..., y no lo eche usted a mala parte, que no soy pretendiente importuno, sino amigo de verdad. Ya sabe usted cómo digo yo las cosas.

Oía la dama la voz del artillero y al par otra interior que zumbaba confusamente:

–Confíale algo ..., al menos indícale tu situación ... Ideas estrafalarias las tiene, y a veces es poco práctico, pero es leal ... No corres peligro, no ... Así te desahogarás ... Tal vez te aconseje bien. Anda, boba ... ¿No hace él confianza en ti? Además ... no creas que callando le engañas ... ¡Quítale ya la escama del tarjetero!

A pesar de las excitaciones de la voz indiscreta, la señora, en alto, decía tan sólo:

–¿Conque la chica le quería a usted algo? ¿Sin saberlo? ¡Eso es muy particular! ¿Y cómo lo explica usted?

–¡Ay, Paquita! He renunciado a explicar cosa alguna ... No hay explicación que valga para los fenómenos del corazón. Cuanto más se quieren entender, más se obscurecen. Hay en nosotros anomalías tan raras, contradicciones tan absurdas ... Y a la vez cierta lógica fatal. En esto de la simpatía sexual, o del amor, o como usted guste llamarle, es en lo que se ven mayores extravagancias. Luego, a los caprichos y las desviaciones y los brincos de esta víscera que tenemos aquí, sume usted la maraña de ideas con que la sociedad complica los problemitas psicológicos. La sociedad ...

–Contigo tengo la tema, morena ... –interrumpió Asís festivamente–. Usted le echa a la sociedad todas las culpas. Ahí que no duele. Ya no sé cómo tiene espaldas la infeliz.

False. She didn't hate me, and what's more, she would have loved me with all her heart after a little time... Only she herself didn't manage to work it out. When she met me she was engaged to another man ... whose social class ... no... Anyway, who had no hope of being her husband. And when she convinced herself of this, the unhappy girl believed that her world had come to an end and that her only refuge was a convent. Ah, Paquita! If you knew what grief ... what a tragedy! It's amazing that after certain events one can live again as before ... and go to social gatherings and make jokes, and look at women again, and like them too ... as I like you, for example ... and don't get me wrong, because I'm not a troublesome suitor, but a true friend. You know I say things as they are.'

The lady heard the artilleryman's voice together with another interior voice that resounded confusingly:

'Confide in him ... at least tell him about your situation... He's got weird ideas, and at times he's not very practical, but he's loyal... You're not running any risk, not... You'll get it off your chest that way... Perhaps he'll give you good advice. Go on, you fool... Doesn't he confide in you? Besides ... don't think that you'll fool him by saying nothing... Get rid of his suspicion about the card case!'

Despite the rousing nature of the indiscreet voice, the lady merely said out loud:

'So the girl loved you a bit? Without realising? That's very strange! And how do you explain it?'

'Ah, Paquita! I've given up explaining anything... There's no worthy explanation for things of the heart. The more you want to understand, the more confused they become. There are such strange anomalies in us, such absurd contradictions... And at the same time a certain fatal logic. As for sexual sympathy, or love, or whatever you like to call it, that's where the greatest extravagances are seen. And then, to the whims and aberrations and leaps of this organ we've got here, add the entanglement of ideas with which society complicates the psychological problems. Society...'

'You're always insisting on the same thing,' Asís interrupted humorously. 'You blame society for everything. That way it doesn't hurt. I don't know how that contention can still stand.'

–Pues, figúrese usted, paisana. Como que de mi tragedia únicamente es responsable la sociedad. Por atribuir exagerada importancia a lo que tiene mucha menos ante las leyes naturales. Por hacer lo principal de lo accesorio. En fin, punto en boca. No quiero escandalizarla a usted.

–Paisano … Pero si me da mucha curiosidad eso que iba usted diciendo … No me deje a media miel … Todas las cosas pueden decirse, según como se digan. No me escandalizaré, vamos.

–Bien, siendo así … Pero ya no sé en qué estábamos … ¿Usted se acuerda?

–Decía usted que lo principal y lo accesorio … Eso será alguna herejía tremenda, cuando no quiso usted pasar de ahí.

–Sí, señora … Verá usted, la herejía … Yo llamo accesorio a lo que en estas cuestiones suele llamarse principal … ¿Se hace usted cargo?

Asís no respondió, porque pasaba un mozalbete silbando un aire de zarzuela y mirando de reojo y con malicia al sospechoso grupo. Cuando se perdió de vista, pronunció la dama:

–¿Y si me equivoco?

–¿No se asusta usted si lo expreso claramente?

La verdad, desde cierta distancia aquello parecía un diálogo amoroso. Acaso la valla que existía para que ni pudiese serlo ni llegase a serlo jamás, era un delgado y breve trozo de piel inglesa, la cubierta de un tarjetero.

–No, no me asusto … Vamos a hablar como dos amigos … francamente.

–¿Quedamos en eso? ¡Magnífico! Pues conste que ya no tiene usted derecho para reñirme si se me va la lengua … Procuraré, sin embargo … En fin, entiendo por accesorio … aquello que ustedes juzgan irreparable. ¿Lo pongo más claro aún?

–No, ¡basta! –gritó la señora–. Pero entonces, ¿qué es lo principal según usted?

–Una cosa que abunda menos …, en cambio, vale más … La realidad de un cariño muy grande entre dos … ¿Qué le parece a usted?

–¡Caramba! –exclamó la señora, meditabunda.

–Le voy a proponer a usted una demostración de mi teoría … Ejemplo; como dicen los predicadores. Imagínese que en vez de estar en el Prado,

'Well, just think, my friend. About how society alone is responsible for my tragedy. By attributing an exaggerated importance to what has far less according to the laws of nature. By making something incidental into the main thing. Anyway, mum's the word. I don't want to scandalise you.'

'Dear compatriot... How you excite my curiosity with what you were saying... Don't leave me hanging... You can say anything, depending on how it's said. Come on, I won't be scandalised.'

'Very well, in that case... But I don't know where we were any more... Do you remember?'

'You were talking about the main thing and the incidental... It must be some terrible heresy that you refused to go down that path.'

'Yes... You'll see the heresy... I call incidental what in these matters is usually called the main thing... Do you understand?'

Asís didn't reply, because a young lad was passing by whistling a song from a *zarzuela* and looking furtively and mischievously at the suspicious pair. When he was out of sight, the lady declared:

'And if I'm wrong?'

'You won't be afraid if I express things clearly?'

To be honest, from a certain distance it would have looked like a lovers' dialogue. Perhaps the barrier which prevented it from being one, or ever becoming one, was a short, thin piece of English leather, the cover of a card case.

'No, I'm not afraid... Let's talk like two friends ... openly.'

'Do we agree on that? Magnificent! Well, then, acknowledge that you have no right to reprimand me if I talk too much ... I shall try, though... Anyway, by accessory, I understand ... what you judge irreparable. Shall I put it even more clearly?'

'No, enough!' the lady shouted. 'But what, then, is the main thing for you?'

'A thing less common ... but more valuable... The reality of a very great affection between two... What do you think?'

'Good gracious!' exclaimed the lady thoughtfully.

'I'm going to propose a demonstration of my theory to you ... An example, as preachers say. Imagine that instead of being in the Prado

estamos en Tierra de Campos, a dos leguas de un poblachón; que yo soy un bárbaro; que me prevalgo de la ocasión, y abuso de la fuerza, y le falto a usted al respeto debido ... ¿Hay entre nosotros, dos minutos después, algún vínculo que no existía dos minutos antes? No señora. Lo mismo que si ahora se trompica usted con una esquina ..., se hace daño ..., procura apartarse y andar con más cuidado otra vez ... y acabóse.

–Pintado el lance así ..., lo que habría, que usted me parecería atroz de antipático y de bruto.

–Eso sí ... pero vamos a perfeccionar el ejemplo, y pido a usted perdón de antemano por una conversación tan *shocking*. Pues no señora: suponga usted que yo no abuso de la fuerza ni ese es el camino. Lo que hago es explotar con maña la situación y despertar en usted ese germen que existe en todo ser humano ... Nada de violencia: si acaso, en el terreno puramente moral ... Yo soy hábil y provoco en usted un momento de flaqueza ...

Fortuna que era de noche y estaba lejos el farol, que si no, el sofoco y el azoramiento de la dama se le meterían por los ojos al comandante. –Lo sabe, lo sabe–, calculaba para sí, toda trémula y en voz alterada y suplicante, exclamó interrumpiendo:

–¡Qué horror! ¡Don Gabriel!

–¿Qué horror? ¡Mire usted lo que va de ustedes a nosotros! Ese horror, Paquita del alma, no les parece horrible a los caballeros que usted trata y estima: al marqués de Huelva con su severidad de principios y su encomienda de Calatrava que no se quita ni para bañarse ..., al papá de usted tan amable y francote ..., yo ..., el otro ..., toditos. Es valor entendido y a nadie le extraña ni le importa un bledo. Tratándose de ustedes es cuando por lo más insignificante se arma una batahola de mil diablos, que no parece sino que arde por los cuatro costados Madrid. La infeliz de ustedes que resbala, si olfateamos el resbalón, nos arrojamos a ella como sabuesos, y o puede casarse con el *seductor*, o la matriculamos en el gremio de las mujeres galantes hasta la hora de la muerte. Ya puede después de su falta llevar vida más ejemplar que la de una monja: la hemos fallado ..., no nos la pega más. O bodas, o es usted una corrida, una perdida de profesión

we're in Tierra de Campos,[37] two leagues from any one-horse town; that I'm a brute, that I take advantage of the situation, and abuse my strength, and fail to show you due respect... Is there, two minutes afterwards, any bond between us which didn't exist two minutes before? No. The same if you stumble now in a corner ... hurt yourself ... try to move away and walk more carefully again ... and that's it.'

'Describing the incident like this ... the thing is, you'd seem atrociously unpleasant and brutish.'

'Yes indeed ... but let's finish the example, and I beg your pardon in advance for a conversation so *épatant*. Well, no: suppose that I don't abuse my strength, or anything of the sort. What I do is skilfully exploit the situation and revive in you that germ which exists in every human being... No violence, except maybe in the purely moral field... I'm skilful and I bring about a moment of weakness in you...'

Fortunately it was night and the streetlamp was in the distance, otherwise the lady's shame and embarrassment would have betrayed her to the major. 'He knows, he knows,' she realised, trembling and in a disturbed and imploring voice, interrupted with an exclamation:

'How awful! Don Gabriel!'

'How awful? Just look at the difference between you and us! This horror, my dear Paquita, doesn't seem horrible to the men you know and respect: the Marquis of Huelva with his stern principles and his Calatrava cross, which he doesn't take off even when has a bath ... your nice, forthright dad ... me ... the others ... all of us. It's an accepted value and nobody is surprised by it or gives a damn about it. They use the polite 'usted' form of address whilst, even for the most trivial thing, creating an uproar that makes it seem like the whole of Madrid is on fire. We only have to get a whiff of a lapse for us to throw ourselves like bloodhounds upon the unfortunate woman who slips up, and either she gets married to the *seducer* or we register her in the association of wanton women until the hour of her death. After her slip she can lead a more exemplary life than a nun: we have passed judgement on her ... and she will deceive us no more. It's either marriage or you're a promiscuous woman, a loose woman by

---

37   A vast, desolate plain that includes parts of the provinces of León, Zamora, Valladolid and Palencia.

… ¡Bonita lógica! Usted, niña inocente, que cae víctima de la poca edad, la inexperiencia y la tiranía de los afectos y las inclinaciones naturales, púdrase en un convento, que ya no tiene usted más camino … Amiga Asís … ¡Tonterías!

Mientras hablaba el comandante, su fantasía, en vez de los plátanos del jardincillo, le representaba otras masas sombrías de follaje, robles y castaños; y el olor fragante de las flores de acacia le parecía el de las silvestres mentas que crecen al borde de los linderos en el valle de Ulloa. La dama que tenía a su lado, por otro fenómeno de óptica interior, veía el rebullicio de una feria, una casita al borde del Manzanares, un cuartuco estrecho, un camastro, una taza de té volcada …

–Tonterías –prosiguió don Gabriel sin fijarse en la gran emoción de Asís–, pero que se pagan caras a veces … Sucede que se nos imponen, y que por obedecerlas, una mujer de instintos nobles se juzga manchada, vilipendiada, infamada por toda su vida a consecuencia de un minuto de extravío, y, de no poder casarse con aquel a quien se cree ligada para siempre jamás, se anula, se entierra, se despide de la felicidad por los siglos de los siglos amén … Es monja sin vocación, o es esposa sin cariño … Ahí tiene usted donde paran ciertas cosas.

Al murmurar con amargura estas palabras, el comandante, en lugar de la silueta gentil del Museo, veía las verdosas tapias del convento santiagués, las negras rejas de trágicos recuerdos, y tras de aquellas rejas comidas de orín una cara pálida, con obscuros ojos, muy semejante a la de cierta hermana suya que había sido el cariño más profundo de su vida.[37]

---

37 El narrador hace referencia a Nucha, hermana de Gabriel y madre de Manuela Moscoso.

profession… Great logic! You, innocent child, a victim of youth, inexperience and the tyranny of passions and natural preferences, go and rot in a convent because you've no other path to go down… My friend Asís… What rubbish!'

While the major was speaking, fancy showed him, instead of the plane trees of the Prado, other, sombre masses of foliage, oak and chestnut trees; and the fragrant smell of the acacias seemed to him like the wild mint that grows at the edge of the limits in the Valley of Ulloa. By another phenomenon of inner optics, the woman by his side could see the tumult of a fair, a little house on the banks of the Manzanares, a narrow little room, a ramshackle bed, a cup of tea knocked over…

'Rubbish,' continued Don Gabriel without noticing Asís's strong emotion, 'but we pay dearly at times… It happens that they command our respect, and that in order to obey them a woman of noble instincts judges herself tarnished, vilified, infamous for her whole life as a result of a minute's transgression, and not being able to marry the man to whom she believes herself eternally bound, she renounces everything, hides herself away, says goodbye to happiness forever, amen… She's a nun without vocation, or a wife without affection… And there you have it, where certain things lead.'

As he bitterly murmured these words, instead of the graceful silhouette of the Prado Museum, the major could see the greenish walls of the Santiago convent, the black bars of tragic memories, and behind those rusted bars a pale face with dark eyes very similar to those of a certain sister of his who had been the most profound love of his life.

XIV

–Vaya, Pardo … Es usted terrible. ¿Me quiere usted igualar la moral de los hombres con la de las mujeres?

–Paquita …, dejémonos de *clichés* –(Pardo usaba muy a menudo esta palabrilla para condenar las frases o ideas vulgares)–. Tanto jabón llevan ustedes en las suelas del calzado como nosotros. Es una hipocresía detestable eso de acusarlas e infamarlas a ustedes con tal rigor por lo que en nosotros nada significa.

–¿Y la conciencia, señor mío? ¿Y Dios?

La dama argüía con cierta afectada solemnidad y severidad, bajo la cual velaba una satisfacción inmensa. Iban pareciéndole muy bonitos y sensatos los detestables sofismas del comandante, que así pervierte la pasión el entendimiento.

–¡La conciencia! ¡Dios! –exclamó él remedando el tono enfático de la señora–. Otro registro. Bueno: toquémoslo también. ¿Se trata de pecadores creyentes? ¿Católicos, apostólicos, romanos?

–Por supuesto. ¿Ha de ser todo el mundo hereje como usted?

–Pues si tratamos de creyentes, la cuestión de conciencia es independiente de la de sexo. Aunque me llama usted hereje, todavía no he olvidado la doctrina; puedo decirle a usted de corrido los diez mandamientos … y se me figura que rezan igual con ustedes que con nosotros. Y también sé que el confesor las absuelve y perdona a ustedes igualito que a nosotros. Lo que pide a la penitente el ministro de Dios, es arrepentimiento, propósito de enmienda. El mundo, más severo que Dios, pide la perfección absoluta, y si no … O todo o nada.

–No, no; mire usted que también el confesor nos aprieta más las clavijas. Para ustedes la manga se ensancha un poquito … –repuso Asís, saboreando el deleite de aducir malas razones para saborear el gusto de verlas refutadas.

–Hija, si eso hacen, es por prudencia, para que no desertemos del confesionario si nos da por frecuentarlo … En el fondo ningún confesor le dirá a usted que hay un pecado más para las hembras. Es decir que la cosa queda reducida a las consecuencias positivas y exteriores, … al criterio social. En salvando éste, en no sabiéndose nada, el asunto no

14

'Come on, Pardo… You're dreadful. Do you want to make men's moral standards the same as women's?'

'Paquita… Let's drop the *clichés.*' (Pardo very often used this little word to condemn commonplace phrases or ideas). 'We are all made of the same clay. It's terrible hypocrisy to accuse and discredit women with such rigour for what means nothing in us men.'

'And conscience, my friend? And God?'

The lady argued with a certain affectation of solemnity and severity beneath which she concealed an immense satisfaction. The major's detestable sophisms, that passion perverts understanding in this way, began to seem very nice and sensible to her.

'Conscience! God!' he exclaimed, imitating the lady's emphatic tone. 'Another topic to be explored. All right, let's touch on that too. Is it about sinners who are believers, Catholic, apostolic, Roman?'

'Of course. Has everybody got to be a heretic like you?'

'Well, if we're talking about believers, the question of conscience is independent of sex. Even though you call me a heretic, I still haven't forgotten the catechism; I can tell you the ten commandments off by heart … and I think that they apply as much to you as us. And I also know that your confessor absolves you and pardons you the same as us. What the minister of God asks of the penitent is repentance, determination to make amends. The world, severer than God, demands absolute perfection, and if not… All or nothing.'

'No, no. Look, the confessor tightens the screws with us. They're a bit more lenient with you men', replied Asís, savouring the delight of providing poor reasons to savour the pleasure of hearing them refuted.

'If they do that, it's by way of precaution, so that we men do not abandon the confessional if we feel like going there… Basically, no priest will tell you that there's a special sin for women. So the matter is reduced to positive and external consequences … to the social criterion. If this is saved, if no one knows anything, it's no worse for

tiene más trascendencia en ustedes que en nosotros ... Y en nosotros
... ¡ayúdeme usted a sentir! (Al argüir así, el comandante castañeteaba
los dedos.) Ahora, si usted me ataca por otro lado ...

–Yo ... –balbució la señora, sin pizca de ganas de atacar.

–Si me sale usted con el respeto y la estimación propia ..., con lo
que cada cual se debe a sí mismo ...

–Eso ..., lo que cada cual se debe a sí mismo –articuló Asís hecha
una amapola.

–Convendré en que eso siempre realza a una mujer; pero, en gran
parte, depende del criterio social. La mujer se cree infamada después
de una de esas caídas ante su propia conciencia, porque le han hecho
concebir desde niña que lo más malo, lo más infamante, lo irreparable,
es eso; que es como el infierno, donde no sale el que entra. A nosotros
nos enseñan lo contrario; que es vergonzoso para el hombre no tener
aventuras, y que hasta queda humillado si las rehúye ... De modo, que
lo mismo que a nosotros nos pone muy huecos, a ustedes las envilece.
Preocupaciones hereditarias emocionales, como diría Spencer. Y vaya
unos terminachos que le suelto a usted.

–No, si yo con su trato ya me voy haciendo una sabia. Todos los
días me aporrea usted los oídos con cada palabrota ...

–¿Y si yo le dijese a usted –prosiguió Pardo echándose a disertar–,
que *eso* que llamé accesorio en las aventurillas, me parece a mí que en
el cariño verdadero, cuando están unidas así, así, como si las pegasen
con argamasa, las voluntades, llega a ser más accesorio aún? Es el
complemento de otra cosa mucho más grande, que dura siempre, y
que comprende eso y todo lo demás ... Lo estoy embrollando, paisana.
Usted se ríe de mí: a callar.

Asís oía, oía con toda su alma, pareciéndole que nunca había tenido
su paisano momentos tan felices como aquella noche, ni hablado tan
discreta y profundamente. Los dichos del comandante, que al pronto
lastimaban sus convicciones adquiridas, entraban, sin embargo, como
bien disparadas saetas hasta el fondo de su entendimiento y encendían
en él una especie de hoguera incendiaria, a cuya destructora luz

you than for us... And as for us ... help me here!' (As he argued in this way, the major snapped his fingers.) 'Now, if you attack me from the other side ...'

'I...,' stammered the lady, without the slightest desire to attack. 'If you come out with respect and self-esteem ... what each one of us owes himself...'

'That's it ... what each one owes himself,' uttered Asís, as red as a beetroot.

'I'll agree that that always elevates a woman; but it depends largely on the social criterion. Women believe they have lost their honour after one of these falls before their own conscience, because from childhood they have been made to conceive of it as the worst, the most shameful, the most irreparable thing; that it's like hell, where anyone who enters doesn't leave. We men are taught the opposite; that it's shameful for a man not to have any flings, and even that it's humiliating if he avoids them... So, the very same thing that makes us proud degrades you. Hereditary emotional worries, as Spencer would say.[38] What ugly words I'm hurling at you.'

'No, my dealings with you are making me into a wise woman. Day in day out you bash my ears with every coarse expression...'

'And if I told you,' continued Pardo, starting to lecture, 'that what I called an accessory in little flings becomes, in my opinion, even more of an accessory in real love when minds are united like this, as if stuck together with mortar. It's the complement of something else much bigger, that lasts forever, including that and everything else ... I'm complicating it. You're laughing at me: time to shut up.'

Asís was listening, listening with all her soul, thinking that her compatriot had never had moments of such success as that night, nor spoken so prudently, so profoundly. The major's remarks, which at first offended the convictions she had acquired, nevertheless entered into the very depths of her understanding like well-aimed arrows and kindled in it a kind of incendiary bonfire by whose destructive light she

---

38 Herbert Spencer (1820–1903) was an English sociologist, philosopher, biologist and anthropologist, best remembered for his doctrine of social Darwinism, according to which the principles of evolution, including natural selection, apply equally to human societies, social classes and individuals.

veía tambalearse infinitas cosas de las que había creído más sólidas y firmes hasta entonces. Era como si le arrancasen del espíritu una muela dañada: dolor y susto al sentir el frío del instrumento y el tirón; pero después, un alivio, una sensación tan grata viéndose libre de aquel cuerpo muerto … Anestesia de la conciencia con cloroformo de malas doctrinas, podría llamarse aquella operación quirúrgico-moral.

–Es un extravagante este hombre –pensaba la operada–. Decir me está diciendo cosas estupendas … Pero se me figura que le sobra la razón por encima de los pelos. Habla por su boca la justicia. ¿Va una a creerse criminal por unos instantes de error? Siempre estoy a tiempo de pararme y no reincidir … ¡Claro que si por sistema …! Ni él tampoco dice eso, no … Su teoría es que ciertas cosas que suceden así …, qué sé yo cómo, sin iniciativa ni premeditación por parte de uno, no han de mirarse como manchas de esas que ya nunca se limpian … El mismo padre Urdax de fijo que no es tan severo en eso como la sociedad hipocritona … ¡Ay Dios mío! … Ya estoy como mi paisano, echándole a la sociedad la culpa de todo.

Al llegar aquí de sus reflexiones la dama, la molestó un cosquilleo, primero entre las cejas, luego en la membrana de la nariz … ¡Aaach! Estornudó con ruido, estremeciéndose.

–¡Adiós! Ya se me ha resfriado usted –exclamó su amigo–. No está usted acostumbrada a estas vagancias al sereno … Levántese usted y paseemos.

–No, si no es el rocío lo que me acatarra a mí … He tomado sol.

–¿Sol? ¿Cuándo?

–Ayer …, digo, anteayer …, yendo …, sí, yendo a misa a las Pascualas. No crea usted: desde entonces ando yo … regular, nada más que regularcita. Cuando jaquecas, cuando mareos …

–De todos modos … guíese usted por mí: andemos, ¿eh? Si sobre la insolación le viene a usted un pasmo … o coge usted unas intermitentes de estas de primavera en Madrid …

–No me asuste usted … Tengo poco de aprensiva –contestó la dama levantándose y envolviéndose mejor en el abrigo.

–¿A su casa de usted?

–Bien …, sí, vamos hacia allá despacio.

No siguió el comandante explanando sus disolventes opiniones

could see rocking an infinite number of things which up until then she had believed to be firm and solid. It was as if a rotten tooth were being extracted from her mind: pain and fear on feeling the cold instrument and the tug, but afterwards relief, such a pleasant sensation being free from that dead body… That surgical moral operation could be called anaesthesia of the conscience by chloroform of evil doctrines.

'This man is bizarre,' thought the patient. 'He's certainly saying some astonishing things… But I think he's absolutely right. What comes from his mouth makes sense. Should you think of yourself as a criminal for the sake of a brief error? There's still time for me to stop and not reoffend… Of course, if one behaves that way as a rule… Nor does he say that, no… His theory is that certain things that happen like this … how shall I say, without initiative or premeditation on one's part, shouldn't be seen as indelible stains… Even Father Urdax is definitely not as strict on these matters as our hypocritical society… Oh my God! … I'm just like my compatriot, blaming society for everything.'

When the lady's thoughts reached this point she was troubled by a tickling sensation, at first between her eyebrows and then in her nasal membrane … Achoo! She sneezed noisily, shivering.

'Why, you've caught a cold,' her friend exclaimed. 'You're not used to roaming about in the open air… Get up, let's go for a walk.'

'No, it's not the dew that's giving me a cold… It's too much sun.'

'Sun? When?'

'Yesterday … I mean the day before yesterday … going … yes, going to mass at Las Pascualas. Since then I've been so-so, nothing more than so-so… At times a headache, other times feeling sick…'

'Anyway … be guided by me. Let's walk, eh? If you get a chill on top of sunstroke … or one of those intermittent spring fevers from Madrid…'

'Don't frighten me … I'm not a hypochondriac,' answered the lady as she stood up and wrapped herself warmly in her coat.

'Shall we go to your house?'

'All right … yes, we'll go slowly in that direction.'

The major desisted from elucidating his analytical opinions right

hasta la misma puerta de la señora. Al abrirla Imperfecto, Asís convidó a su amigo a que descansase un rato; él se negó; necesitaba darse una vuelta por el Círculo Militar, leer los periódicos extranjeros y hablar con un par de amigos, a última hora, en Fornos. Deseó respetuosamente las buenas noches a la señora y bajó las escaleras a paso redoblado. Con el mismo echó calle abajo aquel gran despreocupado, nihilista de la moral: y nos consta que iba haciendo este o parecido soliloquio, parecidísimo al que en igualdad de circunstancias haría otra persona que pensase según todos los *clichés* admitidos:

–Me ha engañado la viuda ... Yo que la creía una señora impecable. Un apabullo como otro cualquiera. No he mirado las iniciales del tarjetero: serían ... ¡vaya usted a saber! Porque en realidad, ni nadie murmura de ella, ni veo a su alrededor persona que ... En fin, cosas que suceden en la vida: chascos que uno se lleva. Cuando pienso que a veces se me pasaba por la cabeza decirle algo formal ... No, esto no es un *caballo muerto*, ¡qué disparate!, es sólo un tropiezo del caballo ... No he llegado a caerme ... ¡Así fuesen los desengaños todos! ...

Siguió caminando sin ver los árboles del Retiro, que se agrupaban en misteriosas masas a su derecha. Ni percibía el olor de las acacias. Pero él seguía oliendo, no a los cortesanos y pulidos vegetales de los paseos públicos, sino a otros árboles rurales, bravíos y libres: los que producen la morena castaña que se asa en los magostos de noviembre, en el valle de los Pazos.

up to the lady's very door. When Imperfecto opened it, Asís invited her friend to rest a while, but he refused; he needed to have a stroll around the Military Club, read the foreign newspapers and have a chat later with a couple of friends at the Café de Fornos.[39] He wished the lady a respectful good night and descended the stairs at the double. That great broad-minded, moral nihilist went down the street at the same pace; and there is evidence that he was soliloquising like this or in a similar way, as would anyone who, in the same circumstances, thought according to all the accepted *clichés*:

'The widow has deceived me... And I thought her an impeccable lady. A crushing blow like any other. I didn't see the initials on the card case. They must be ... who knows! Because in reality nobody whatsoever gossips about her, nor can I see anyone near her who... Well, such things happen in life, disappointments we have to bear. When I think that at times I have been close to saying something serious to her... No, this isn't flogging a dead horse – how absurd! – it's only a setback ... I haven't had a fall... If all disappointments were like this!'

He carried on walking without seeing the trees of the Retiro grouped together in mysterious clumps to his right. Nor did he smell the acacias. But he carried on smelling, not the courtly, manicured plants of the public avenues, but other rural trees, wild and free: those which produce the dark chestnuts roasting on the open fires of November in the Valley of Los Pazos.

---

39 A famous *café de tertulia* situated on the corner of the Calle de Alcalá y Peligros.

XV

La tarde del día siguiente la dedicó Asís a pagar visitas. Tarea maquinal y enfadosa, deber de los más irritantes que el pacto social impone. Raro es que nadie se someta a él sin murmurar, por fuera o por dentro, del mundo y sus farsas. Menos mal cuando las visitas se hacen, como las hacía la dama, en pies ajenos. Entonces lo arduo de la faena empieza en las porterías. ¡Si todas las casas fuesen como la de Sahagún o la de Torres-Nobles, por ejemplo! Allí, antes de llegar, ya llevaba Asís en la mano la tarjeta con el pico dobladito,[38] y al sentir rodar el coche, ya estaba asomándose al ancho vano del portón el portero imponente, patilludo, correcto, amabilísimo, que recogía la tarjeta preguntando: —¿Adónde desea ir la señora?— para transmitir la orden al cochero. Los Torres-Nobles, los Sahagún, los Pinogrande y otras familias así, de muy alto copete, no recibían sino de noche alguna vez, y el llegarse a su casa para dejar la tarjeta representaba una fórmula de cortesía facilísima de cumplir al bajar al paseo o al volver de las tiendas. Pero si entre las relaciones de Asís las había tan granadas, otras eran de muchísimo menos fuste, y algunas, procedentes de Vigo, rayaban en modestas. Y allí era el entrar en portales angostos, el parlamentar con porteras gruñonas, la desconsoladora respuesta: —Sí, señora, me parece que no ha salío en to el día de casa … Tercero con entresuelo, primero y principal … a mano izquierda—. Y la ascensión interminable, el sobrealiento, el tedio de subir por aquel caracol obscuro, con olores a cocina y a todas las oficinas caseras, y la cerril alcarreña que abre, y la acogida embarazosa, las empalagosas preguntitas, los chiquillos sucios y desgreñados, los relatos de enfermedades, la chismografía viguesa agigantada por la óptica de la distancia … Vamos, que era para renegar, y Asís renegaba en su interior, consultando sin embargo la lista de la cartera y diciendo con un suspiro profundo: —¡Ay! … Aún falta la viuda de Pardiñas … la madre del médico de Celas …, y Rita, la hermana de Gabriel Pardo … Y esa sí que es urgente … Ha tenido al chiquillo con difteria …

---

38 Para anunciar o solicitar una visita, la tarjeta tenía la esquina superior derecha doblada.

15

Asís spent the following afternoon paying visits, a mechanical and burdensome task that was one of the most irritating duties imposed by the social compact. Rarely does anybody submit to it without muttering inwardly or outwardly about the world and its farces. What a relief when, as was the case with the lady's visits, someone else takes you. Then the arduous nature of the task begins at the caretaker's lodge. If only all the houses were like those of Sahagún and Torres-Nobles, for example. There, before she arrived, Asís would already be holding in her hand the card with a corner turned down, and as soon as the impressive, pleasing and polite doorman heard the approaching carriage he would appear in the wide doorway and take the card, asking, 'Where does madam wish to go?' so as to pass on the order to the coachman. The Torres-Nobles, Sahagúns, Pinograndes and other such prominent families didn't receive except occasionally at night, and going over to their house to leave a card was a courtesy formula that was very easy to carry out on the way down for a stroll or coming back from the shops. But if some of Asís's acquaintances were very distinguished, others were of a much lower social standing, and some from Vigo bordered on having a very modest standard of living. And there, going into narrow doorways to converse with grumpy porters, the disheartening reply: 'Yes, madam, I b'lieve she ain't left the house all day... Third floor counting the mezzanine level, and the first and second floors ... on the left-hand side.' And the never-ending ascension, the difficulty breathing, the boredom of going up that dark spiral staircase, with smells from the kitchen and all the utility rooms, and the coarse woman from the Alcarria at the door, and the awkward reception, the sickly sweet little questions, the dirty, dishevelled kids, the accounts of illnesses, the Vigo gossip exaggerated by the distant viewpoint... Come on, it was detestable, and in her heart Asís detested it, nevertheless consulting the list in her purse and saying with a deep sigh: 'Oh! ... Pardiñas's widow is still to do ... the mother of the doctor from Celas ... and Rita, Gabriel Pardo's sister... And that really is urgent... Her kid's had diphtheria ...'[40]

40   Pardiñas's widow is Esclavitud Lamas in *Morriña* (1889). Rita Pardo had

Por lo mismo que el ajetreo de las visitas había sido tan cargante, que a la mayor parte se las encontrara en casa y que no le sacaron sino conversaciones capaces de aburrir a una estatua de yeso, la dama regresaba a su vivienda con el espíritu muy sosegado. A semejanza de los devotos que si les hurga la conciencia se imponen la obligación de rezar tres rosarios seguidos en una serie considerable de padrenuestros, Asís, sintiéndose reo de perturbación social, o al menos de amago de este delito, se consagraba a cumplir minuciosamente los ritos de desagravio, y como le habían producido tan soberano fastidio, juzgaba saldada más de la mitad de su cuenta. Por otra parte, encontrábase decidida —más que nunca— a cortar las irregularidades de su conducta presente. Tenía razón el comandante: la falta, bien mirado, no era tan inaudita; pero si trascendía al público, ¡ah!, ¡entonces! Evitar el escándalo y la reincidencia, garantizar lo venidero …, y se acabó. Cortar de raíz, eso sí (la dama veía entonces la virtud en forma de grandes y afiladísimas tijeras, como las que usan los sastres). Y bien podía hacerlo, porque, la verdad ante todo, su corazón no estaba interesado … —Vamos a ver —argüía para sí la señora—. Supongamos que ahora viniesen a decirme: Diego Pacheco se ha largado esta mañana a su tierra, donde parece que se casa con una muchacha preciosa … Nada: yo tan fresca, sin echar ni una lágrima. Hasta puede que diese gracias a Dios, viéndome libre de este grave compromiso. Pues la cosa es bien sencilla: ¿se había de ir él? Soy yo quien se larga. Así como así, días arriba o abajo, ya estaba cerca el de irse a veranear … Pues adelanto el veraneo un poquillo … y corrientes. —¡Qué descanso tomar el tren! Se concluían aquellos recelos incesantes, aquel volver el rostro cuando la Diabla le preguntaba alguna cosa, aquella tartamudez, aquella vergüenza, vergüenza tonta en una viuda, que al fin y al cabo era libre y no tenía que dar a nadie cuenta de sus actos …

Pensaba en estas cosas cuando se apeó y empezó a subir la escalera de su casa. Aún no estaba encendida la luz, caso frecuente en las tardes veraniegas. Al segundo tramo … ¡Dios nos asista! Un hombre que se destaca del obscuro rincón … ¡Pacheco!

For the very reason that the round of visits had been so irksome, because most of the ladies had been at home and all you could get from them were conversations capable of boring a plaster statue, Asís went home with a very peaceful mind. Just as devout people, when their consciences are pricked, force themselves to recite the rosary three times in a row with many a Lord's Prayer, Asís, feeling herself guilty of social disorder, or at least a hint of this crime, devoted herself in minute detail to making amends, and as this had caused her such supreme annoyance, she judged that more than half of what she owed was settled. On the other hand, she was more determined than ever to bring to an end the erratic nature of her present conduct. The major was right: all things considered, her fault wasn't so unheard of, but if it became public …. ah, then! Avoid scandal and relapse, guarantee the future … and that's it. Nip it in the bud, indeed (at that moment the lady could see virtue in the shape of large, sharp scissors, like those used by tailors). And she could easily do it, because in truth her heart wasn't in it… 'Let's see,' thought the lady to herself. 'Let's suppose they came right now to tell me that Diego Pacheco had gone back home this morning, where it appears he is marrying a charming girl… Nothing, cool as cucumber, I wouldn't shed a single tear. I might even thank God for finding myself free from this serious commitment. Well it's really quite simple: why should he be going? I'm the one who's leaving. Anyway, give or take a few days, going off for summer was already close … I'll just bring the holiday forward a bit … and agreed. What a relief to take the train! To put an end to the constant suspicion, looking the other way when Diabla asked anything, that stammering, that embarrassment, stupid embarrassment for a widow who, at the end of the day, was free and didn't have to answer to anybody for her actions…

She was thinking about these things when she got out of the carriage and started going up the stairs in her house. The light was as yet unlit, which was often the case in summer evenings. At the second flight of stairs… Heaven preserve us! A man standing out in the dark corner… Pacheco!

---

already appeared in *Los Pazos de Ulloa* (1886) and reappears in *Morriña*. Celas is a parish in La Coruña.

Reprimió el chillido. El meridional le cogía ambas manos con violencia.

–¿Cómo está mi niña? Tres veces he venido y siempre te negaron … Lo que es una de ellas juro que estabas en casa … Si no quieres verme, dímelo a mí, que no vendré … Te miraré de lejitos en el paseo o en el teatro … Pero no me despidas con una criada, que se ríe de mí al darme con la puerta en las narices.

–No … pero si yo … –contestaba aturdida la señora.

–¿No se había negado la nena para mí?

–No, para ti no … –afirmó rápidamente Asís con acento de sinceridad: tan espontáneo e inevitable suele ser en ciertas ocasiones el engaño.

–Pues, entonces, vengo esta noche. ¿Sí? Esta noche a las nueve.

Hizo la dama un expresivo movimiento.

–¿No quieres? ¿Tienes compromiso de salir, de ir a alguna parte? La verdad, chiquilla. Me largaré como aquel a quien le han dado cañaso, pero no porfiaré. Me sabe mal porfiar. Por mí no has de tener tú media hora de disgusto.

Asís titubeaba. Cosa rara y sin embargo explicable dentro de cierto misterioso ilogismo[39] que impone a la conducta femenina la difícil situación de la mujer: lo que decidió su respuesta afirmativa fue cabalmente la resolución de poner tierra en medio que acababa de adoptar en el coche.

–Bueno, a las nueve … (Pacheco la apretó contra sí.) ¿Pero … te irás a las diez?

–¿A las diez? Es tanto como no venir … Tú tienes que hacer hoy: dímelo así, clarito.

–Que hacer no … Por los criados. No me gusta dar espectáculo a esa gente.

–El chico no importa, es un bausán … La chica es más avispada. Mándala con un recado fuera … Hasta pronto.

Y Pacheco ocultó la cara en el pelo de la señora, descomponiéndolo y echándole el sombrero hacia atrás. Ella se lo arregló antes de llamar, lo cual hizo con pulso trémulo.

Iba muy preocupada, mucho. Se desnudó distraídamente, dejando una prenda aquí y otra acullá; la Diabla las recogía y colgaba, no sin

---

39 Otro neologismo de Pardo Bazán: contrario a la lógica.

She repressed a scream. The southerner violently grabbed both her hands.

'How's my little girl? I've come three times and they always denied you were in... But one of those times I swear you were at home... If you don't want to see me, tell me and I won't come... I'll look at you from a distance in the street or in the theatre... But don't dismiss me through a servant who laughs at me as she shuts the door in my face.'

'No ... but I...,' answered the bewildered lady.

'Was the refusal not for me, darling?'

'No, not for you...,' Asís asserted quickly with a tone of sincerity. At certain times deception usually is that spontaneous and inevitable.

'I'll come tonight, then. Yes? Tonight at nine o'clock?'

The lady made an expressive movement.

'Don't you want me to? Have you arranged to go out, are you going somewhere? Tell me the truth, dear. I'll be off like someone who's been let down, but I won't insist. I don't like insisting. You won't have to bother yourself for half an hour on my account.'

Asís hesitated. An unusual yet understandable fact in the context of a certain mysterious illogicality which the difficult situation of women imposes on feminine conduct: what decided her assent was the very resolution to get away quickly which she had just adopted in the carriage.

'All right, nine o'clock...' (Pacheco squeezed her against himself.)

'But ... will you go at ten?'

'At ten? I might as well not come... You've got something on today. Tell me honestly.'

'No, nothing... It's the servants. I don't like making a spectacle of myself in front of them.'

'Never mind the lad, he's a simpleton... The lass is sharper. Send her out on an errand... See you later.'

And Pacheco hid his face in the lady's hair, disarranging it and pushing her hat backwards. She sorted it out before ringing, which she did with a trembling hand.

She was really worried, very worried indeed. She absent-mindedly got undressed, leaving articles of clothing here, there and everywhere.

haberlas sacudido y examinado con un detenimiento que a Asís le pareció importuno. ¿Por qué no rehusar firmemente la dichosa cita? ... Sí, sería mejor; pero al fin, para el tiempo que faltaba ... Volvióse hacia la doncella.

–Mira, revisarás el mundo grande ...: creo que tiene descompuestas las bisagras. Acuérdate mañana de ir a casa de madama Armandina ...: puede que ya estén los sombreros listos ... Si no están, le das prisa. Que quiero marcharme pronto, pronto.

–¿A Vigo, señorita? –preguntó la Diabla con hipócrita suavidad.

–¿Pues adónde? También te darás una vuelta por el zapatero ... y a ver si en la plazuela del Ángel tienen compuesto el abanico.

Dictando estas órdenes se calmaba. No, el rehusar no era factible. Si le hubiese despedido esta noche, él querría volver mañana. Disimulo, transigir ... y, como decía él ..., *najensia*.

Comió poco; sentía esa constricción en el diafragma, inseparable compañera de las ansiedades y zozobras del espíritu. Miraba frecuentemente para la esfera del reloj, la cual no señalaba más que las ocho al levantarse la señora de la mesa.

–Oye, Ángela ...

Faltábale saliva en la boca; la lengua se le pegaba al velo del paladar.

–Oye, hija ... ¿Quieres ... irte a pasar esta noche con tu hermana, la casada con el guardia civil? ¿Eh?

–¡Ay señorita! ... Yo, con mil amores ... Pero vive tan lejos: el cuartel lo tienen allá en las Peñuelas ... Mientras se va y se viene ...

–Es lo de menos ... Te pago el tranvía ... o un simón.[40] Lo que te haga falta ... Y aunque vuelvas después de ... media noche ¿eh?, no dejarán de abrirte. Come a escape ... Mira, ¿no tiene tu hermana una niña de seis años?

–De ocho, señorita, de ocho ... Y un muñeco de trece meses que anda con la dentición.

---

40   Abreviatura de 'coche de don Simón', por referencia a un alquilador de coches.

Diabla gathered them and hung them up, not without shaking them and examining them with a meticulousness which Asís found annoying. Why not refuse the confounded meeting in no uncertain terms? ... Yes, that would be better; but after all, for the time that was left... She turned towards the maid.

'Look, you check the large trunk ... I think the hinges are broken. Remember tomorrow to go to Madam Armandina's house ... the hats might be ready now... If not, make her get a move on. I want to be off quickly, quickly.'

'To Vigo, miss?' asked Diabla with hypocritical sweetness.

'Where else? You can go to the shoemaker's as well ... and the Plazuela del Ángel[41] to see if they've mended my fan.'

Giving these orders calmed her down. No, it wasn't feasible to refuse. If she'd said goodbye to him that evening, he would want to come back in the morning. Dissimulation, make concessions ... and, as he would say ... *scarper*.

She ate little dinner, feeling that constriction in her diaphragm which always accompanied anxiety and nervous tension. She kept looking at the clock, which was only pointing to eight o'clock when she got up from the table.

'Hey, Ángela...'

Her mouth was dry, and her tongue was sticking to the roof of her mouth.

'Hey... Do you want ... to go and spend the evening with your sister, the one married to the civil guard officer? Eh?'

'Oh, miss ... I'd love to ... but she lives so far away. The barracks are over there in the Peñuelas ... To get there and back...'

'That's not a problem ... I'll pay for the tram ... or hire a carriage. Whatever you need... And they'll let you in, even if you get back after ... midnight, eh? Hurry up and eat... Look, hasn't your sister got a six-year-old daughter?'

'Eight, madam, eight... And a baby thirteen months old that's teething.'

---

41 The old Plazuela del Ángel, now known as the Plaza del Ángel, apparently took its name from the guardian angel (Ángel de la Guarda) decorating the front of one of its buildings.

–Bien: a la niña podrá servirle, arreglándola ... Le llevas aquella ropa de Marujita que hemos apartado el otro día ...

–Dios se lo pague ... ¿También el sombrero de castor blanco, con el pájaro?

–También ... Anda ya.

El sombrero de castor produjo excelente efecto. Imaginaba siempre la señora que, de algunos días a esta parte, su doncella se atrevía a mirarla y hablarla ya con indefinible acento severo, ya con disimulada entonación irónica; pero después de tan espléndida donación, por más que aguzó la malicia, no pudo advertir en el gracioso semblante de la criada sino júbilo y gratitud. Comió la Diabla en tres minutos: ni visto ni oído: y a poco se presentó a su ama muy maja y pizpireta, con traje dominguero, el pelo rizado a tenacilla, botas que cantaban.

–Vete, hija, ya debe de ser tarde ... Las nueve menos cuarto ...

–No, señorita ... Las ocho y veinticinco por el comedor ... ¿Tiene algo que mandar? ¿Quiere alguna cosa? ...

–Nada, nada ... Que lo pases bien ... ¡Qué elegante te has puesto! ... ¿Allí habrá gente, eh? ¿Guardias civiles? ¿Jóvenes?

–Algunos ... Hay uno de nuestra tierra ... de la provincia de Pontevedra, de Marín ... alto él, con bigote negro.

–Bien, hija ... Pues lo que es por mí, ya puedes marcharte.

¿Qué haría aquella maldita Diabla, que un cuarto de hora después de recibidas semejantes despachaderas aún no había tomado el portante? Con el oído pegado a la puertecilla falsa de su dormitorio, que caía al pasillo, Asís espiaba la salida de su doncella, mordiéndose los labios de impaciencia nerviosa. Al fin sintió pasitos, taconeo de calzado flamante, oyó una risotada, un *¡a divertirse y gastar poco!* que venía de la cocina ... La puerta se abrió, hizo ¡puum!, al cerrarse ... ¡Ay, gracias a Dios!

Así que se fue la condenada chica, parecióle a la señora que todo el piso se había quedado en un silencio religioso, en un recogimiento inexplicable. Hasta la lámpara del saloncito alumbraba, si cabe, con luz más velada, más dulce que otras noches. Eran las nueve menos cuarto: Pacheco aún tardaría cosa de veinte minutos ... Se oyó un campanillazo sentimental, tímido, como si la campanilla recelase pecar de indiscreta ...

'All right, it might be of use to the girl... You can take Marujita's clothes, those we put aside the other day...'

'God bless you... And the white beaver hat with the feather as well?'

'As well. Off you go.'

The beaver hat produced an excellent effect. For some time now the lady had imagined that her maid was daring to look at her and speak to her one minute with an indefinable, severe tone, the next with a sly and ironic haughtiness; but after such a splendid donation, however much malice it stirred up, she noticed nothing but jubilant gratitude in the maid's amusing expression. Diabla ate her dinner in three minutes, like lightning, and in no time presented herself before her mistress, all nice and cheerful, in her Sunday best, her hair curled with a curling iron, her boots resounding.

'Off you go, it must be late... A quarter to nine...'

'No, madam ... twenty-five past eight by the dining room clock... Any orders? Do you want anything?'

'Nothing, nothing... Have a good time. How elegant you look!... Will there be people there? Civil guards? Young men?'

'Some... There's one from our part of the world ... from the province of Pontevedra, from Marín ... tall, with a black moustache.'

'Good... Well for my part you can go now.'

What was that wretched Diabla up to, that a quarter of an hour after receiving her dismissal she still hadn't cleared off? With her ear glued to the false door of the bedroom, which was in the corridor, Asís was listening for her maid's departure, biting her lips with nervous impatience. At last she could hear steps, the clicking of new shoes, a loud laugh, a parting, 'Have a good time and don't spend too much' coming from the kitchen... The door opened, then shut with a bang... Ah, thanks be to God!

As soon as the damned girl left it seemed to the lady that the whole upstairs was left in a religious silence, an inexplicable peace and quiet. Even the lamp in the room shone, if it's possible, with a light that was more veiled, softer than other nights. It was a quarter to nine; Pacheco would be another twenty minutes or so... A tinkle could be heard, sentimental and timid, as if the bell were afraid of being too indiscreet...

XVI

Era Pacheco, envuelto en su capa de embozos grana, impropia de la estación, y de hongo. Detúvose en la puerta como irresoluto, y Asís tuvo que animarle:

–Pase usted …

Entonces el galán se desembozó resueltamente y se informó de cómo andaba la salud de Asís.

En los primeros momentos de sus entrevistas, siempre se hablaban así, empleando fórmulas corteses y preguntando cosas insignificantes; su saludo era el saludo de ordenanza en sociedad; estrecharse la mano. Ni ellos mismos podrían explicar la razón de este procedimiento extraño, que acaso fuese la cortedad debida a lo reciente e impensado de su trato amoroso. No obstante, algo especial y distinto de otras veces notaría el andaluz en la señora, que al sentarse en el diván a su lado, murmuró después de una embarazosa pausa:

–¡Qué fría me recibes! ¿Qué tienes?

–¡Qué disparate! ¿Qué voy a tener?

–¡Ay prenda, prenda! A mí no se me engaña … Soy perro viejo en materia de mujeres. Estorbo. Tú tenías algún plan esta noche.

–Ninguno, ninguno –afirmó calurosamente Asís.

–Bien, lo creo. Eso sí que lo has dicho como se dicen las verdaes. Pero, en plata: que no te pinchaban a ti las ganas de verme. Hoy me querías tú a cien leguas.

Aseveró esto metiendo sus dedos largos, de pulcras uñas, entre el pelo de la señora, y complaciéndose en alborotar el peinado sobrio, sin postizos ni rellenos, que Asís trataba de imitar del de la Pinograde, maestra en los toques de la elegancia.

–Si no quisiese recibirte, con decírtelo …

–Así debiera ser …: el corasonsillo en la mano …; pero a veces se le figura a uno que está comprometido a pintar afecto ¿sabes tú?, por caridad o qué sé yo por qué … Si yo lo he hecho a cada rato, con un ciento de novias y de querías … Harto de ellas por cima de los pelos … y empeñado en aparentar otra cosa … porque es fuerte eso

16

It was Pacheco, wrapped in his scarlet cloak, which was unsuitable for the time of year, and with a bowler hat. He stopped irresolutely in the doorway, and Asís had to encourage him:

'Come in...'

Upon that the young gentleman uncovered his face determinedly and asked after Asís's health.

During the first moments when they met they always spoke like this, using polite expressions and asking trivial questions. Their greeting was the official society greeting: shaking hands. Not even they themselves would be able to explain the reason for this strange procedure, which perhaps was shyness due to the recent and unexpected nature of their relationship. However, the Andalusian noticed something special and different from the other times about the lady, and as he sat down on the divan beside her he muttered after an awkward pause:

'You're so cold with me! What's wrong?'

'How absurd! What could be wrong?'

'Oh darling, darling! You can't fool me ... I'm an old hand when it comes to women. I'm a hindrance. You had other plans for this evening.'

'Nothing, nothing,' Asís declared ardently.

'Okay, I believe you. You said that as if you meant it. But be frank, you had no desire to see me. You wished I were a hundred leagues away today.'

As he said this he ran his long fingers with exquisite nails through the lady's hair, taking pleasure in disturbing the simple hairdo, devoid of hairpieces or fillers, in which Asís tried to imitate the style of Mrs Pinogrande, an authority on the final touch of elegance.

'If I didn't want to receive you, I'd only have to say...'

'That's how it should be ... hand on heart ... but sometimes one feels committed to put on a show, you know, out of compassion or who knows what? I've done it all the time with many a girlfriend and lover... Sick to the back teeth of them ... and trying to feign

de estamparle a un hombre o a una hembra en su propia cara: «Ya me tiene usted hasta aquí …, no me hace usted ni tanto de ilusión».

–¿Quién sabe si eso te estará pasando a ti conmigo? –exclamó Asís festivamente, echándolas de modesta.

No contestó el meridional sino con un abrazo vehemente, apretado, repentino, y un –¡*ojalá!*– salido del alma, tan ronco y tan dramático, que la dama sintió rara conmoción, semejante a la del que, poniendo la mano sobre un aparato eléctrico, nota la sacudida de la corriente.

–¿Por qué dices *ojalá*? –preguntó, imitando el tono del andaluz.

–Porque esto es de más; porque nunca me vi como me veo; porque tú me has dado a beber zumo de hierbas desde que te he conocío, chiquilla … Porque estoy mareado, chiflado, loco, por tus pedasos de almíbar … ¿Te enteras? Porque tú vas a ser causa de la perdición de un hombre, lo mismo que Dios está en el sielo y nos oye y nos ve … Terroncito de sal, ¿qué tienes en esta boca, y en estos ojos, y en toda tu persona, para que yo me ponga así? A ver, dímelo, gloria, veneno, sirena del mar.

La señora callaba, aturdida, no sabiendo qué contestar a tan apasionadas protestas; pero vino a sacarla del apuro un estruendo inesperado y desapacible, el alboroto de una de esas músicas ratoneras antes llamadas *murgas*, y que en la actualidad, por la manía reinante de elevarlo todo, adoptan el nombre de *bandas populares*.

–¡Oiga! ¿Nos dan cencerrada ya los vecinos del barrio? –gritó Pacheco levantándose del sofá y entreabriendo las vidrieras–. ¡Y cómo desafinan los malditos! … Ven a oír, chiquilla, ven a oír. Verás cómo te rompen el tímpano.

En el meridional no era sorprendente este salto desde las ternezas más moriscas al más prosaico de los incidentes callejeros: estaba en su modo de ser la transición brusca, la rápida exteriorización de las impresiones.

otherwise … because it's hard to say to a man or woman's face: "I'm up to here with you … I get no enjoyment from you".'

'Who knows if that's what you're going through with me?' Asís exclaimed jovially, with boastful modesty.

The southerner made no answer other than a quick, tight and impassioned embrace along with the words 'If only!' from his very soul, so hoarse and dramatic that the lady felt a strange tremor, similar to putting one's hand on an electrical appliance and feeling the current.

'Why do you say *if only?*' she asked, imitating the Andalusian's tone of voice.

'Because this is too much, because I've never felt like this, because you've given me a love potion from the moment I met you, darling… Because I feel dizzy, mad, crazy for you, for your sweetness… Do you realise? Because you're goin' to be the cause of a man's perdition, just as God's in heaven where He can hear and see us… Sugar pie, what have you got in that mouth and those eyes and your whole body for me to get like this? Come on, tell me, my love, my poison, my siren.'

The lady was silent, astonished, not knowing what to say in answer to such impassioned outbursts, but a sudden, unpleasant din got her out of the mess, the racket of one of those groups that used to be known as *murgas*[42] and which, with the prevailing craze nowadays for elevating everything, adopt the name of *popular bands.*

'Listen! Are the neighbours playing us a charivari[43] already?' cried Pacheco getting up from the sofa and half-opening the glass windows. 'They're devilishly out of tune! Come 'ere, darling, come and listen. See if they don't burst your eardrum.'

In the southerner this jump from tender words to the most prosaic of street incidents was not surprising. Sudden change was part of his being, the rapid externalisation of impressions.

---

42   According to the Real Academia Española, a *murga* is 'Compañia de músicos malos, que en Pascuas, cumpleaños, etc., toca a las puertas de las casas acomodadas, con la esperanza de recibir algún obsequio (A band of unskilled musicians who at Easter, on birthdays etc., knock on the doors of well-to-do houses, in the hope of receiving a tip).

43   A serenade of 'rough music', with kettles, pans, tea trays and the like, in mockery and derision of incongruous or unpopular marriages, and of unpopular persons generally.

–Mira, ven … –continuó–. Te pongo aquí una butaca y nos recreamos. ¿A quién le dispararán la serenata?

–A un almacén de ultramarinos que se ha estrenado hoy –contestó Asís recordando casualmente chismografías de la Diabla–. En la otra acera, pocas casas más allá de la de enfrente. Aquella puerta … allí. ¡Ya tenemos música para rato!

Pacheco arrastró un sillón hacia la ventana y se sentó en él.

–¡Desatento! –exclamó riendo la señora–. ¿Pues no decías que era para mí?

–Para ti es –respondió el amante cogiéndola por la cintura y obligándola quieras no quieras a que se acomodase en sus rodillas. Se resistió algo la dama, y al fin tuvo que acceder. Pacheco la mecía como se mece a las criaturas, sin permitirse ningún agasajo distinto de los que pueden prodigarse a un niño inocente. Por forzosa exigencia de la postura, Asís le echó un brazo al cuello, y después de los primeros minutos, reposó la cabeza en el hombro del andaluz. Un airecillo delgado, en que flotaban perfumes de acacia y ese peculiar olor de humo y ladrillo recaliente de la atmósfera madrileña en estío, entraba por las vidrieras, intentaba en balde mover las cortinas, y traía fragmentos de la música chillona, tolerable a favor de la distancia y de la noche, hora que tiene virtud para suavizar y concertar los más discordantes sonidos. Y la proximidad de los dos cuerpos ocupando un solo sillón, estrechaba también, sin duda, los espíritus, pues por vez primera en el curso de aquella historia, entablóse entre Pacheco y la dama un cuchicheo íntimo, cariñoso, confidencial.

No hablaban de amor: versaba el coloquio sobre esas cosas que parecen muy insignificantes escritas y que en la vida real no se tratan casi nunca sino en ocasiones semejantes a aquella, en minutos de imprevista efusión. Asís menudeaba preguntas exigiendo detalles biográficos: ¿Qué hacía Pacheco? ¿Por dónde andaba? ¿Cómo era su familia? ¿La vida anterior? ¿Los gustos? ¿Las amistades? ¿La edad justa, justa, por meses, días y no sé si horas?

–Pues yo soy más vieja que tú –murmuró pensativa, así que el gaditano hubo declarado su fe de bautismo.

–¡Gran cosa! Será un añito, o medio.

–No, no, dos lo menos. Dos, dos.

'Look, come here…,' he continued. 'I'll put a chair here for you and we'll enjoy ourselves. In whose honour is this serenade?'

'The grocery store that opened today,' answered Asís, happening to remember Diabla's gossip. 'On the other side, a few houses down. That door … there. There'll be music for a while!'

Pacheco pulled an armchair towards the window and sat down on it.

'Manners!' exclaimed the lady with a laugh. 'Didn't you just say it was for me?'

'It is for you,' replied the lover, grabbing her by the waist and forcing her, like it or not, to settle down on his lap. The lady resisted a little, but in the end had to give in. Pacheco rocked her as you rock children, without allowing himself any sign of affection different from those that can be lavished on an innocent child. As a result of the inevitable requirement of her position, Asís put an arm around his neck, and after the first few moments laid her head on his shoulder. A gentle breeze, on which the perfume of acacias and that strange smell of smoke and heated brick of the Madrid atmosphere in summer came in through the windows, tried in vain to move the curtains, and brought in fragments of shrill music, tolerable thanks to the distance and the night, a time which has the virtue of toning down and harmonising the most discordant sounds. And the proximity of the two bodies occupying a single chair also undoubtedly brought their spirits closer, because for the first time in the course of this affair, Pacheco and the lady began whispering in an intimate, affectionate and confidential way.

They didn't speak about love: the conversation concerned those things which seem very trivial when written down and which in real life are hardly ever dealt with, except at times like this, in moments of extemporaneous effusions. Asís repeated questions demanding biographical details. What did Pacheco do? Where did he go? What were his family like? His life up until now? His tastes? His friends? His exact age, down to the very month, day and even hour?

'Well I'm older than you,' she murmured thoughtfully, as soon as he had declared his certificate of baptism.

'Not much! It can only be a year, or even half.'

'No, no, two at least. Two, two.'

–Corriente, sí, pero el hombre siempre es más viejo, cachito de gloria, porque nosotros vivimos, ¿te enteras?, y vosotras no. Yo, en particular, he vivido por una docena. No imaginarás diablura que yo no haya catado. Soy maestro en el arte de hacer desatinos. ¡Si tú supieses algunas cosas mías!

Asís sintió una curiosidad punzante unida a un enojo sin motivo.

–Por lo visto eres todo un perdis, buena alhaja.

–¡Quia! ... ¿Perdis yo? Di que no, nena mía. Yo galanteé a trescientas mil mujeres, y ahora me parece que no quise a ninguna. Yo hice cuanto disparate se puede hacer, y al mismo tiempo no tengo vicios. ¿Dirás que cómo es ese milagro? Siendo ... ahí verás tú. Los vicios no prenden en mí. Ninguno arraiga, ni arraigará jamás. Aún te declaro otra cosa: que no sólo no se me puede llamar vicioso, sino que si me descuido acabo por santo. Es según los lados a que me arrimo. ¿Me ponen en circunstancias de ser perdío? No me quedo atrás. ¿Qué tocan a ser bueno? Nadie me gana. Si doy con gente arrastrada, ¿qué quieres tú?

–¿Hasta en lo tocante a la honra te dejarías llevar? –preguntó algo asustada Asís.

El gaditano se echó atrás como si le hubiese picado una sierpe.

–¡Hija! Vaya unas cosillas que me preguntas. ¿Me has tomado por algún secuestrador? Yo no secuestro más que a las hembras de tu facha. Pero ya sabes que en mi tierra, las pendencias no se cuentan por delitos ... He *enfriado* a un infeliz ... que más quisiera no haberle tocado al pelo de la ropa. Dejémoslo, que importa un pito. Fuera de esas trifulcas, no ha tenío el diablo por donde cogerme: he jugado, perdiendo y ganando un dinerillo ... regular; he bebío ..., vamos, que no me falta a mí saque; de novias y otros enredos ... De esto estaría muy feo que te contase ná. Chitito. ¿Un cariño a tu rorro?

–Vamos, que eres la gran persona –protestó escandalizada Asís, desviándose en vez de acercarse como Pacheco pretendía.

–No lo sabes bien. Eso es como el Evangelio. Yo quisiera averiguar pa qué me ha echado Dios a este mundo. Porque soy, además de tronerilla, un haragán y un zángano de primera, niña del alma ... No hago cosa de provecho, ni ganas de hacerla. ¿A qué? Mi padre, empeñao el buen señor en que me luzca y en que sirva al país, y dale

'Agreed, yes, but the man is always older, darling, because we live and you don't. Do you get me? And 'specially me, I've lived for a dozen men. You couldn't dream up any mischief I haven't sampled. I'm a master in the art of doing crazy things. If only you knew some of my deeds!'

Asís felt a pang of curiosity mixed with irrational annoyance.

'It would appear that you're an out and out rake, a fine one.'

'Never! Me a rake? Not at all, my darling. I've wooed three hundred thousand women, but now I believe that I didn't love any of 'em. Every stupid thing that can be done, I've done it, but at the same time I've no vices. You may ask how this miracle can be? It's ... here I'll tell you. Vices don't take root in me. None of 'em takes hold, nor ever will. And I'll tell you something else too: not only can I not be called sinful, but also if I don't watch out I'll end up a saint. It's a question of the direction in which I'm drawn. Put me in a position to be a lost soul and I won't lag behind. It's time to be good? No one can beat me. If I find myself with rascals, what do you expect?'

'Even where honour is concerned you'd go with the tide?' asked Asís, somewhat alarmed.

The man from Cádiz drew back as if a big snake had bitten him.

'Good lord, you do ask some questions. Do you take me for some kidnapper? I only kidnap women like you. But you know full well that where I come from fights don't count as crimes ... I *bumped off* one poor guy ... I wish I'd never laid a finger on him. Let's leave it, it's of no importance. Outside of these squabbles, the devil has got no hold on me. I've gambled, lost and won a bit of money ... average amount. I've drunk ... well, I'm not lacking in that area. Girlfriends and other love affairs... It'd be very bad to tell you anythin' about that. Hush. A caress for your little boy?'

'That's enough, you're a fine one,' protested a shocked Asís, turning away instead of moving closer as Pacheco hoped.

'You don't know the half of it. It's the gospel truth. I'd like to find out why God put me on Earth. Because, my dear girl, as well as being a libertine, I'm a layabout and a first-class idler ... I don't do anythin' useful, nor wish to do so. Why should I? My father, he's a good person determined to see me shine and serve the country, with the crazy notion

con la chifladura de que me meta en política, y tumba con que salga diputao, y vaya a hacer el bu al Congreso … ¡En el Congreso yo! A mí, lo que es asustarme, ni el Congreso ni veinte Congresos me asustan. La farsa aquella no me pone miedo. Te aviso que en todo cuanto me propongo salir avante, salgo y sin grandes fatigas: ¡qué! Pero a decir verdad, no me he tomado nunca trabajos así enormes, como no fuese por alguna mujer guapa. No soy memo ni lerdo, y si quisiese ir allí a pintar la mona como Albareda, la pintaría, figúrate. ¿Que se me ha muerto mi abuelita? ¡Si es la pura verdad! Sólo que too eso porque tanto se descuaja la gente, no vale los sudores que cuesta. En cambio … ¡una mujer como tú …!

Díjolo al oído de la dama, a quien estrechó más contra sí.

–Sólo esto, terrón de azúcar, sólo esto sabe bien en el mundo amargo … Tener así a una mujer adorándola … Así, apretadica, metida en el corasón … Lo demás … pamplina.

–Pero eso es atroz –protestó severamente Asís, cuya formalidad cantábrica se despertaba entonces con gran brío–. ¿De modo que no te avergüenzas de ser un hombre inútil, un mequetrefe, un cero a la izquierda?

–¿Y a ti qué te importa, lucerito? ¿Soy inútil pa quererte? ¿Has resuelto no enamorarte sino de tipos que mangoneen y anden agarraos a la casaca de algún ministro? Mira … Si te empeñas en hacer de mí un personaje, una notabilidad … como soy Diego que te sales con la tuya. Daré días de gloria a la patria: ¿no se dice así? Aguarda, aguarda …, verás qué registros saco. Proponte que me vuelva un Castelar o un Cánovas del Castillo, y me vuelvo … ¡Ole que sí! ¿Te creías tú que alguno de esos panolis vale más que este nene? Sólo que ellos largaron todo el trapo y yo recogí velas … Por no deslucirlos. Modestia pura.

No había más remedio que reírse de los dislates de aquel tarambana, y Asís lo hizo; al reírse hubo de toser un poco.

–¡Ea!, ya te me acatarraste –exclamó el gaditano consternadísimo–. Hágame usté el obsequio de ponerse algo en la cabeza … Así, tan desabrigada … ¡Loca!

that I go into politics and become a member of parliament and frighten the Congress... Me in Congress! When it comes to frightening me, neither one nor twenty congresses frighten me. That farce doesn't scare me. I'm tellin' you that as soon as I propose to get ahead, I do so without great hardship! But to tell the truth, I've never taken the trouble to do much unless it be for some beautiful woman. I'm not stupid or slow-witted, and if I wanted to go there and do nothing of importance like Albareda, I would. You think I'm blowing me own trumpet? It's the pure truth! Only that all the things people work so hard for are not worth the sweat they cause. Whereas ... a woman like you!'

This he said in her ear, pressing her closer to himself.

'It's just that, my sugar pie, that's the only thing that tastes sweet in this bitter world... To have a woman you adore like this... Pressed close like this, deep in your heart... The rest ... nonsense.'

'But that's atrocious,' protested Asís sternly, her Cantabrian seriousness awakening then with great brio. 'So you're not ashamed of being a hopeless man, a good-for-nothing, a total nonentity.'

'And what does it matter to you, my little star? Am I unfit to love you? Have you made up your mind to fall in love only with meddlesome guys who go about hanging on the coattails of some politician? Look... If you insist on making a somebody of me, a notable person ... as sure as my name's Diego you'll get your way. Days of glory shall I bequeath my country. Isn't that how they put it? Just you wait ... you'll see. Tell me to become a Castelar or a Cánovas del Castillo, 'n' I'll do it[44] ... Yes, indeed! Did you think any one of those chumps is worth more than this child? It's just that they gave it their all whilst I gave up... So as not to show them up. Pure modesty.'

There was nothing for it but to laugh at that crackpot's nonsense, and Asís did so. When she laughed she coughed a little.

'Eh! You've already caught a cold,' exclaimed the man from Cádiz, completely dismayed. 'Do me the courtesy of putting something on your head... It's so exposed like that... Crazy!'

---

44 Emilio Castelar y Ripoll (1832–99), a champion of Spanish republicanism, was president of the First Spanish Republic. Antonio Cánovas del Castillo (1828–97), Spanish Prime Minister and historian, played a key role in supporting the restoration of the Bourbon monarchy to the Spanish throne and was assassinated by the Italian anarchist Michele Angiolillo.

–Pero si nunca me pongo nada, ni … No soy enclenque.

–Pues hoy te pondrás, porque yo lo mando. Si aciertas a enfermar, me suicido.

Saltó Asís de brazos de su adorador muerta de risa, y al saltar perdió una de sus bonitas chinelas, que por ser sin talón, a cada rato se le escurrían del pie. Recogióla Pacheco, calzándosela con mil extremos y zalamerías. La dama entró en su alcoba, y abriendo el armario de luna empezó a buscar a tientas una toquilla de encaje para ponérsela y que no la marease aquel pesado. Vuelta estaba de espaldas a la poca luz que venía del saloncito, cuando sintió que dos brazos la ceñían el cuerpo. En medio de la lluvia de caricias delirantes que acompañó a demostración tan atrevida, Asís entreoyó una voz alterada, que repetía con acento serio y trágico:

–¡Te adoro! … ¡Me muero, me muero por ti!

Parecía la voz de otro hombre, hasta tenía ese *trémolo* penoso que da al acento humano el rugir de las emociones extraordinarias comprimido en la garganta por la voluntad. Impresionada, Asís se volvió soltando la toquilla.

–Diego … –tartamudeó llamando así a Pacheco por primera vez.

–¿Por qué no dices *Diego mío, Diego del alma*? –exclamó con fuego el andaluz deshaciéndola entre sus brazos.

–Qué sé yo … Cuando uno habla así … me parece cosa de novela o de comedia. Es una ridiculez.

–¡Prueba … prueba …! ¡Ay! ¡Cómo lo has dicho! *¡Diego mío!* – prorrumpió él remedando a la señora, al mismo tiempo que la soltaba casi con igual violencia que la había cogido–. ¡Pedazo de hielo! ¡Vaya unas hembras que se gastan en tu país …! ¡Marusiñas! ¡Reniego de ellas todas! ¡Que las echen al carro e la basura!

–Mira –dijo la dama tomándolo otra vez a risa– eres un cómico y un orate … No hay modo de ponerse seria con un tipo como tú. A ver: aquí está un señorito que ha tenido cuatrocientas novias y dos mil líos gordos, y ahora se ha prendado de mí como el Petrarca de la señora Laura … De mí nada más: privilegio exclusivo, patente del Gobierno.

'But I never put anything on, not even ... I'm not sickly.'

'Well today you'll put something on, because I say so. If you succeed in falling ill, I'll kill myself.'

Asís sprang out of her admirer's arms in fits of laughter, and in doing so lost one of her pretty slippers, which, because they had no heel, kept slipping off her feet. Pacheco picked it up, putting it on her with extreme care and fawning. The lady went into her bedroom and, opening the mirrored wardrobe, began to look in the dark for a lace shawl to put on and stop that pest going on at her. With her back turned again to the faint light coming from the small room, she felt two arms encircle her. In the midst of the shower of frenzied caresses that accompanied such a bold demonstration, Asís half-heard a voice that had changed, repeating in a serious, tragic tone:

'I adore you ... I'm dying, dying for you!'

It sounded like the voice of another man. It even had that painful *tremolo* given to human utterances by the roar of exceptional emotions wilfully held back in the throat. Asís, deeply touched, turned round whilst undoing her shawl.

'Diego...,' she stammered, calling Pacheco this for the first time.

'Why don't you say, "My Diego, Diego my love"?' exclaimed the Andalusian fierily, making her melt in his arms.

'I don't know... When anyone talks like that ... it seems to me like something from a novel or a play. It's ridiculous.'

'There's the proof, there's the proof! Ay! How you said it! "My Diego!"' he burst out, imitating the lady, simultaneously releasing her almost as violently as he had grabbed her. 'You block of ice! What strange women you have in your region! So prim 'n' proper! I renounce them all! Put them on a wagon 'n' throw 'em away!'

'Look,' said the lady, treating it as a joke again, 'you're an actor and a lunatic... There's no way of being serious with a guy like you. Let's see. Here's a young man who's had four hundred girlfriends and two thousand major love affairs, and now he's fallen in love with me like Petrarch with his lady Laura...[45] With me no less. Exclusive privilege, royal patent.'

---

45   A reference to Petrarch's *Il Canzionere*, which contain 366 poems with the central theme of the author's love for Laura (i.e. just one lady).

–Tómalo a guasa …
Pues es tan verdad como
que ahora te agarro la
mano. Yo tuve un millón
de devaneos, conformes;
pero en ninguno me
pasó lo que ahora. ¡Por
estas, que son cruces!
Quebraeros de cabesa
míos, novias y demás, me
las encuentro en la calle y
ni las conozco. A ti … te
dibujaría, si fuese pintor, a
obscuras. Tan clavadita te tengo. De aquí a cincuenta años, cayéndote
de vieja, te conocería entre mil viejas más. Otras historias las seguí por
vanidad, por capricho, por golosina, por terquedad, por matar el tiempo
… Me quedaba un rincón aquí, donde no ha puesto el pie nadie, y tenía
yo guardaa la llave de oro para ti, prenda morena … ¿Que lo dudas?
Mira, haz un ensayo … Por gusto.

Arrastró a la dama hacia el salón y se recostó en el diván; tomó
la mano de Asís y la colocó extendida sobre el lado izquierdo de su
chaleco. Asís sintió un leve y acompasado vaivén, como de péndulo
de reloj. Pacheco tenía los ojos cerrados.

–Estoy pensando en otras mujeres, chiquilla … Quieta …, atención
…, observa bien.

–No late nada fuerte –afirmó la señora.

–Déjate un rato así … Pienso en mi última novia, una rubia que
tenía un talle de lo más fino que se encuentra en el mundo … ¿Ves qué
quietecillo está el pájaro? Ahora … dime tú … ¡si puedes! alguna cosa
tierna … Mas que no sea verdá.

Asís discurría una gran terneza y buscaba la inflexión de voz para
pronunciarla. Y al fin salió con esta eterna vulgaridad:

–¡Vida mía!

Bajo la palma de la señora, el corazón de Pacheco, como espíritu
folleto que obedece a un conjuro, rompió en el más agitado baile que
puede ejecutar semejante víscera. Eran saltos de ave azorada que embiste

'Take it as a joke… Well it's as true as I'm holding your hand now. I've had a million affairs, agreed; but nothing happened to me like it is now. By all that is holy! Headaches of mine, girlfriends and all the rest, I bump into them in the street and I don't even know them. You … if I were a painter I could draw you in the dark, you're so fixed in my mind. Fifty years from now, when you're falling apart with age, I'd pick you out amongst a thousand other old women. Those other flings I pursued out of vanity, caprice, greed, obstinacy, to kill time… There remained a corner here, where nobody has set foot, and I've got the golden key kept for you, my gorgeous brunette. Do you doubt it? Look, do a test … for the fun of it.'

He pulled the lady towards the room and lay down on the sofa; he took Asís's hand and stretched it out on the left side of his waistcoat. Asís felt a slight, steady vibration like the pendulum of a clock. Pacheco had his eyes closed.

'I'm thinking of other women, my dear… Keep still … pay attention … observe carefully.'

'Nothing beating strongly there,' declared Asís.

'Stay like that a while… I'm thinking of my last girlfriend, a blonde with the finest figure in the world… Can you see how still the bird is? Now … if you can, say something affectionate to me… Even if it isn't true.'

Asís thought up some term of endearment and tried to give her voice the proper inflection. And finally she came out with this common expression.

'My love!'

Under the lady's palm, like a crazy spirit obeying a spell, Pacheco's heart broke into the most agitated dance that any such organ can perform. They were like leaps of a flustered bird charging its prison bars… The

contra los hierros de su cárcel … El meridional entreabrió las azules
pupilas; su tez tostada había palidecido algún tanto; con extraña prisa
se levantó del sofá y fue derecho al balcón, donde se apoyó como para
beber aire y rehacerse de algún trastorno físico y moral. Asís, inquieta,
le siguió y le tocó en el brazo.

–Ya ves qué majadero soy … –murmuró él volviéndose.

–¿Pero te pasa algo?

–Na … –El gaditano se apartó del balcón, y viniendo a sentarse en
un *puf* bajito, y rogando a Asís con la mirada que ocupase el sillón,
apoyó la cabeza en el regazo de la dama–. Con sólo dos palabritas que
tú me dijiste … Haz favor de no reírte, mona, porque donde me ves
tengo mal genio … y puede que soltase un desatino. Desde que me
he entontecido por ti, estoy echando peor carácter. Calladita la niní …
Deje dormir a su rorro.

Pacheco cruzó el umbral de aquella casa antes de sonar la media
noche. La Diabla no había regresado aún. Cuando el gaditano, según
costumbre hasta entonces infructuosa, se volvió desde la esquina de
la calle mirando hacia los balcones de Asís, pudo distinguir en ellos
un bulto blanco. La señora exponía sus sofocadísimas mejillas al aire
fresco de la noche, y la embriaguez de sus sentidos y el embargo de
sus potencias empezaban a disiparse. Como náufrago arrojado a la
costa, que volviendo en sí toca con placer el cinto de oro que tuvo
la precaución de ceñirse al sentir que se hundía el buque, Asís se
felicitaba por haber conservado el átomo de razón indispensable para
no acceder a cierta súplica insensata.

–¡Buena la hacíamos! Mañana estaban enterados vecinos, servicio,
portero, sereno, el diablo y su madre. ¡Ay Dios mío …! ¡Me sigue, me
sigue el mareo aquel de la verbena … y lo que es ahora no hay álcali
que me lo quite! … ¡Qué mareo ni qué …! Mareo, alcohol, insolación
… ¡Pretextos, tonterías! … Lo que pasa es que me gusta, que me va
gustando cada día un poco más, que me trastorna con su palabrería
…, y punto redondo. Dice que yo le he dado bebedizos y hierbas …
Él sí que me va dando a comer sesos de borrico … y nada, que no
me desenredo. Cuando se va, reflexiono y caigo en la cuenta; pero en
viéndole … acabóse, me perdí.

southerner half-opened his blue eyes; his tanned skin had turned a little pale. With surprising speed he got up from the sofa and went straight to the balcony, where he leaned out as if to drink the air and recover from some physical and moral trauma. Asís anxiously followed him and touched him on the arm.

'Now you can see how foolish I am...,' he murmured as he turned round.

'Is anything wrong?'

'Noth–' The man from Cádiz moved away from the balcony and, sitting down on a very low pouffe and begging Asís with a look to be seated in the easy chair, leaned his head on the lady's lap. 'With just those two little words you said to me... Please don't laugh, dear, for as you can see I'm suffering ... and I might come out with some foolish remark. Since I went crazy for you my temper's been less equable. Don't say anything, my darling... Let your baby boy sleep.'

Pacheco crossed the threshold of that house before midnight struck. Diabla still hadn't returned. When the man from Cádiz, following his hitherto fruitless custom, turned round at the corner of the street to look towards Asís's balcony, he could make out a white shape on it. The lady was exposing her burning cheeks to the cool night air, and the intoxication of her senses and the paralysis of her will power began to dissipate. Like a castaway dumped on the shore who, as he is coming round, is delighted to feel the gold lifebelt he had taken the precaution to strap on when he felt his ship sinking, Asís was glad to have retained the modicum of reason necessary not to agree to a certain stupid request.

'A fine thing that would be! Tomorrow the neighbours, servants, night watchman, the world and his uncle would be in the know. Oh, good lord...! It's still there, I can still feel the dizziness of the fair ... and as for now there's no medicine that will get rid of it! What do you mean dizziness! Dizziness, alcohol, sunstroke... Pretexts, nonsense! The truth is I like him, that I'm getting to like him a bit more every day, that he's driving me crazy with his prattle ... end of discussion. He says I've given him love potions and herbs... He's the one who's cast a spell on me ... and there's nothing for it, I can't extricate myself. When he goes off, I think about it and the penny drops; but as soon as I see him ... it's finished, I'm lost.'

Llegada a este capítulo, la dama se dedicó a recordar mil pormenores, que reunidos formaban lindo mosaico de gracias y méritos de su adorador. La pasión con que requebraba; el donaire con que pedía; la gentileza de su persona; su buen porte, tan libre del menor conato de gomosería impertinente como de encogimiento provinciano; su rara mezcla de espontaneidad popular y cortesía hidalga; sus rasgos calaverescos y humorísticos unidos a cierta hermosa tristeza romántica (conjunto, dicho sea de paso, que forma el hechizo peculiar de los *polos, soleares* y demás canciones andaluzas), eran otros tantos motivos que la dama se alegaba a sí propia para excusar su debilidad y aquella afición avasalladora que sentía apoderarse de su alma. Pero al mismo tiempo, considerando otras cosas, se increpaba ásperamente.

–No darle vueltas: aquí no hay nada superior, ni siquiera bueno: hay un truhán, un vago, un perdis … Todo eso que me dice de que sólo a mí … Ardides, trapacerías, costumbre de engañar, mañitas de calavera. En volviendo la esquina … (Pacheco acababa de verificar, hacía pocos minutos, tan sencillo movimiento) ya ni se acuerda de lo que me declama. Estos andaluces nacen actores … Juicio, Asís …, juicio. Para estas tercianas, hija mía, píldoras de camino de hierro[41] … y extracto de Vigo, mañana y tarde, durante cuatro meses. ¡Bahía de Vigo, cuándo te veré!

El airecillo de la noche, burlándose de la buena señora, compuso con sus susurros delicados estas palabras:

–Terronsito e asúcar …, gitana salá.

---

41   Calco del francés *chemin de fer* (vía férrea).

Having reached this point, the lady devoted herself to recalling a thousand details, which together made up a beautiful mosaic of her admirer's charms and merits. His passionate wooing, his graceful way of asking a favour, his kindness and fine demeanour, as free from the least attempt at impertinent affectation as from provincial reserve; his rare mixture of popular spontaneity and noble courtesy; his rakish, humorous characteristics united with a certain beautiful and romantic melancholy (a combination, incidentally, which makes up the peculiar charm of *polos*, *soleares* and the other Andalusian songs), were the many reasons put forward by the lady to excuse her own weakness and the overwhelming inclination she felt take possession of her soul. But at the same time, bearing other things in mind, she reproached herself bitterly.

'Don't think about him: there's nothing superior about him, nothing even good. He's a rogue, an idler, a cad... All that about my being the only one... Ruses, deceits, the habit of misleading, a rake's tricks. As soon as he turns the corner...' (Pacheco had just performed this very simple movement a few minutes previously) 'he can't even remember what he declared to me. These Andalusians are born actors... Be sensible, Asís, be sensible. For this tertian fever, my good girl, railway pills ... and extract of Vigo, night and morning, for four months. Bay of Vigo, when shall I see you?'

The night breeze, making fun of the good lady, delicately whispered these words:

'Sugar pie ... you charmin' gypsy.'

XVII

Muy atareadas estaban la marquesa viuda de Andrade y su doncella en revisar mundos, sacos y maletillas, operación necesaria cuando se va a emprender un viaje. Y mire usted que parece cosa del mismo enemigo. Siempre en los últimos momentos han de faltar las llaves de los baúles. Por mucho que uno las coloque en sitio determinado, diciendo para sí: –En este cajón se queda la llavecita; no olvidar que aquí la puse; le ato un estambre colorado, para acordarme mejor; no sea que el día de la marcha salgamos con que se ha obscurecido –viene el instante crítico, la busca uno, y ... ¡echarle un galgo! Nada, no parece: venga el cerrajero, tiznado, sucio, preguntón, insufrible; haga una nueva, y lléveselo todo la trampa.

Nerviosa y displicente, daba Asís a la Ángela estas quejas. El ajetreo del viaje la ponía de mal humor: ¡son tan cargantes los preparativos! ¡Qué babel, qué trastorno! Nunca sabe uno lo que conviene llevar y lo que debe dejarse; cree no necesitar ropa de abrigo, porque al fin se viene encima la canícula, pero ¡fíese usted de aquel clima gallego, tan inconstante, tan húmedo, tan lluvioso, que tiene seis temperaturas diferentísimas en cada veinticuatro horas! Se quedan aquí las prendas en el ropero, muertas de risa, y allá tirita uno o tiene que envolverse en mantones como las viejas ... Luego las fiestecitas, los bailes dichosos de la Pastora, que obligan a ir provisto de trajes de sociedad, porque si uno se presenta sencillo, de seda cruda, les choca y se ofenden y critican ... Nada, que la última hora es para volverse loco. ¿A que no se había acordado Ángela de pasarse por casa de la Armandina, a ver si tiene lista la pamela de la niña y el pajazón? ¿Apostamos a que el impermeable aún está con los mismos botones, que lastiman y en todo se prenden? ¿Y el alcanfor para poner en el abrigo de nutria? ¿Y la pimienta para que no se apolillase el tapiz de la sala?

Atarugada y dando vueltas de aquí para allí, la Diabla contestaba lo mejor posible al chaparrón de advertencias, reconvenciones y preguntas de su señora. La hábil muchacha, después de los primeros pases,

17

The Marchioness of Andrade and her maid were very busy checking large trunks, bags and small suitcases, a necessary operation when about to undertake a journey. And it's always the same devilish thing. At the last moment the keys to the trunks are bound to be missing. However much you put them in a particular place, saying to yourself: 'The key's in this drawer; don't forget I put it here; I'll tie some red worsted to help me remember, so that it won't be hidden from view on the day of departure', the critical moment arrives, you look for it, and … fat hope! Nothing, no sign of it. Send for the grimy, dirty, nosey, unbearable locksmith to make a new one, and time wasted.

These are the complaints which Asís, who was agitated and out of sorts, was making to Ángela. The drudgery of packing put her in a bad mood. The preparations are such a pain! What bedlam, what a nuisance! You never know what to take and what you should leave behind. You think you don't need heavy clothing because at last the dog days are nearly upon us, but trust that Galician climate, so changeable, damp and rainy, with six totally different temperatures every twenty-four hours! Your articles of clothing stay here in the wardrobe, dying of laughter, and you're there shivering or having to wrap up in shawls like old women... Then the festivals, the happy Pastora[46] balls where you have to go in evening dress because if you turn up in plain silk, it shocks them and they are offended and criticise... The last hours are enough to drive you mad. I bet Ángela didn't remember to go round to Armandina's house to see if she's got the girl's sun hat ready and the straw hat. We bet the raincoat still has those same buttons which damage and catch on everything. And the camphor to put on the otter fur coat? And the pepper to stop the carpet in the room getting moth-eaten?

Diabla, ashamed and going round and round everywhere, answered as best she could the lady's barrage of warnings, reprimands and questions. After the first feints, the skilful girl knew how to stab her

---

46   The Pazo de la Pastora is a stately house in Vigo where high society went to celebrate dances and other events.

conocía una estocada certera para su ama: si los preparativos de viaje andaban algo retrasados, era que la señorita aquel año había dispuesto la marcha un mes antes que de costumbre, por lo menos; también a ella (la Diabla) se le quedaba sin alistar un vestido de percal, y calzado, y varias menudencias; ella creía que hasta mediados de junio, hacia el día de San Antonio ... ¿Cómo se le había de ocurrir que se largaban tan de prisa y corriendo? La señora contestaba con reprimido suspiro, callaba dos minutos, y luego, redoblando su gruñir, corría del cuarto-ropero al dormitorio, de la leonera o cuarto de los baúles al saloncito, y aún se determinaba a entrar en la cocina y el comedor, para regañar a Imperfecto que no le había traído a su gusto papel de seda, bramante, puntas de París, algodón en rama ... Imperfecto, con la boca abierta y la fisonomía estúpida, subía y bajaba cien veces la escalera haciendo recados: las puntas eran gordas, se precisaban otras más chiquitas; el algodón no convenía blanco, sino gris: era para rellenar huecos en ciertos cajones y que no se estropease lo que iba dentro ... En una de estas idas y venidas del criado, la señora cruzaba el pasillo, cuando repicó la campanilla. Impremeditadamente fue a abrir —cosa que no hacía nunca— y se encontró cara a cara con su Diego.

El primer movimiento fue de despecho y contrariedad mal encubierta. ¿Quién contaba con Pacheco a tales horas (las diez y media de la mañana)? No estaba Asís lo que se llama hecha un pingo, con traje roto y zapatos viejos, porque ni en una isla desierta se pondría ella en semejante facha; pero su bata de chiné blanco tenía manchas y visos obscuros, y aun no sé si alguna telaraña, indicio de la lidia con los baúles de la leonera; su peinado, revuelto sin arte, con rabos y mechones saliendo por aquí y por acullá, parecía obra de peluquería gatuna; y en la superficie del pelo y del rostro se había depositado un sutil viso polvoriento, que la señora percibía vagamente al pestañear y al pasarse la lengua por los labios, y que la impacientaba lo indecible. Y en cambio el galán venía todo soplado, con una camisa y un chaleco como el ampo de la nieve, el ojal guarnecido de fresquísimo clavel, guantes de piel de perro flamantitos y, en suma, todas las señales de haberse acicalado mucho. En la mano traía el pretexto de la visita madrugadora: dos libros medianamente gruesos.

—Las novelas francesas que le prometí ... —dijo en voz alta después

mistress in the back: if the preparations for the journey were somewhat behind it was because that year the lady had arranged to go off at least a month earlier than usual. In addition, she, Diabla, still hadn't got ready her percale dress, footwear and various trifles; she reckoned on up until the middle of June, about Saint Anthony's Day... Why should it occur to her that they would run off in such a hurry? The lady replied with a repressed sigh, remained silent for two minutes, and then, grumbling twice as much, ran from the walk-in wardrobe to the bedroom, from the junk room or storage room to the living room and even decided to go into the kitchen and dining room to scold Imperfecto for not bringing her the right silk paper, twine, small pins, raw cotton... With his stupid face and mouth wide open, Imperfecto went up and down the stairs running errands a hundred times: the pins were too big, smaller ones were needed; the cotton should be grey, not white; it was to fill holes in certain drawers and stop what went inside them from getting ruined... In one of the comings and goings of the servant, the lady was crossing the hall just as the doorbell rang. Quite unpremeditatedly, she went to open the door – something she never did – and found herself face to face with Diego.

Her first reaction was one of spite and badly hidden annoyance. Who could have expected Pacheco at such a time, half past ten in the morning? Asís wasn't what you'd call dressed in rags, with a torn dress and old shoes, because not even on a desert island would she look like that; but her white *chiné* silk dressing gown had stains and a dark appearance, and maybe even a cobweb, the sign of a struggle with the trunks in the junk room. Her hair, tied up clumsily and with stray curls protruding here and there, looked like the work of a salon for cats; and on the surface of her hair and skin a subtle layer of dust had settled, something the lady was vaguely aware of when she blinked and licked her lips, and which exasperated her terribly. Her suitor, on the other hand, was all spruced up, with shirt and waistcoat as white as the driven snow, the buttonhole adorned with a fresh carnation, brand-new dog-skin gloves and, in short, all the signs of having really dressed up. In his hand he had the pretext for the early morning visit: two quite thick books.

'The French novels I promised you...,' he said in a loud voice after

del cambio de saludos, porque la dama le había hecho seña con el mirar de que había moros en la costa–. Si está usted ocupada, me retiro … Si no, entraré diez minutos …

–Con mucho gusto … A la sala: el resto de la casa está imposible … no quiero que se asuste usted del estado en que se encuentra.

Entró Pacheco en la sala; pero por aprisa que Ángela cerrase las puertas de las habitaciones interiores, el gaditano pudo ver baúles abiertos, con las bandejas fuera, ropa desparramada, cajas, sacos …

–¿Está usted de mudanza … o de viaje? –preguntó quedándose de pie en medio del saloncito, con voz opaca, pero sin emplear tono de reconvención ni de queja.

–No … –tartamudeó Asís–, tanto como de viaje precisamente … no. Es que estoy guardando la ropa de invierno, poniéndole alcanfor … Si uno se descuida, la polilla hace destrozos …

Pacheco se acercó a la dama, y bajando el diapasón, con las inflexiones dolientes y melancólicas que solía adoptar a veces, le dijo:

–A mí no se me engaña, te lo repito. Antes de venir sabía que te ibas. Tú no me conoces; tú te has creído que me la puedes dar. Aún no pasaron las ideas por esa cabecita y ya las he olfateado yo. Siento que gastes conmigo tapujos. Al fin no te valen, hija mía.

La señora, no acertando a responder nada que valiese la pena, bajó los ojos, frunció la boca e hizo un mohín de disgusto.

–No amoscarse. Si no me enfado tampoco. La nena mía es muy dueña de irse a donde quiera. Pero mientras está aquí, ¿por qué me huye? Ayer me dijiste que no podíamos vernos, por estar tú convidada a comer …

Movidos por el mismo impulso, Asís y don Diego miraron en derredor. Las puertas, cerradas; al través de la que comunicaba con los cuartos interiores, pasaba amortiguado el ruido del ir y venir de la Diabla. Y sin concertarse, a un mismo tiempo, se acercaron, para cruzar mejor esas explicaciones que el corazón adivina antes de pronunciadas.

–Hazte cargo … Los criados … Es una atrocidad … Yo nunca tuve de estas …, vamos …, de estas historias … No sé lo que me pasa. Por favor te pido …

greetings had been exchanged, because the lady had signalled with a glance that the coast wasn't clear. 'If you're busy, I'll leave... If not, I'll come in for ten minutes...'

'Be my guest ... come into the living room. The rest of the house is out of the question ... I don't want you to be alarmed about the state it's in.'

Pacheco went into the living room, but no matter how quickly Ángela closed the doors of the connecting rooms, the man from Cádiz could see open trunks, with the trays outside, clothes scattered, boxes, bags...

'Are you moving ... or going away?' he asked in a gloomy voice, standing in the middle of the little room, without any trace of reprimand or complaint.

'No...,' Asís stammered, 'not exactly on holiday. It's just that I'm putting away my winter clothes, putting camphor on them... If you're not careful, the moths wreak havoc...'

Pacheco moved close to the lady and, lowering his voice, said to her with the sorrowful, melancholic inflections he often used:

'I'll tell you again, you can't fool me. Before I came here I knew you were goin' away. You don't know me, you thought you could deceive me. I've already sniffed out your thoughts before they've come into that little head of yours. I'm sorry that you use false excuses with me. You're better than that, my dear.'

Not managing to find a suitable reply, the lady lowered her eyes, pursed her lips and gave a look of displeasure.

'Don't be cross. It's not as if I'm angry. My love can go exactly where she wants. But while she's here, why is she avoiding me? Yesterday you said we couldn't meet because you were invited for lunch...'

Moved by the same impulse, Asís and Don Diego looked round about. The doors were shut, but from the one connecting to the inner rooms came the muffled sound of Diabla to-ing and fro-ing. And they spontaneously moved closer, the better to exchange those explanations which the heart divines before they have been uttered.

'Be careful... The servants... It's awful... Never have I had ... well ... anything like this ... I don't know what's happening to me. I beg you, please...'

–¡Bendita sea tu madre, niña! Si ya lo sé ... ¿Te crees que no me informo yo de los pasos en que anduvo mi reina? Estoy enterao de que nadie consiguió de ti ni esto. Yo el primerito ... ¡Ay!, te deshago ... Rica, gitana ... ¡Cielo!

–Chist ... La chica ... Si pesca ... Es más curiosa ...

–Un favor te pido no más. Vente a almorsá conmigo. Que te vienes.

–Estás tocado ... Quita ... Chist ...

–Que te vienes. Palabra, no lo sabrá ni la tierra. Se arreglará ..., verás tú.

–¿Pero cómo? ¿Dónde?

–En el campo. Te vienes, te vienes. ¡Ya pronto te quedas libre de mí ...! La despedía. Al reo de muerte se le da, mujer.

¿Cómo cedió y balbució *que sí*, prometiendo, si no por la Estigia, por algún otro juramento formidable? ¡Ah! Aunque la observación ya no resulte nueva, cedió obedeciendo a los dos móviles que, desde la memorable insolación de San Isidro, guiaban, sin que ella misma lo notase, su voluntad; dos resortes que podemos llamar de goma el uno y de acero el otro: el resorte de goma era la debilidad que aplaza, que remite toda gran resolución hasta que la ampare el recurso de la fuga; el resorte de acero, todavía chiquitín, menudo como pieza de reloj, era el sentimiento que así, a la chiticallando, aspiraba nada menos que a tomar plenísima posesión de sus dominios, a engranar en la máquina del espíritu, para ser su regulador absoluto, y dirigir su marcha con soberano imperio.

Fiado en la palabra solemne de la señora, Pacheco se marchó, pues no convenía, por ningún estilo, que los viesen salir juntos. Asís entró en su cuarto a componerse. La Diabla la miraba con su acostumbrada curiosidad fisgona y aun le disparó tres o cuatro preguntas pérfidas referentes a la interrumpida tarea del equipaje.

–¿Se cierra el mundo?[42] ¿Se clavan los cajones? ¿La señorita quiere que avise a la Central para mañana?

¿Cómo había de responder la señora a interrogaciones tan impertinentes? Claro que con alguna sequedad y no poco enfado secreto. Además, otros incidentes concurrían a exasperarla: por culpa

---

42 Baúl grande.

'God bless your mother! I know only too well... Do you think I don't know about the path my queen has trodden? I know that nobody's managed even this from you. I'm the very first... Ah! I'll make you melt... My gypsy beauty... My love!'

'Shh... The girl... If she catches on... She's very inquisitive...'

'One favour is all I'm asking. Come 'n' have breakfast with me. Please come.'

'You're crazy... Leave... Shh...'

'Please come. On my word, not a soul shall know. It'll work out... you'll see.'

'But how? Where?'

'In the country. Go on, come with me. You'll soon be free of me! A parting gift. That's what they give a person condemned to death.'

Why did she give in and stutter *yes*, swearing, if not on the River Styx, some other formidable oath?[47] Ah! Even if there is nothing new about the observation, she yielded to the two motives which, since the memorable sunstroke at Saint Isidro, had guided her will without her noticing; two springs, one that we might call rubber and the other steel. The rubber spring was the weakness that postpones, puts off every big decision until it is protected by the resort of flight; the steel spring, still very small like a tiny piece from a watch, was the feeling that silently aspired in this way to take nothing less than full possession and control, to connect with the mental mechanism in order to be in complete control, and direct its operation with supreme authority.

Trusting the lady's solemn word, Pacheco set off, because on no account was it advisable for them to be seen leaving together. Asís went into her room to dress up. Diabla looked at her with her customary nosey curiosity and even fired three or four perfidious questions at her concerning the interrupted task of packing.

'Does the trunk need closing? Should the boxes be fastened? Does madam want me to notify the station office for tomorrow?'

How should the lady respond to such impertinent questions? Clearly with some curtness and much secret anger. Moreover, other incidents

---

47 The Styx is a sacred river that separates the land of the living from the Underworld. In Homer's *Iliad* and *Odyssey*, the gods swear by the water of the Styx as their most binding oath.

del revoluto del equipaje, ni había cosa con cosa, ni parecía lo más indispensable de vestir: para dar con unos guantes nuevos tuvo que desbaratar el baúl más chico: para sacar un sombrero, desclavó dos cajones. Más peripecias: la hebilla del zapato inglés, descosida: al abrochar el cuerpo del traje, salta un herrete; al cepillarse los dientes, se rompe el frasco del elixir contra el mármol del lavabo …

–¿Almuerza fuera la señorita? –preguntó la incorregible Diabla.

–Sí … En casa de Inzula.

–¿Ha de venir a buscarla Roque?

–No … Pero le mandas que esté con la berlina allí, a las siete …

–¿De la tarde?

–¿Había de ser de la mañana? ¡Tienes cosas …!

La Diabla sonrió a espaldas de su señora y se bajó para estirarle los volantes del vestido y ahuecarle el polisón. Asís piafaba, pegando taconacitos de impaciencia. ¿El pericón? ¿El gabán gris, por si refresca? ¿Pañuelo? ¿Dónde se habrá metido el velo de tul? Estos pinguitos parece que se evaporan … Nunca están en ninguna parte … ¡Ah! Por fin … Loado sea Dios …

combined to exasperate her: because of the disorder of the luggage, nothing was in its place, and the most essential items of clothing failed to turn up. To find some new gloves she had to mess up the smallest trunk; to get out a hat she unfastened two boxes. Additional incidents: the buckle of her English shoe falls off; a tag comes off while doing up her dress; while brushing her teeth the bottle of mouthwash breaks against the marble of the basin…

'Is madam having lunch out?' asked the incorrigible Diabla.

'Yes… At Inzula's house.'

'Will Roque need to fetch you?'

'No… But tell him to be there with the carriage at seven…'

'In the evening?'

'Could it be in the morning? The things you come out with!'

Diabla smiled behind her mistress's back and bent down to smooth out the flounces of her skirt and plump up the crinoline. Asís stomped her feet, stamping her heels with impatience. My fan? My grey overcoat, in case it gets cold? My handkerchief? Where can my tulle veil be? These little things seem to vanish into thin air… They're never there… Ah! At last… Praise the Lord…

XVIII

Salvó la escalera como pájaro a quien abren el postigo de su penitenciaría, y con el mismo paso vivo, echó calle abajo hasta Recoletos. La cita era en aquel sitio señalado donde Pacheco había tirado el puro: casi frente a la Cibeles. Asís avanzaba protegida por su antucá, pero bañada y animada por el sol, el sol instigador y cómplice de todo aquel enredo sin antecedentes, sin finalidad y sin excusa. La dama registró con los ojos las arboledas, los jardincillos, la entrada en la Carrera y las perspectivas del Museo, y no vio a nadie. ¿Se habría cansado Diego de esperar? ¡Capaz sería …! De pronto a sus espaldas una voz cuchicheó afanosa:

–Allí … Entre aquellos árboles … El simón.

Sin que ella respondiese, el gaditano la guió hacia el destartalado carricoche. Era uno de esos clarens[43] inmundos, con forro de gutapercha resquebrajado y mal oliente, vidrios embazados y conductor medio beodo, que zarandean por Madrid adelante la prisa de los negocios o la clandestinidad del amor. Asís se metió en él con escrúpulo, pensando que bien pudiera su galán traerle otro simón menos derrotado. Pacheco, a fin de no molestarla pasando a la izquierda, subió por la portezuela contraria, y al subir arrojó al regazo de la dama un objeto … ¡Qué placer! ¡Un ramillete de rosas, o mejor dicho un mazo, casi desatado, mojado aún! El recinto se inundó de frescura.

–¡Huelen tan mal estos condenaos coches! –exclamó el meridional como excusándose de su galantería. Pero Asís le flechó una ojeada de gratitud. El indecente vehículo comenzaba a rodar: ya debía de tener órdenes.

–¿Se puede saber adónde vamos o es un secreto?

–A las Ventas del Espíritu Santo.

–¡Las Ventas! –clamó Asís alarmada–. ¡Pero si es un sitio de los más públicos! ¿Vuelta a las andadas? ¿Otro San Isidro tenemos?

–Es sitio público los domingos: los días sueltos está bastante solitario. Que te calles. ¿Te iba yo a llevar a donde te encontrases en

---

43 Coche con capota, tirado por caballos, con cuatro asientos.

18

She flew down the staircase like a bird whose prison cage has just been opened and with the same lively step went down the street towards Recoletos. Their meeting was in the very place where Pacheco had thrown away his cigar, almost opposite the Cibeles fountain. Asís walked along protected by her parasol, but bathed and animated by the sun – the sun, instigator and accomplice of all that romance without precedent, purpose and excuse. The lady surveyed the groves, little gardens, the entrance to the Carrera and views of the Prado Museum, and couldn't see anybody. Had Diego tired of waiting? He was quite capable of that! Suddenly an eager voice whispered:

'There... Between those trees... The carriage.'

Without her replying, the man from Cádiz guided her towards the rickety coach. It was one of those dirty Clarence carriages, with cracked, evil-smelling gutta-percha lining, shaded windows and half-drunk driver, that rattle through Madrid with the rush of business or clandestine romance. Asís got in warily, thinking that her gallant might well have brought a less shabby carriage. Pacheco, so as not to disturb her by getting in on the left side, climbed in through the opposite door, and as he got in he threw something into the lady's lap... How nice! A bunch of roses, or rather a loosely-tied bundle, still wet! The enclosed space became flooded with freshness.

'These damn coaches smell so bad!' exclaimed the southerner, as if to excuse his gallantry. But Asís darted him a glance of gratitude. The filthy vehicle began to roll along: the order must have already been given.

'Any chance of knowing our destination or is it a secret?'

'Las Ventas del Espíritu Santo.'[48]

'Las Ventas?' exclaimed Asís in alarm. 'But it's such a public place! Back to your old ways? Are we going to have another Saint Isidro?'

'It's public on Sundays. On working days it's fairly empty. Just keep quiet. Would I take you to a place where you'd be embarrassed? Before

---

48   Las Ventas del Espíritu Santo, on the east side of Madrid, was an area with lots of snack bars and restaurants, a popular destination for Madrilenians.

un bochorno? Antes de convidarte, chiquilla, me he enterado yo de toas las maneras de almorsá en Madrid ... Se puede almorsá en un buen *restaurant* o en cafés finos, pero eso es echar un pregón pa que te vean. Se puede ir a un colmado de los barrios o a una pastelería decente y escondía, pero no hay cuartos aparte: tendrías que almorsá en pública subasta, a la vera de alguna chulapa o de algún torero. Fondas, ya supondrás ... No quedaban sino las Ventas o el puente de Vallecas. Creo que las Ventas es más bonito.

¡Bonito! Asís miró el camino en que entraban. Dejándose atrás las frondosidades del Retiro y las construcciones coquetonas de Recoletos, el coche se metía, lento y remolón, por una comarca la más escuálida, seca y triste que puede imaginarse, a no ser que la comparemos al cerro de San Isidro. Era tal la diferencia entre la zona del Retiro y aquel arrabal de Madrid, y se advertía tan de golpe, que mejor que transición parecía sorpresa escenográfica. Cual mastín que guarda las puertas del limbo, allí estaba la estatua de Espartero, tan mezquina como el mismo personaje, y la torre mudéjar de una escuela parecía sostener con ella competencia de mal gusto. Luego, en primer término, escombros y solares marcados con empalizadas; y allá en el horizonte, parodia de algún grandioso y feroz anfiteatro romano, la plaza de toros. En aquel rincón semidesierto –a dos pasos del corazón de la vida elegante– se habían refugiado edificios heterogéneos, bien como en ciertas habitaciones de las casas se arrinconan juntas la silla inservible, la máquina de limpiar cuchillos y las colgaduras para el día de Corpus: así, después del circo taurino y la escuela, venía una fábrica de galletas y bizcochos, y luego un barracón con este rótulo: *Acreditado merendero de la Alegría*.

Las lontananzas, una desolación. El fielato parecía viva imagen del estorbo y la importunidad. A su puerta estaba detenido un borrico cargado de liebres y conejos, y un tío de gorra peluda buscaba en

inviting you along, I found out about all the different ways of having breakfast in Madrid... You can go to a good restaurant or fine cafés, but that's making an announcement to be seen. You can go to a snack bar in the suburbs or a baker's that's respectable and hidden away, but there are no private rooms: you'd have to have breakfast at a public auction, next to some working-class Madrid girl or a bullfighter. Small restaurants, you can well imagine... All that was left was Las Ventas or the Puente de Vallecas.⁴⁹ I think Las Ventas is prettier.'

Pretty! Asís looked at the road they were entering. Leaving behind the luxuriance of the branches and leaves of Retiro Park and the coquettish buildings of the Recoletas, the carriage slowly and leisurely went into the most dingy, parched and sad district imaginable, unless we compare it to the hill of Saint Isidro. Such was the difference between the area of the Retiro Park and that slum of Madrid, and so sudden, that it seemed more like a theatrical surprise than a transition. Like a mastiff guarding the gates of Limbo stood the statue of Espartero,⁵⁰ as miserable as the personage himself, and the Mudejar tower of a school seemed to compete in bad taste with it. Then, in the foreground, rubble and undeveloped plots of land marked off with fences; and there on the horizon, a parody of some grandiose, ferocious Roman amphitheatre, the bullring.⁵¹ In that semi-desert, two steps from the heart of fashionable life, heterogeneous buildings had taken refuge, just like useless chairs, knife-cleaning machines and hangings for Corpus Christi day are put in the corner of some room in a house. In the same way, after the taurine circus and school came a biscuit and cake factory and then a big hut with this sign: *Reputable snack bar of Joy.*

In the distance, desolation. The tollhouse looked like the living image of hindrance and importunity. A donkey laden with hares and rabbits was hitched to its door, and a guy with a furry cap was looking

---

49 Puente de Vallecas, in the south-east of Madrid, was an area where people went for entertainment and to see bullfights.

50 Pablo Giber's statue of Baldomero Espartero (1793–1879), a Spanish general and statesman associated with the progressive wing of Spanish liberalism, was erected in 1886.

51 This is a reference to la Plaza de Toros de las Ventas, a famous bullring in the east of Madrid designed by José Espeliú in the neo-Mudejar style.

su cinto los cuartos de la alcabala. Más adelante, en un descampado amarillento, jugaban a la barra varios de esos salvajes que rodean a la Corte lo mismo que los galos a Roma sitiada. Y seguían los edificios fantásticos: un castillo de la Edad Media hecho, al parecer, de cartón y cercado de tapias por donde las francesillas sacaban sus brazos floridos; un parador, tan desmantelado como teológico (dedicado al Espíritu Santo nada menos); un merendero que se honraba con la divisa *tanto monta*, y por último, una franja rojiza, inflamada bajo la reverberación del sol: los hornos de ladrillo. En los términos más remotos que la vista podía alcanzar, erguía el Guadarrama sus picos coronados de eternas nieves.

Lo que sorprendió gratamente a Asís fue la ausencia total de carruajes de lujo en la carretera. Tenía razón Pacheco, por lo visto. Sólo encontraron un domador que arrastraban dos preciosas tarbesas;[44] un carromato tirado por innumerable serie de mulas; el tranvía, que cruzó muy bullanguero y jacarandoso, con sus bancos atestados de gentes; otro simón con tapadillo, de retorno, y un asistente, caballero en el alazán de su amo. ¡Ah! Un entierro de angelito, una caja blanca y azul que tambaleándose sobre el ridículo catafalco del carro se dirigía hacia la sacramental sin acompañamiento alguno, inundado de luz solar, como deben de ir los querubines camino del Empíreo …

Poco hablaron durante el trayecto los amantes. Llevaban las manos cogidas; Asís respiraba frecuentemente el manojo de rosas y miraba y remiraba hacia fuera, porque así creía disminuir la gravedad de aquel contrabando, que en su fuero interno –cosa decidida– llamaba *el último*, y por lo mismo le causaba tristeza sabiéndole a confite que jamás, jamás había de gustar otra vez.

Llegaron al puente, y detúvose el simón ante el pintoresco racimo

---

44   Yeguas de la raza propia de Tarbes en Francia.

in his belt for money for the excise tax. Further on, in a yellowish area of open space, many of those savages who surround Madrid, like the Gauls did Rome when it was besieged, were playing at tossing the bar. And the fantastic buildings carried on: a medieval castle made to all appearances from cardboard and surrounded by a wall through which buttercups threw out their florid arms; an inn, as dilapidated as it was theological (dedicated to no less than the Holy Spirit); a snack bar which was honoured with the motto *it makes no difference*,[52] and finally a reddish strip ignited beneath the reverberation of sunlight: the brick ovens. In the most remote distance that sight can reach, the Guadarrama Mountains raised their peaks crowned with eternal snow.

What gave Asís a pleasant surprise was the total absence of luxury carriages on the road. Pacheco, it would seem, had been right. They only met one luxurious carriage dragged by two beautiful *tarbais* horses, a wagon pulled by an interminable succession of mules, a tram with its benches full of people passing by with rowdy jollity, another carriage with a cover on its return journey and an orderly mounted on his master's chestnut horse. Ah! A child's funeral, a blue-and-white coffin jolting about on the absurd open hearse, was making its way towards the cemetery[53] without any accompaniment, bathed in sunshine like the cherubim must be as they go towards the Empyrean...

During the journey the lovers didn't speak much. They held hands, Asís frequently smelling the bunch of roses and repeatedly staring outside, because she believed this would lessen the seriousness of this illicit escapade, which in her heart of hearts she had decided to designate *the last*, and for that reason it made her sad since it tasted of a sweetness she would never ever taste again.

They reached the bridge and the coach stopped in front of the

---

52   According to one story, when Alexander the Great arrived in the Phrygian capital of Gordium, he encountered an ancient wagon whose yoke was tied with so many knots that it was impossible to see how they were fastened. An oracle had declared that any man who could unravel the knots would become the ruler of the whole of Asia. After trying but failing to do this, Alexander stepped back, proclaimed that it made no difference how they were loosed, drew his sword and sliced the knot in half.

53   The San Isidro cemetery in Madrid.

de merenderos, hotelitos y jardines que constituye la parte nueva de las Ventas.

–¿Qué sitio prefieres? ¿Nos apeamos aquí? –preguntó Pacheco.

–Aquí … Ese merendero … Tiene trazas de alegre y limpio –indicó la dama, señalando a uno cuya entrada por el puente era una escalera de palo pintada de verde rabioso.

Sobre el frontis del establecimiento podía leerse este rótulo, en letras descomunales imitando las de imprenta, y sin gazapos ortográficos: – *Fonda de la Confianza. –Vinos y comidas. –Aseo y equidad.–* El aspecto era original y curioso. Si no cabía llamar a aquello los jardines aéreos de Babilonia, cuando menos tenían que ser los merenderos colgantes. ¡Ingenioso sistema para aprovechar terreno! Abajo una serie de jardines, mejor dicho, de plantaciones entecas y marchitas, víctimas de la aridez del suburbio matritense; y encima, sostenidos en armadijos de postes, las salas de baile, los corredores, las alcobas con pasillos rodeados de una especie de barandas, que comunicaban entre sí las viviendas. Todo ello –justo es añadirlo para evitar el descrédito de esta Citerea suspendida– muy enjabelgado, alegre, clarito, flamante, como ropa blanca recién lavada y tendida a secar al sol, como nido de jilguero colgado en rama de arbusto.

Un mozo frisando en los cincuenta, de mandil pero en mangas de camisa, con cara de mico, muequera,[45] arrugadilla y sardónica, se adelantó apresurado al divisar a la pareja.

–Almorsá –dijo Pacheco lacónicamente.

–¿Dónde desean los señoritos que se les ponga el almuerzo?

El gaditano giró la vista alrededor y luego la convirtió hacia su compañera: ésta había vuelto la cara. Con la agudeza de la gente de su oficio el mozo comprendió y les sacó del apuro.

–Vengan los señoritos … Les daré un sitio bueno.

Y torciendo a la izquierda, guió por una escalera angosta que sombreaba un grupo de acacias y castaños de Indias, llevándoles a una especie de antesala descubierta, que formaba parte de los consabidos corredores aéreos. Abriendo una puertecilla, hízose a un lado y murmuró con unción:

---

45 Que hace muecas (neologismo).

picturesque cluster of snack bars, small hotels and gardens which constitute the new part of Las Ventas.

'Which place do you prefer? Shall we get off here?' Pacheco asked.

'Here... That snack bar... It looks clean and cheerful,' stated the lady, pointing out one whose entrance via the bridge was a wooden staircase painted bright green.

On the façade of the establishment this sign, in enormous letters like printing blocks and without spelling mistakes, could be seen: *Inn of Confidence. Wine and food. Clean and reasonably priced.* The appearance was original and curious. If you couldn't call this the Hanging Gardens of Babylon, they at least had to be the hanging open air cafés. What an ingenious system of utilising the land! Below, a series of gardens, or rather of sickly, withered plantations, victims of the dryness of the Madrid suburb; and above, supported on a framework of posts, the dance halls, dining rooms, corridors and bedrooms, all connected by passageways enclosed with a kind of handrail. It's fair to add, in order to avoid damaging the reputation of this hanging Cytherea,[54] that it was all very whitewashed, bright and clear, splendid, like white clothes recently washed and pegged out to dry in the sun, like a goldfinch's nest hanging on the branch of a bush.

A waiter getting on for fifty, wearing an apron but in shirtsleeves, with the face of a monkey, grimacing, wrinkled and sardonic, hurried forward when he saw the couple.

'Breakfast,' said Pacheco laconically.

'Where do you want me to set the table?'

The man from Cádiz looked all around and then turned his gaze towards his companion, who had averted her face. With the shrewdness of those in his profession, the waiter understood and got them out of the predicament.

'Follow me ... I'll find you a good spot.'

And turning to the left, he led the way up a narrow staircase shaded by a group of acacias and horse chestnut trees, taking them to a kind of open-air antechamber which formed part of the renowned hanging corridors. Opening a little door, he stepped aside and murmured unctuously:

---

54   A small Greek island in the Gulf of Laconia where, according to one version of her birth, the goddess Aphrodite first landed and where she had a celebrated temple.

–Pasen, señoritos, pasen.

La dama experimentó mucho bienestar al encontrarse en aquella salita. Era pequeña, recogida, misteriosa, con ventanas muy chicas que cerraban gruesos postigos y enteramente blanqueada; los muebles vestían también blanquísimas fundas de calicó. La mesa, en el centro, lucía un mantel como el armiño; y lo más amable de tanta blancura era que al través de ella se percibía, se filtraba, por decirlo así, el sol, prestándole un reflejo dorado y quitándole el aspecto sepulcral de las cosas blancas cuando hace frío y hay nubes en el cielo. Mientras salía el mozo, el gaditano miró risueño a la señora.

–Nos han traído al palomar –dijo entre dientes.

Y levantando una cortina nívea que se veía en el fondo de la reducida estancia, descubrió un recinto más chico aún, ocupado por un solo mueble, blanco también, más blanco que una azucena …

–Mira el nido –añadió tomando a Asís de la mano y obligándola a que se asomase–. Gente precavida … Bien se ve que están en todo. No me sorprende que vivan y se sostengan tantos establecimientos de esta índole. Aquí la gente no viene un día del año como a San Isidro; pero digo yo que habrá abonos a turno. ¿Nos abonamos, cacho de gloria?

No sé cómo acentuó Pacheco esta broma, que en rigor, dada la situación, no afrentaba; lo cierto es que la señora sintió una sofoquina … vamos, una sofoquina de esas que están a dos deditos de la llorera y la congoja. Parecíale que le habían arañado el corazón. La mujer es un péndulo continuo que oscila entre el instinto natural y la aprendida vergüenza, y el varón más delicado no acertará a no lastimar alguna vez su invencible pudor.

'This way, this way.'

The lady had a feeling of real well-being when she found herself in that little room. It was small, secluded, mysterious, with very small windows protected by large shutters, and completely whitewashed; the furniture was also covered in pure white calico. The table in the centre was sporting a cloth like ermine; and the most agreeable thing about all this whiteness was that you could see the sun through it, filtered as it were, casting a golden reflection and neutralising the sepulchral appearance white things have when it's cold and there are clouds in the sky. As the waiter was going out, the man from Cádiz looked at the lady with a smile.

'They've brought us to the dovecot,' he said under his breath.

And raising a snowy curtain that could be seen at the back of the little room, he disclosed a still smaller recess, occupied by a single piece of furniture that was also white, whiter than a Madonna lily…

'Look at the nest,' he added, taking Asís by the hand and making her lean over. 'Cautious people… You can clearly see they're on top of everything. I'm not surprised that so many establishments of this kind exist and keep going. People don't come here for a single day in the year as at Saint Isidro, there must be season tickets is what I say. Shall we take out a subscription, darling?'

I don't know what tone Pacheco gave to this joke which, strictly speaking and under the circumstances, wasn't insulting. What was certain was that the lady felt a real shock … well, the sort of shock that is within an inch of a fit of tears and anguish. She felt like her heart had been clawed out. Women are a continuous pendulum swinging between natural instinct and a learned sense of shame, and not even the most attentive man will manage to avoid hurting their invincible modesty at some time or other.

XIX

Al colarse en el palomar los dos tórtolos, no lo hicieron sin ser vistos y atentamente examinados por una taifa de gente humilde, que a la puerta de la cocina del merendero fronterizo se dedicaba a aderezar un guisote de carnero puesto, en monumental cazuela, sobre una hornilla. Es de saber que ambos enseres domésticos los alquilaba el dueño del *restaurant* por módica suma en que iba comprendido también el carbón: en cuanto al carnero y al arroz de añadidura, lo habían traído en sus delantales las muchachas, que por lo que pueda importar, diremos que eran operarias de la Fábrica de tabacos.

Capitaneaba la tribu una vieja pitillera, morena, lista, alegre, más sabidora que Merlín; y dos niñas de ocho y seis años travesaban alrededor de la hornilla, empeñadas en que les dejasen cuidar el guisado, para lo cual se reconocían con superiores aptitudes. Toda esta gentuza, al pasar la marquesa viuda de Andrade y su cortejo, se comunicó impresiones con mucho parpadeo y meneo de cabeza, y susurrados a media voz dichos sentenciosos. Hablaban con el seco y recalcado acento de la plebe madrileña, que tiene alguna analogía con lo que pudo ser la parla de Demóstenes si se le ocurriese escupir a cada frase una de las guijas que llevaba en la boca.

–Ay ... Pus van así como asustaos ... Ella es guapotona, colorá y blanca.

–Valiente perdía será.

–Se ve caa cosa ... Hijas, la mar son estos señorones de rango.

–Puee que sea arguna del Circo. Tié pinta de franchuta.

–Que no, que este es un belén gordo, de gente de calidá. Mujer de algún menistro lo menos. ¿Qué vus pensáis? Pus una conocí yo, casaa

19

When the two turtle doves slipped into the dovecot, they didn't do so without being seen and closely examined by a group of poor people next to the kitchen door of the snack bar opposite, who were busily preparing a mutton stew in a huge earthenware cooking pot over a stove. Let it be known that the owner of the *restaurant* hired both these domestic utensils for a modest sum which also included the charcoal. As for the mutton and rice, the girls had brought it in their aprons and, for what it's worth, we'll mention that they were workers at the tobacco factory.[55]

The tribe was headed by an old female cigarette maker, dark-haired, intelligent, cheerful, wiser than Merlin; and two girls, six and eight years old, were romping around the stove, determined to be allowed to look after the stew, something for which they believed themselves to have a great aptitude. When the Marchioness of Andrade and her escort went by, the whole mob communicated impressions with lots of winking, shaking of heads and whispered sententious remarks. They spoke with the dry, clipped accent of the Madrid working classes, which must be similar to how Demosthenes[56] might have spoken if he had thought with each sentence to spit out one of the pebbles he had in his mouth.

'Oh... They look nervous... She's a beauty, all rosy 'n' pale.'

'A fine 'un she must be.'

'Ya can see it all... These high-ranking big shots.'

'She might as well be one of 'em from the Circus. She's gorra Froggy look.'

'Not at all, this is the real deal: 'igh class people. Wife o' some minister at least. What d'ya think? I knew one, married tuh one o' dem

---

55 The tobacco factory was built in 1790 in the Calle Embajadores. For two months Emilia Pardo Bazán spent mornings and afternoons at the tobacco factory in La Coruña in order to immerse herself in the working environment. She depicts the world of cigar makers in *La Tribuna* (1883).

56 Demosthenes, a statesman and orator of fourth-century Greece, apparently practised giving speeches with his mouth full of pebbles.

con un presonaje de los más superfarolíticos ... de mucho coche, una casa como el Palacio Rial ... y andaba como caa cuala, con su apaño. ¡Qué líos, Virgen!

–No, pus muy amartelaos no van.

–¿Te quies callar? Ya samartelarán dentro. Verás tú las ventanas y las puertas atrancás, como en los pantiones ... Pa que el sol no los queme el cutis.

Desmintiendo las profecías de la experta matrona, los postigos y vidrieras del palomar se abrieron, y asomó la cabeza de la dama, sin sombrero ya, mirando atentamente hacia el merendero.

–Miala, miala ..., la gusta el baile.

En efecto, el corredor aéreo de enfrente ofrecía curiosa escena coreográfica. Un piano mecánico soltaba, con la regularidad que hace tan odiosos a estos instrumentos, el duro chorro de sus martilleadoras tocatas: *Cádiz* hacía el gasto: paso doble de *Cádiz*, tango de *Cádiz*, coro de majas de *Cádiz* ... y hasta una veintena de cigarreras, de chiquillas, de fregonas muy repeinadas y con ropa de domingo, saltaba y brincaba al compás de la música, haciendo a cada zapateta temblar el merendero ... Asís veía pasar y repasar las caras sofocadas, las toquillas azul y rosa; y aquel brincoteo, aquel tripudio suspendido en el aire, sin hombres, sin fiesta que lo justificara, parecía efecto escénico, coro de zarzuela bufa. Asís se imaginó que las muchachas cobraban de los fondistas algún sueldo por animar el cuadro.

–¡Calla! –secreteó minutos después el grupo dedicado a vigilar la cazuela del guisote–. ¡Pus si también han abierto la puerta! Chicas ... quien que se entere too el mundo.

–Estas tunantas ponen carteles.

El mozo subía y bajaba, atareado.

–Mia lo que los llevan. Tortilla ... Jamón ... Están abriendo latas de perdices ... ¡Aire!

–No se las cambio por mi rico carnero. A gloria huele.

–¡Chist! –mandó el mozo, imponiéndose a aquellas cotorras–. Cuidadito ... Si oyen ... Son gente ... ¡uf!

Al expresar la calidad de los huéspedes, el mozo hizo una mueca indescriptible, mezcla de truhanería y respeto profundo a la propina que ya olfateaba. La vieja cigarrera, de repente, adoptó cierta diplomática gravedad.

real refined people … whoppin' coach, 'ouse like the Royal Palace … and carried on like ev'ryone else, with 'er fancy boy. Holy mother, what fun!'

'No, they ain't deeply in love.'

'Will ya keep quiet? They'll be all lovey-dovey in there now. You'll see the windows and doors closed and bolted, like in vaults… So as the sun don't burn their skin.'

Giving the lie to the expert matron's prophecies, the dovecot shutters and windows opened and the lady appeared bare-headed, looking attentively towards the snack bar.

'Look at 'er, look at 'er … she likes the dancing.'

Indeed, the hanging corridor opposite offered a curious choreographic scene. A pianola, with the regularity that makes these instruments so odious, was banging out the harsh stream of its hammering toccatas. *Cádiz* monopolised the repertoire: *Cádiz paso doble*, *Cádiz* tango, *Cádiz* street girls' chorus … and up to about twenty cigar makers, children and kitchen maids all dolled up and in their Sunday best leaped and jumped in time to the music, making the snack bar shake with each jump and slap on the shoe … Asís saw the burning faces go round and round with blue and pink shawls; and that jumping, that dance in mid-air, without men, without a fiesta to justify it, was like a stage effect, a chorus from a comic opera. Asís imagined that the girls were paid something by the restaurant owners for livening up the scene.

'Be quiet!' the group supervising the stew whispered minutes later. 'They've opened the door as well! Girls … they wan' us all tuh see.'

'These brazen hussies are puttin' up posters of themselves.'

The waiter was busily going up and down.

'Let's see what they're gettin'! Omelette… Ham… They're openin' tins o' partridges. Get out!'

'I wouldn't swap them for my delicious mutton stew. It smells divine.'

'Shh!' ordered the waiter, asserting his authority over those chatterboxes. 'Be careful… If they hear… They're the sort of people… Phew!'

In describing the quality of his guests, the waiter made an indescribable grimace, a mixture of buffoonery and deep respect for the tip he was already smelling out. The old cigar maker suddenly took on a certain diplomatic gravity.

–Y pué que sean gente tan honrá como Dios Padre. No sé pa qué ha de condenar una su arma echando malos pensamientos. Serán argunos novios recién casaos, u dos hermanos, u tío y sobrina. Vayasté a saber. Oigasté, mozo …

Se apartó y secreteó con el mozo un ratito. De esta conferencia salió un proyecto habilísimo, madurado en breves minutos en el ardiente y optimista magín de la señá Donata, que así se llamaba la pitillera, si no mienten las crónicas. Arriba dama y galán empezaban a despachar los apetitosos entremeses, las incitantes aceitunas y las sardinillas, con su ajustada túnica de plata. Aunque Pacheco había pedido vinos de lo mejor, la dama rehusaba hasta probar el *Tío Pepe* y el amontillado,[46] porque con sólo ver las botellas, le parecía ya hallarse en la cámara de un trasatlántico, en los angustiosos minutos que preceden al mareo total. Como la señora exigía que puertas y ventanas permaneciesen abiertas, el almuerzo no revelaba más que la cordialidad propia de una luna de miel ya próxima a su cuarto menguante. Pacheco había perdido por completo su labia meridional, y manifestaba un abatimiento que, al quedar mediada la botella de *Tío Pepe*, se convirtió en la tristeza humorística tan frecuente en él.

–¿Te aburres? –preguntaba la dama a cada vuelta del mozo.

–Ajogo las peniyas, gitana –respondía el meridional apurando otro vaso de jerez, más auténtico que la famosa manzanilla del Santo.

Acababa el mozo de dejar sobre la mesa las perdices en escabeche, cuando en el marco de la puerta asomó una carita infantil, colorada, regordeta, boquiabierta, guarnecida de un matorral de rizos negrísimos. ¡Qué monada de chiquilla! Y estaba allí hecha un pasmarote, si entro si no entro. Asís le hizo seña con la mano; el pájaro se coló en el nido sin esperar a que se lo dijesen dos veces. Y las preguntas y los halagos de cajón: –Eres muy guapa … ¿Cómo te llamas? ¿Vas a la escuela? … Toma pasas … Cómete esta aceitunita por mí … Prueba el jerez … ¡Huy qué gesto más salado pone al vino! … Arriba con él … ¡Borrachilla! ¿Dónde está tu mamá? ¿En qué trabaja tu padre?

De respuesta, ni sombra. El pajarito abría dos ojos como dos espuertas, bajaba la cabeza adelantando la frente como hacen los

---

46 *Tío Pepe*: marca de vino de jerez; *amontillado*: vino blanco de alta graduación, parecido al de Montilla.

'And they might be people as honest as God the Father. I dunno why we should condemn us souls thinkin' evil thoughts. They're probably a newly-wed couple, or brother and sister, or uncle and niece. Find out about 'em. Listen, waiter…'

She moved aside and whispered with the waiter for a short while. A very accomplished plan emerged from this conversation, matured for a few moments in the ardent, optimistic imagination of Señora Donata, for such was the cigarette maker's name if the chronicles are to be believed. Upstairs the lady and her lover were beginning to dispose of the tasty *hors d'oeuvres*, the enticing olives and the sardines with their close-fitting silver tunics. Although Pacheco had ordered the choicest wines, the lady refused to taste the Tío Pepe and Amontillado, because just seeing the bottles made her feel like she was in the cabin of an Atlantic steamer, in those moments of anguish preceding total seasickness. As the lady demanded that doors and windows remain open, the breakfast only showed the cordiality typical of a honeymoon already close to its last quarter. Pacheco had completely lost his southern glibness, and exhibited a dejection which, when the bottle of Tío Pepe was half-empty, became the humorous sadness so frequently seen in him.

'Are you bored?' asked the lady every time the waiter turned round.

'I'm drowndin' me sorrows, gypsy,' replied the southerner, draining another glass of sherry that was better than the famous *manzanilla* of Saint Isidro.

The waiter had just placed the tinned partridges on the table when a little red, chubby face, mouth wide open and bedecked with a shock of jet-black curls, appeared in the door frame. What a little beauty! And she was there like a dummy, whether to go in or not. Asís beckoned her with her hand; the bird sneaked into the nest without waiting to be told twice. And the usual questions and flattery: 'You're very pretty… What's your name? … Do you go to school? … Take some raisins … Eat this baby olive for me… Try the sherry… Wow, what a funny face at the wine! … Bottoms up! … Little drunkard! Where's your mum? What does your father do?'

Not even the trace of a response. The little bird opened two eyes as big as saucers, lowered her head and bringing her forehead forward

niños cuando tienen cortedad y al par se encuentran mimados, picaba golosinas y daba con el talón del pie izquierdo en el empeine del derecho. A los tres minutos de haberse colado el primer gorrión migajero en el palomar, apareció otro. El primero representaba cinco años; el segundo, más formal pero no menos asustadizo, tendría ya ocho lo menos.

–¡Hola! Ahí viene la hermanita … –dijo Asís–. Y se parecen como dos gotas … La pequeña es más saladilla … pero vaya con los ojos de la mayor … Señorita, pase usted … Ésta nos enterará de cómo se llama su padre, porque a la chiquita le comieron la lengua los ratones.

Permanecía la mayor incrustada en la puerta, seria y recelosa, como aquel que antes de lanzarse a alguna empresa erizada de dificultades, vacila y teme. Sus ojazos, que eran realmente árabes por el tamaño, el fuego y la precoz gravedad, iban de Asís a Diego y a su hermanita: la chiquilla meditaba, se recogía, buscaba una fórmula, y no daba con ella, porque había en su corazón cierta salvaje repugnancia a pedir favores, y en su carácter una indómita fiereza muy en armonía con sus pupilas africanas. Y como se prolongase la vacilación, acudióle un refuerzo, en figura de la señá Donata, que con la solicitud y el enojo peor fingidos del mundo, se entró muy resuelta en el gabinete refunfuñando:

–¡Eh!, niñas, corderas, largo, que estáis dando la gran jaqueca a estos señores … A ver si vus salís afuera, u sino …

–No molestan … –declaró Asís–. Son más formalitas … A esa no hay quien la haga pasar, y la chiquitilla … ni abre la boca.

–Pa comer ya la abren las tunantas …

Pacheco se levantó cortésmente y ofreció silla a la vieja. El gaditano, que entre gente de su misma esfera social pecaba de reservado y aun de altanero, se volvía sumamente campechano al acercarse al pueblo.

–Tome usted asiento … Se va usted a bebé una copita de Jerés a la salú de toos.

¡Oídos que tal oyeron! ¡Señá Donata, fuera temor, al ataque, ya que te presentan la brecha franca y expedito el rumbo! Y tan expedito, que Pacheco, desde que la vieja puso allí el pie, pareció sacudir sus

like children do when they are bashful and being pampered, nibbled sweets and stood with the heel of her left foot on the instep on her right foot. Three minutes after the first crumb-eating sparrow had flown into the dovecot, another one appeared. The first one looked five years old; the second one, more responsible but no less easily frightened, must have already been at least eight.

'Hello! Here comes her sister...' said Asís. 'And they're like two peas in a pod... The little one is more amusing ... but look at the older one's eyes... Come in, young lady... This one will tell us what her father's called, being as the cat's got the little one's tongue.'

The elder girl stood fixed in the doorway, serious and suspicious, like someone who is hesitant and afraid before pitching into an enterprise bristling with difficulties. Her large eyes, which in size, fire and precocious seriousness were really Moorish, went from Asís to Diego and her little sister. The little girl meditated, withdrew, looked for a set phrase but couldn't find one, because in her heart she had a certain wild aversion to asking favours, and in her character an indomitable ferocity very much in harmony with her African eyes. And as her hesitation became prolonged, reinforcement came in the shape of Señora Donata, who, with the most badly feigned devotion and annoyance in the world, entered the private room in a purposeful manner and grumbled:

'Hey, girls, clear off, you're bothering this lady and gentleman... Out you go, or else...'

'They're no trouble,' declared Asís. 'They're very well-behaved... That one won't come in for anybody, and the little one ... she won't even open her mouth.'

'The little scamps open it when it comes to food...'

Pacheco stood up politely and offered the old woman a seat. The man from Cádiz, who was guilty of being reserved and even arrogant with people of his own social sphere, became extremely good-natured when he got closer to the lower classes.

'Take a seat... You can have a little glass o' sherry to everyone's good health.'

Did she really hear this? Señora Donata, since the breach is open and the course clear, abolish fear, go on the attack! And as soon as the old woman set foot there, Pacheco seemed very promptly to shake his

penosas cavilaciones y recobrar su cháchara, diciendo los mayores desatinos del mundo. Como que se puso muy formal a solicitar a la honrada matrona, proponiéndole un paseíto a solas por los tejares. Oía la muy lagarta de la vieja, y celebraba con carcajadas pueriles, luciendo una dentadura sana y sin mella; pero al replicar, iba encajando mañosamente aquella misión diplomática que bullía en su mente fecunda desde media hora antes. Tratábase de que ella, ¿se hacen ustés cargo?, trabajaba en la Frábica de Madrí ... y tenía cuatro nietecicas, de una hija que se murió de la tifusidea, y el padre de gomitar sangre, así, a golpás ..., en dos meses se lo llevó la tierra, ¡señores!, que si se cuenta, mentira parece. Las dos nietecicas mayores, colocaas ya en los talleres; pero si la suerte la deparase una presona de suposición pa meter un empeño ..., porque en este pícaro mundo, ya es sabío, too va por las amistaes y las enfluencias de unos y otros ... –Llegada a este punto, la voz de la señá Donata adquiría inflexiones patéticas– «¡Ay Virgen de la Paloma! No premita el Señor que ustés sepan lo que es comer y vestir y calzar cinco enfelices mujeres con tristes ocho u nueve riales ganaos a trompicones ... Si la señorita, que tenía cara de ser tan complaciente y tan cabal, conociese por casualidá al Menistro ... o al Menistraor de la Frábica ..., o al contaor ..., o algún presonaje de estos que too lo regüerven ... pa que la chiquilla mayor, Lolilla, entrase de aprendiza también ... ¡Sería una caridá de las grandes, de las mayores! Dos letricas, un cacho de papel ...»

Pacheco respondía a la arenga con mucha guasa, sacando la cartera, apuntando las señas de la pitillera detenidamente, y asegurándole que hablaría al presidente del Consejo, a la infanta Isabel (íntima amiga suya), al obispo, al nuncio ... Enredados se hallaban en esta broma, cuando tras la abuela pedigüeña y las nietecillas mudas, se metieron en el gabinete las dos chicas mayores.

–Miren mis otras huerfanicas enfelices –indicó la señá Donata.

Imposible imaginarse cosa más distinta de la clásica orfandad enlutada y extenuada que representan pintores y dibujantes al cultivar el sentimentalismo artístico. Dos mozallonas frescas, sudorosas porque acababan de bailar, echando alegría y salud a chorros, y

tormented ruminations and get back his patter, coming out with the biggest load of nonsense in the world. With mock formality he requested the honourable matron the pleasure of a little stroll on their own around the brick and tile factories. The sly old woman listened and revelled with childish laughter that showed off a set of healthy teeth without any gaps; but in her replies she was craftily putting in place that secret mission which had been seething in her fertile brain for the last half hour. The thing was, she worked in the Madrid factory, do you get me? … and she had four little granddaughters from a daughter who had died of typhoid and the father a-coughin' up blood 'n' all in fits 'n' starts … in two months he was under the sod, which is hard to believe. The two eldest granddaughters were already in the workshops; but if luck would provide someone in a position to use his influence … because, as we all know, in this crooked world everything hinges on the friendship and influence of others… At this point, Señora Donata's voice acquired moving inflections: 'Ah! Our Lady o' the Dove. Heav'n forbid that you ever know what it is to feed, clothe and previde footwear for five fulorn women on eight or nine *reals* earned on 'n' off… If the young woman, who had such an obliging and just face, should 'appen to know the menister … or the fact'ry menistra'or … or the accountant … or any one o' them important people who get ev'rythin' movin' … so as the older girl, Lolilla, could enter as an apprentice too… It'd be a charity indeed, one o' the greatest! A couple o' words, a piece o' paper…'

Pacheco responded to the harangue with great humour, pulling out his card case, carefully making a note of the cigarette maker's address, and assuring her that he would speak to the President of the Council, Princess Isabel (his close friend),[57] the bishop, the nuncio… In the midst of this pleasantry two fully grown girls came into the private room behind the demanding grandmother and the silent grandchildren.

'These are my other fulorn orphans,' stated Señora Donata.

It is impossible to imagine anything more different from the classic orphan, black-robed and emaciated, which painters and sketchers depict when they cultivate artistic sentimentality. Two fresh, strapping girls, sweaty because they had just been dancing, overflowing with

---

57 La Infanta Isabel (1851–1931) was the sister of Alfonso XII, and the daughter of Isabel II and Francisco de Paula. She became known as 'La Chata' (snub nose).

saliéndoles la juventud en rosas a los carrillos y a los labios; para más, alborotadas y retozonas, dándose codazos y pellizcándose para hacerse reír mutuamente. Viendo a semejantes ninfas, Pacheco abandonó a la señá Donata, y con el mayor rendimiento se consagró a ellas, encandilado y camelador como hijo legítimo de Andalucía. Todas las penas *ajogadas* por el *Tío Pepe* se fueron a paseo, y el gaditano, entornando los ojos, derramando sales por la boca y ceceando como nunca, aseguró a aquellas principesas del Virginia que desde el punto y hora en que habían entrado, no tenía él sosiego ni más gusto que comérselas con los ojos.

–¿Vienen ustés de bailar? –les preguntó risueño.

–Pus ya se ve –contestaron ellas con chulesco desgarro.

–¿Sin hombres? ¿Sin pareja?

–Ni mardita la falta.

–Pan con pan …[47] Eso es más soso que una calabasa, prendas. Si me hubiesen ustés llamao …

–¿Que iba usté a venir? Somos poca cosa pa usté.

–¿Poca cosa? Son ustés … dos peasito del tersiopelo de que está forraa la bóveda seleste. ¡Ea!, ¿echamos o no ese baile? Ahora me empeñé yo … ¡A bailar!

Salió como una exhalación; dio la vuelta al pasillo aéreo; cruzó el puente que a los dos merenderos unía, y en breve, al compás del horrible piano mecánico, Pacheco bailaba ágilmente con las cigarreras.

---

47 *Pan con pan, comida de tontos*: resulta muy monótona la reunión entre personas que piensan igual, o bien personas del mismo sexo.

joy and health, their cheeks and lips glowing with the flush of youth; in addition, excited and playful, lots of nudging and pinching to make each other laugh. Seeing such nymphs, Pacheco abandoned Señora Donata and devoted himself to them with his best performance, fascinated and seductive like a true son of Andalusia. All the sorrows *drowned* by the Tío Pepe went away, and the man from Cádiz, half-closing his eyes, spouting forth witticisms and lisping more than ever, assured these princesses of Virginia tobacco that, from the very moment they had come in, he had no peace, his only pleasure being to devour them with his eyes.

'Have you been dancin'?' he asked them with a smile.

'Sure looks that way,' they answered with cocky impudence.

'Without men? Without a partner?'

'No need for 'em.'

'All bread and no butter… That's more insipid than a pumpkin, me darlings. If you'd called me…'

'And you'd have come? We're not much use to you.'

'Not much? You're … two little pieces o' the velvet the firmament is lined with. Come, are we havin' that dance or not? I insist on it now… Let's dance!'

He flashed out, round the airy corridor, across the bridge which connected the two snack bars, and before long Pacheco was nimbly dancing in time to the awful pianola with the cigar makers.

XX

Entre las condiciones de carácter de la marquesa viuda de Andrade, y de los gallegos en general, se cuenta cierto don de encerrar bajo llave toda impresión fuerte. Esto se llama *guardarse* las cosas, y si tiene la ventaja de evitar choques, tiene la desventaja de que esas impresiones archivadas y ocultas se pudren dentro. Cuando el andaluz regresó después de haber pegado cuatro saltos, enjugándose la frente con su pañuelo y abanicándose con el hongo, halló a la señora aparentemente tranquila y afable, ocupada en obsequiar con queso, bizcochos y pasas a las dos gorrioncillas, y muy atenta a la charla de la vejezuela, que refería por tercera vez las *golpás* de sangre causa de la defunción de su yerno. Pero el camarero, que era más fino que el oro y más largo que la cuaresma, se dio cuenta con rápida intuición de que *aquello* no iba por el camino natural de almuerzos semejantes, y adoptando el aire imponente de un bedel que despeja una cátedra, intimó a toda la bandada la orden de expulsión.

–¡Ea! bastante han molestado ustedes a los señores. Me parece regular que se larguen.

–Oigasté … ¡El tío este! Si yo he entrao aquí, fue porque los señores me lo premitieron, ¿estamos? Yo soy así, muy franca de mi natural …, y me arrimo aonde veo naturalidá, y señoritos llanos y buenos mozos, sin despreciar a nadie.

–¡Ole las mujeres principales! –contestó con la mayor formalidad Pacheco, pagando el requiebro de la señá Donata. La cual no soltó el sitio hasta que don Diego y la señora prometieron unánimes acordarse de su empeño y procurar que Lolilla entrase en los talleres. Las gorrionas se dejaron besar y se llevaron las manos atestadas de postres, pero ni con tenazas se les pudo sacar palabra alguna. No piaron hasta que fueron a posarse en el salón de baile.

El camarero también salió anunciando que «dentro de un ratito» traería café y licores. Al marcharse encajó bien la puerta, e inmediatamente los ojos de Pacheco buscaron los de su amiga. La vio de pie, mirando a las paredes. ¿Qué quería la niña? ¿Eh?

20

Among the character traits of the widowed Marchioness of Andrade, and those of Galicians in general, is a certain gift for keeping all strong feelings locked away. This is called *keeping things to oneself*, and if it has the advantage of avoiding shocks, it has the disadvantage that those feelings secretly filed at the back of one's mind rot away inside. When the Andalusian returned after having danced a bit, mopping his brow with a handkerchief and fanning himself with his bowler hat, he found the lady apparently tranquil and affable, busy feeding the two little sparrows with cheese, sponge cake and raisins, and listening very attentively to the little old woman's chatter, referring for the third time to the *fits 'n' starts* of bloodied vomit which had been the cause of her son-in-law's decease. But the waiter, who was very vigilant and very astute, quickly intuited that *this* wasn't following the natural path of similar breakfasts and, adopting the imposing air of a beadle clearing out a seminar room, intimated to the whole party that they must be off.

'Hey! That's enough bothering the lady and gentleman. I think you should clear off.'

'Listen… That fellow! If I came in here, it was because the lady and gentleman gave me promission, right? I'm like that, very outspoken by nature … and I'm drawn towards wherever I see naturalness, and straightforward people and good young men, without scorning anyone.'

'Bravo, illustrious women!' Pacheco answered with the greatest politeness, returning the compliment, and Señora Donata didn't decamp until Don Diego and the lady promised in unison to remember her determination, and endeavour to get Lolilla into the factory. The sparrows let themselves be kissed and left with their hands full of sweets, but you couldn't get a single word out of them even with pincers. They didn't chatter until they were perched in the dance hall.

The waiter left as well, announcing that he would bring coffee and liqueurs "in a little while". When he went he shut the door carefully, and Pacheco's eyes immediately sought out those of his companion. He saw her standing, looking at the walls. What did the girl want, eh?

–Un espejo.

–¿Pa qué? Aquí no hay. Los que vienen aquí no se miran a sí mismos. ¿Espejo? Mírate en mí. ¿Pero cómo? ¿Vas a ponerte el sombrero, chiquilla? ¿Qué te pasa?

–Es por ganar tiempo … Al fin, en tomando el café hemos de irnos …

El meridional se acercó a Asís, y la contempló cara a cara, largo rato … La señora esquivaba el examen, poniendo, por decirlo así, sordina a sus ojos y un velo impalpable de serenidad a sus facciones. Le tomó Pacheco la cintura, y sentándose en el sofá, la atrajo hacia sí. Hablaba y reía y la acariciaba tiernamente.

–¡Ay, ay, ay! … ¿Esas tenemos? Mi niña está celosa. ¡Celosita, celosita! ¡Celosita de mí la reina del mundo!

Asís se enderezó en el sofá, rechazando a Pacheco.

–Tienes la necedad de que todo lo conviertes en substancia. La vanidad te parte, hijo mío. Yo no estoy celosa, y si me apuras, te diré …

–¿Qué? ¿Qué me dirás? –prorrumpió Pacheco algo inmutado y descolorido.

–Que … es algo imposible eso de estar celoso cuando …

–¡Ah! –interrumpió el meridional, más que pálido, lívido, con voz que salía a *golpás*, según diría la señá Donata–. No necesitas ponerlo más claro … Enterado, mujer, enterado, si yo adivino antes que hables. Pa miserables tres horas o cuatro que nos faltan de estar juntos, y probablemente serán las últimas que nos hemos de ver en este mundo perro, ya pudiste callarte y procurar engañarme como hasta aquí … Poco favor te haces, si viniste aquí no queriéndome algo. Tú te habrás creído que yo me tragaba … ¡Y me llamas necio! Yo seré un vago, un hombre que no sirve para ná, un tronera, un perdido, lo que gustes; ¡pero necio! Necio yo …, ¡y en cuestiones de faldas! ¡Mire usted que es grande! Pero, ¿qué importa? Llámame lo que quieras … y óyeme sólo esto, que te voy a decir una verdá que ni tú la sabes, niña. No me has querío hasta hoy, corriente … Hoy, más que digas por tema lo que te dé la gana, me quieres, me requieres, estás enamoraa de mí … Poquito a poco te ha ido entrando … y así que yo te falte, se te va a

'A mirror.'

'What for? There isn't one here. Those who come here don't look at themselves. Mirror? Look at yourself in my eyes. But why? Are you going to put on your hat, darling? What's wrong?'

'It's to save time... After all, we'll have to go when we've had our coffee...'

The southerner went up to Asís, and contemplated her face to face for a long while... The lady avoided his scrutiny, by muting her eyes, so to speak, and putting an impalpable veil of serenity on her features. Pacheco took her by the waist and, sitting down on the sofa, drew her towards him. He spoke and laughed and caressed her tenderly.

'Dear oh dear! ... Is this what we are? My little girl's jealous. Jealous, jealous! The queen o' the world's jealous of me!'

Asís drew herself up on the sofa, pushing Pacheco away.

'You have the folly to interpret everything in your favour. Your vanity exceeds you, my boy. I'm not jealous, and if you press me I'll tell you...'

'What? What will you tell me?' burst out Pacheco somewhat perturbed and pale.

'That ... being jealous is something impossible when...'

'Oh!' the southerner interrupted, livid more than pale, and with a voice that came out in *fits 'n' starts*, as Señora Donata would say. 'You don't need to be any clearer ... I understand, I understand, I can guess before you speak. For the miserable three or four hours we have left together, which will probably be the last we see of each other in this wretched world, you could have been silent and tried to deceive me like you've done up to now... You're not doing me any favours if you came here without any love for me. You must have thought I believed that... And you call me stupid! I might be an idler, a good-for-nothin', a rake or libertine, whatever you like. But stupid! Me stupid ... and where women are concerned! That's a good one! But what does it matter? Call me what you want ... only listen to this, because I'm goin' tell you something true that even you don't know, my child. You didn't love me until today, agreed... Today, whatever you may want to say, you love me, you need me, you're in love with me... Little by little it's got inside you ... and as soon as I'm gone, your world'll be

acabar el mundo. Esta es la fija ... Ya lo verás, ya lo verás. Y por amor propio y por soberbia sales con la pata e gallo ... ¡Te desdeñas de tener celos de mí! Bien hecho ... Así como así, no hay de qué. Boba serías si tuvieses celos. Algún ratito ha de pasar antes de que yo me pierda por otras mujeres ... ¡Maldita sea hasta la hora en que te vi! ... Dispensa, ¡dispensa! No quiero ofenderte, ¿sabes? ahora ni nunca. No sé lo que me digo ... Pero digo verdad.

Soltaba esta andanada paseando por el pequeño recinto, como las fieras en sus jaulas de hierro; unas veces sepultaba las manos en los bolsillos del pantalón, y otras las desenfundaba para accionar con violencia. Su rostro, descompuesto por la cólera, perdiendo su expresión indolente, mejoraba infinito: se acentuaban sus enjutas facciones, temblaba el bigote dorado, resplandecían los blancos dientes, y los azules ojos se obscurecían, como el agua del Mediterráneo cuando amaga tempestad. El piso retemblaba bajo sus pasos; diríase que el aéreo nido iba a saltar hecho trizas. Aquella tormenta de verano, aquella cólera meridional, no cabía en el cuartuco.

Al encajar la puerta el mozo, los amantes se habían olvidado de que el nido tenía otro boquete, la ventana, abierta por Asís y dejada en la misma situación durante todo el almuerzo. Y la ventana justamente miraba al salón de baile, ocupado por parte de la bandada de gorriones, entretenidísimas a la sazón en atisbar la riña amorosa, mientras abajo Lolilla se consagraba al carnero y al arroz.

–Anda ..., ella está de morros con él ... Está amoscá.

–Porque bailó con nusotras ... Me lo malicié, hijas.

–¡Jesús! Pus no se ha resquemao poco ... ¡Qué gesto!

–¡Ay! ¡Miales! Él le está haciendo cucamonas pa que se le pase ... ¡Ole! ... Hombre, no nos ponga usté el gorro ... Siquiera pa repichonear podían tener la ventana cerrá.

–¿Quién os manda mirar?

–Pa eso tiene una los ojos ... ¡Calle! ... Pus ella, en sus trece ... Que nones ... Las orejas le calienta ahora.

–¡Virgen! ¿Qué cosas le habrá icho, pa que él se enfade así? Mueve los brazos que paecen aspas de molino ... ¿A que le pega?

–¿Que lae pegar, mujer, que lae pegar? Eso a las probes. A estas pindongas de señoronas, los hombres les rinden el pabellón. Y eso

over. This is for sure... You'll see, you'll see. And out of self-respect and arrogance you say something inappropriate... You won't deign to be jealous of me! Well done... Just like that, not at all. You'd be stupid to be jealous. It'll be some time before I fall for other women... Cursed be the hour I set eyes on you! Sorry, sorry! I don't wish to offend you, now or ever, you know? I don't know what I'm saying... But I'm telling the truth.'

He dropped this bombshell pacing around the little enclosure like a wild beast behind iron bars, sometimes burying his hands in his trouser pockets and sometimes pulling them out to gesticulate furiously. His countenance, distorted with rage, lost its indolent expression and looked infinitely better for it. His thin features became more noticeable, his gold moustache trembled, his white teeth gleamed and his blue eyes darkened like the Mediterranean sea when a storm threatens. The floor shook beneath his steps, as if the airy nest was going to fly into pieces. That summer storm, that southern rage, was too big for the pokey little room.

When the waiter closed the door, the lovers had forgotten that the nest had another entrance, the window which had been opened by Asís and left in the same position during the whole breakfast. And the window was in fact facing the dance hall, occupied by the quarrel of sparrows, highly amused at that very moment observing the lovers' tiff, whilst Lolilla below devoted herself to the mutton stew and rice.

'Well I never ... she's cross wiv 'im... She's irritated.'

''Cause he danced wiv us ... I thought as much.'

'Good 'eavens! She's fumin' ... What a face!'

'Goodness! Look at 'em! He's butterin' 'er up so she'll forget... Bravo! Don't embarrass us... They could at least close the window if they're gonna be affectionate.'

'Who's tellin' ya to look?'

'That's what eyes are for... Be quiet! ... She's stickin' to 'er guns... No way... She's tellin' 'im off.'

'Holy Mother! What can she 'ave said to 'im that 'e's so angry? He's wavin' 'is arms round like the blades of a windmill... I bet 'e 'its 'er.'

'He's bound to 'it 'er, bound to 'it 'er. That's for us poor girls. Men lower the flag to these gad-about fine ladies, even though any one of

que cualisquiera de nosotras les pue vender honradez y dicencia. Digo, me paece ...

–No, pus enfadao ya está.

–¿Va que acaba pidiendo perdón como los chiquillos? ¿No lo ije? Miale ... más manso que un cordero ... Ella na, espetá, secatona ..., vuelta a la manía de ponerse el abrigo ... Se quie largar ... ¡Madre e Dios, lo que saben estas tunantas! Me lo maneja como a un fantoche ... ¡Qué compungío que está! ... ¿A que se pone de rodillas, pa que le echen la solución? ¡Ay, qué mujer, paece la leona del Retiro! Empeñá en que me voy ... Y se sale con la suya ... Mia ... ¡Se largan!

La turba se precipitó por la escalera del merendero. Verdad: Asís se largaba, se largaba. Salía tranquilamente, sin prisa ni enojo: hasta sonrió a Lolilla, que armada del soplador de mimbres avivaba el fuego. Con voz serena explicó al mozo, atónito de semejante deserción, que se les hacía tarde, que no podían aguardar ni un minuto más; que avisase al cochero, el cual probablemente estaría con el simón por allí, en alguna sombra. Mientras Pacheco, demudado, con pulso trémulo, buscaba en el portamonedas un billete, Asís trazaba en el piso rayas con la sombrilla, hasta dibujar una celosía complicada y menuda. Al terminarla extendió la mano; cogió una ramita florida de la acacia que sombreaba el merendero, y se la sujetó en el pecho con el imperdible. Acercóse obsequiosa la señá Donata, ofreciendo a sus huérfanas, sus nietecitas, «pa juntar un ramo de cacias y de mapolas, si a la señorita le gustan ...». Dio Asís las gracias rehusando, porque se marchaba acto continuo; y acercándose disimuladamente a la vieja, le deslizó algo en la mano, recia y curtida cual la piel del arenque. Acercóse el simón: sin duda el cochero se había atizado un par de tragos, porque su nariz echaba lumbre, reluciendo al sol como la película roja que viste a los pimientos riojanos. La señora tomó por la escalerilla que bajaba desde el puente; Pacheco la siguió ...

–En el coche harán las paces –piaron las gorrionas mayores–. ¿A que sí?

–La fija. En entrando ...

Grande fue el asombro de aquellas aves más, parleras que canoras, viendo que, tras un corto debate al pie de la portezuela, la señora

us could give 'em points on decency and virtue. Look, it seems to me...'

'No, 'e's still angry.'

'I bet 'e ends up beggin' forgiveness like a little boy. I towd yer, di'n't I? Look at 'im ... as meek as a lamb... Not 'er, stiff, dull ... determined to put on 'er coat... She wants to go... Mother o' God, the things these crafty women know! She's workin' 'im like a puppet... 'E's so full o' remorse! ... I bet 'e goes down on 'is knees to beg for absolution. Oh, what a woman, she's like the lion in Retiro Park! Determined to go... And she's gettin' 'er own way... Look... They're off!'

The mob rushed down the stairs of the snack bar. It was true: Asís was going, leaving. She went out calmly, without haste or anger. She even smiled at Lollila, who was stoking the fire with the wicker fan. She serenely explained to the waiter, astonished by their departure, that they were late, that they couldn't wait even a minute longer and to send for the coachman who would probably be with the carriage somewhere in the shade. While Pacheco, distraught and with a trembling hand, was looking for a note in his wallet, Asís traced lines with her parasol on the floor until she had drawn a small, complicated lattice. When she finished it she stretched out her hand, picked a flowery spray of the acacias shading the snack bar, and fastened it to her breast with a safety pin. Señora Donata approached obsequiously, offering to have her orphans, her little granddaughters, "gather a bunch of acacias and poppies, if the lady likes them...". Asís refused with thanks, because she was leaving immediately; and furtively approaching the old woman, she slipped something into her hand, which was as tough and leathery as the skin of a herring. The carriage approached. The coachman had undoubtedly knocked back a couple of drinks, because his nose was glowing, shining in the sun like the red film that covers peppers from La Rioja. The lady took the steps which went down from the bridge, Pacheco following...

'They'll make it up in the carriage,' cheeped the older sparrows. 'I bet they do.'

'That's for sure. When 'e gets in...'

Great was the astonishment of those birds, more talkative than melodious, seeing the lady, after a short discussion at the carriage

tendió la mano a Pacheco; éste llevó la suya al sombrero saludando, y el simón arrancó a paso de tortuga, bamboleándose sobre la polvorosa carretera.

–Pus ella vence ... Me lo deja plantadito.

–¿A que él se nos vuelve aquí? –indicó la gorriona primogénita, alisando con la palma las grandes peteneras de su peinado, untadas de bandolina.

No volvió el muy ... Ni siquiera torció la cabeza para hacerles un saludo o enviarles una sonrisa de despedida. ¡Fantasioso! Estuvo pendiente del simón mientras éste no traspuso los hornos de ladrillo; luego, cabizbajo, echó a andar a pie.

door, hold out her hand to Pacheco; he tipped his hat, and the carriage set off at a snail's pace, wobbling along the dusty road.

'Well, she wins… She's ditched 'im.'

'I bet 'e'll come back 'ere,' said the first-born sparrow, smoothing down her large bandolined curls with the palm of her hand.

He didn't go back… He didn't even turn round to wave or give them a parting smile. Conceited fellow! He was waiting for the carriage to pass the brick ovens; then, with a dejected air, he set off on foot.

XXI

La buena fe, que debe servir de norma a los historiadores así de hechos memorables como de sucesos ínfimos, obliga a declarar que la marquesa viuda de Andrade se dedicó asiduamente –desde las dos de la tarde, hora en que llegó a su casa, hasta cerca de las nueve de la noche– a la faena del arreglo definitivo de su equipaje, resolviendo la marcha para el siguiente día, sin prórroga. El trajín fue gordo, y aumentó sus fatigas el desasosiego moral de la señora. Anduvo hecha un zarandillo; removió hasta el último trasto de la casa; mareó a la Diabla; aturrulló a los demás criados; y al agitarse así, la impulsaban sus nervios, tirantes como cuerdas de guitarra, al par que sentía una especie de punzada continua en el corazón, un calor extraño en el epigastrio, un saborete amargo en la boca. Después de haber comido –por fórmula y sin ganas– pidióle Ángela licencia, ya que era el último día, para decir adiós a su hermana. La negó en un arranque de cólera; la otorgó dos minutos después. Y así que la chica batió la puerta, la señora, rendida de cuerpo, más encapotada que nunca de espíritu, se retiró a su dormitorio … Tenía que poner el S. D.[48] a un sinnúmero de tarjetas; pero ¡estaba tan molida!, ¡de humor tan perro! Además la punzadita aquella del corazón se iba convirtiendo en dolor fijo, intolerable … ¿Se aplacaría un poco recostándose en la cama? A ver …

Cerró los ojos, mascando unas hieles que tenía entre la lengua y el paladar. ¿A qué venían las hieles dichosas? Ella había obrado bien, mostrándose digna y entera. En realidad, ningún desenlace mejor para la historia. De un modo o de otro ello iba a acabarse; era inevitable, inminente: mejor que se acabase así … Porque si aquella última entrevista fuese muy tierna, qué tristeza y qué … Nada; mejor así, mejor cien veces. Ella había tenido razón sobrada: una cosa son los celos, otra el amor propio y el decoro de que nunca está bien prescindir. Y a quién se le ocurre, allí, en su propia cara, ponerse a bailar con … Veía el salón de baile aéreo, el brincoteo de las gorrionas, los incidentes del

---

48 *Sine die*, una locución latina que significa sin fijar el día, sin fecha determinada.

21

Good faith, which should serve as a standard for historians of memorable facts as much as small events, obliges us to declare that the dowager Marchioness of Andrade, from the time of her arrival home at two in the afternoon until around nine in the evening, devoted herself assiduously to the task of finally arranging her luggage, resolving to leave the following day without deferment. It was a huge chore and the lady's moral anxiety increased her troubles. She was like a cat on a hot tin roof, turning over every little thing, making Diabla dizzy and bewildering the other servants. And when she became agitated like this she was driven on by her nerves, as tight as guitar strings, whilst feeling a kind of continuous stabbing pain in her heart, a strange burning in her epigastrium and a slightly bitter taste in her mouth. After she had eaten perfunctorily, Ángela asked her permission, as it was the last day, to say goodbye to her sister. She refused it in a fit of anger, only to grant it two minutes later. And as soon as the girl had slammed the door behind her, the lady, exhausted in body and gloomier than ever in spirit, retired to her bedroom… She had countless PPC cards to sign,[58] but she was so shattered and in such a foul mood! Moreover, that stabbing pain in her heart was becoming a steady, intolerable ache… Would lying down on the bed alleviate it a bit? Let's see…

She shut her eyes, tasting the bile she had between her tongue and palate. What's this blessed bile all about? She had acted well, showing herself dignified and composed. There was actually no better outcome for the whole business. It was going to finish one way or another; it was inevitable, imminent; better that it finish like this… Because if that last meeting had been affectionate, how sad and how… No, better like this, a hundred times better. She had been more than right: jealousy is one thing; self-esteem and the decorum one should never be without are quite another. And who, right there in front of her eyes, would have thought to start dancing with… She could see the dance hall, the sparrows jumping about, all the breakfast incidents … and the bile

---

58   A borrowing from French (*pour prendre congé*) for a card announcing a person's departure from a town, social event, etc.

almuerzo … y las hieles se volvían más amarguitas aún. Cierto que ella fue quien abrió puertas y ventanas: de todos modos, el proceder de Pacheco … Sí … buen tipo estaba Pacheco. En viendo una escoba con faldas. ¡Ay infeliz de la mujer que se fiase de sus exageraciones y sus locuras! ¡Requebrar a las cigarreras así, delante de …! ¡Y qué fatuo! ¡Pues no había querido convencerla de que estaba enamorada de él! ¿Enamorada? No, no señor, gracias a Dios … Conservaría sí un recuerdo …, un recuerdo de esos que … Allí tenía, en el medallón de oro, junto al pelo de Maruja, una florecita de la acacia blanca … ¡Qué tontera! Lo probable es que a Pacheco no volviese a verle nunca más … Y esta punzada del corazón, ¿qué será? Será enfermedad, o … Parece que lo aprieta un aro de hierro … ¡Jesús, qué cavilaciones más simples!

Bregando con la imaginación y la memoria, se quedó traspuesta. No era dormir profundo, sino una especie de somnambulismo, en que las percepciones de la vida exterior se amalgamaban con el delirio de la fantasía. No era la pesadilla que causa la ocupación de estómago, en que tan pronto caemos de altísima torre como volamos por dilatadas zonas celestes, ni menos el sueño provocado por la acción del calor del lecho sobre los lóbulos cerebrales, donde, sin permiso de la honrada voluntad, se representan imágenes repulsivas … Lo que veía Asís, adormecida o mal despierta, puede explicarse en la forma siguiente, aunque en realidad fuese harto más vago y borroso.

Encontrábase ya en el vagón, con la Diabla enfrente, la maletita y el lío de mantas en la rejilla, el velo de gasa inglesa bien ceñido sobre la toca de paja, calzados los guantes de camino, abrochado hasta el cuello el guardapolvo. El tren adelantaba, unas veces bufando y pitando, otras con perezoso cuneo, al través de las eternas estepas amarillas, caldeadas por un sol del trópico. ¡Oh Castilla la fea, la árida, la polvorosa, la de monótonos aspectos, la de escuetas lontananzas! ¡Oh sombría mole, región desconsolada del Escorial, qué felicidad perderte de vista! ¡Oh calor, calor del infierno, cuándo acabarás! Asís sentía que el sol, al través de las cortinas corridas que teñían con viso azul el departamento, se le empapaba en los sesos como el agua en una esponja, y que en sus venas la sangre se volvía alquitrán, y la punta de cada filete nervioso una aguja candente, y que los ojos se le salían de las órbitas, igual que a los gatos cuando los escaldan … El polvillo de carbón, unido al de los páramos

became even more bitter. Certainly she was the one who had opened the doors and windows; in any case, Pacheco's behaviour... Yes ... a fine guy, Pacheco. When he saw a broomstick in a skirt... Oh, wretched be the woman who believed his exaggerations and madness! Flirting with the cigar makers like that, in front of...! And so conceited! Well, hadn't he wanted to convince her that she was in love with him? In love? No, no, thanks be to God... Yes, she would keep a memory ... one of those memories that... There, in the gold locket next to Maruja's hair, she had a little white acacia flower... What folly! She probably wouldn't ever see him again... And that stabbing pain in her heart, what could it be? It could be illness, or... It seemed like an iron ring pressing her tightly... Good heavens, what stupid thoughts!

Struggling with imagination and memory, she dozed off. It wasn't a deep sleep, but a kind of somnambulism in which perceptions of external reality amalgamated with the delirium of fantasy. It wasn't the nightmare caused by gastric activity, in which as soon as we fall from a very high tower, we fly through extensive celestial zones, nor the sleep provoked by the effect of a warm bed on the lobes of the brain, in which repulsive visions are represented without the sanction of the will... What Asís could see, sleepy or half-awake, can be explained in the following way, even if in reality it was a lot more vague and blurred.

She was on the train, with Diabla opposite, the valise and bundle of blankets in the luggage rack, her English crêpe veil fitted over her straw hat, wearing travelling gloves and her dust coat fastened up to her chin. The train moved forward, sometimes puffing and whistling, at others with a lazy rocking, across the eternal yellow plains scorched by the tropical sun. Oh ugly, arid, dusty Castile, with its monotonous appearance and plain horizons! Oh dark, disconsolate mass of the El Escorial region, what happiness to lose sight of you! Oh heat, infernal heat, when will you cease! Asís felt that the sun, through the drawn curtains which cast a blue tinge over the compartment, was soaking into her brain like water in a sponge, that the blood in her veins was turning into tar and the extremity of every bundle of nerves a red-hot needle, and that her eyes were coming out of their sockets like cats when they're scalded... The fine coal dust, in conjunction with that

castellanos, entraba en remolinos o en ráfagas violentas, cegando, desvaneciendo, asfixiando. No valía manejar desesperadamente el abanico: como toda la atmósfera era polvo, polvo levantaba al agitar el aire, y polvo absorbían los sedientos pulmones. –¡Agua! ¡Agua! ¡Agua por Dios! Ángela, va una botella llena ahí en el cesto ...– Revolvía la Diabla el fondo de la canastilla ..., nada: sin duda el agua se había olvidado. ¡Ah!, una botella ... El vaso plano ... Asís bebía. ¡No es agua, no es agua! Es manzanilla, jerez, brasa líquida, esas ponzoñas que roban el juicio a las gentes ... Venga un río, un río de mi tierra, para agotarlo de un sorbo ... Mientras la señora gemía, el inmenso foco del sol ardía más implacable, como si estuviesen echándole carbón, convertidos en fogoneros, los arcángeles y los serafines. Y así atravesaban la pedregosa tierra de Ávila, con sus escuadrones de enormes cantos, y las llanuras de Palencia, y los severos desiertos de León, y la vieja comarca de la Maragatería. ¡Que me abraso! ... ¡Que me abraso! ... ¡Que me muero! ... ¡Socorro! ...

¡Aah! ¿Qué ocurre? Salimos del país llano ... ¡Montes queridos! Cada túnel es una inmersión en la noche, un baño en un pozo: al volver a la claridad, montañas y más montañas, revestidas de frondosos castañares, y por cuyas laderas ... ¡oh deleite!, se despeñan saltando manantiales, cascaditas, riachuelos, mientras allá abajo, caudaloso y profundo, corre el Sil ... Las mismas rocas sudan humedad; de la bóveda de los túneles rezuman gotas gordas; el suelo se encharca. Al principio, Asís revive como el pez restituido a su elemento: su corazón se dilata, cálmase el hervor de su sangre, se aplaca la horrible sed. Pero los riachuelos van engrosando; los túneles menudean, lóbregos, pantanosos; al término se divisa un cielo color de panza de burro,[49] muy bajo, en el cual se acumulan nubes preñadas de agua, que al fin, abriendo su seno, dejan caer, primero en delgados hilos, luego en cerrada cortina, la lluvia, la eterna lluvia del Noroeste, plomo derretido y glacial, que solloza escurriendo por los vidrios. Y aquella lluvia, Asís la siente sobre el corazón, que se lo infiltra, que se lo reblandece, que se lo ensopa, hasta no poder admitir más líquido, hasta que, anegado de tristeza, el corazón empieza también a chorrear agua, primero gota a gota, luego a borbotones, con fúnebre ruido de botella que se vacía ...

---

49 Color gris oscuro del cielo cubierto de nubes.

of the Castilian waste lands, came in swirls or violent gusts, blinding, suffocating and making her dizzy. There was no point desperately using the fan: as the whole atmosphere was dust, wafting the air brought up dust and thirsty lungs took in dust. 'Water! Water! In God's name, water! Ángela, get a full bottle from the basket...' Diabla rummaged through the bottom of the small basket ... nothing. Doubtless the water had been forgotten. Ah! a bottle... The folding glass... Asís drank. It's not water, it's not water! It's *manzanilla*, sherry, liquid red-hot coal, those poisons which rob people of their senses... Bring a river, a river from my homeland, so I can finish it off in one gulp... While the lady was groaning, the immense solar focal point blazed on more relentlessly, as if the archangels and seraphim, transformed into stokers, were throwing coal on it. And so they traversed the rocky territory of Ávila, with its squadrons of enormous stones, and the plains of Palencia, and the harsh deserts of León, and the old district of La Maragatería.[59] I'm burning! ... I'm burning! ... I'm dying! ... Help! ...

Ah! What's happening? We're leaving the flat country... Beloved mountains! Every tunnel is an immersion in night, a bath in a well. Returning to the light of day, mountains and more mountains, covered with leafy chestnut trees along whose sides – what a delight! – are leaping springs, small waterfalls and streams, whilst down below, full and deep, runs the Sil... The very rocks exude humidity, great drops ooze from the tunnel walls, the ground is waterlogged. At first Asís revives like a fish returned to its native element. Her heart dilates, her boiling blood cools and her terrible thirst is appeased. But the brooks grow larger, the dark and marshy tunnels more frequent; at the end a very low, leaden sky can be seen in which gather rain-laden clouds, which finally open up and release their rain, first in thin streams, then in a thick curtain, the eternal rain of the north-east, glacial molten lead which sobs as it drips down the windowpanes. And Asís feels that rain on her heart, filtering in, softening it, soaking it up, until it can absorb no more liquid and, drowning with sorrow, her heart too begins to spout out water, drop by drop at first, then in gushes, with the mournful noise of a bottle being emptied...

---

59   A historical *comarca* situated in the province of León.

***

Pan, pan. Dos golpes en la puerta de la alcoba ... –¡Jesús! ... ¿Quién? ¿Pero dormía o soñaba o qué es esto? –Y la señora palpaba la almohada–. Húmeda, sí ... Los ojos ... También los ojos ... ¡Lágrimas! ¿Quién está? ... ¿Quién?

–Yo, amiga Asís ... Gabriel Pardo ... ¿He venido a molestar? Por Dios, siga usted con sus preparativos ... Me he encontrado a la chica; me dijo que mañana sin falta salía usted para nuestra tierra ... Cuánto sentiré incomodarla ... Me retiro, me retiro.

–Por Dios ... De ningún modo ... Tome usted asiento ... Salgo en seguida ... Estaba lavándome las manos.

Y en efecto, se oía ruido de chapuzón, de lavaroteo. Pero nos consta que lo que lavaba la señora eran los párpados. Luego se dio polvos, se compuso el pelo, se arregló los encajes de la gola. Apareció muy presentable. Pardo había tomado un periódico, creo que *La Época*, y leía distraído, sin entender: «La dispersión veraniega ha comenzado. Parten hoy para Biarritz en el expreso, el duque de Albares, las lindas señoritas de Amézaga ...»

Apenas habían tenido tiempo los dos paisanos para trocar unas cuantas frases de excusa, cuando se oyó sonar la campanilla y en el corredor retumbaron pasos fuertes, varoniles. De sofocada, la señora se volvió pálida: una sonrisa involuntaria y una luz vivísima cruzaron por sus labios y sus ojos. Pacheco entró, y al verle el comandante Pardo, reprimió el impulso de pegarse un cachete en el hueso frontal.

–¡Ya pareció aquello! ¡Se despejó la incógnita! ¡Y decir que no hará dos semanas que se conocieron en casa de Sahagún! ¡¡Mujeres!! ...

El gaditano –lo mismo que si se propusiese evidenciar lo que Pardo adivinaba– apenas se hubo sentado sacó del bolsillo un tarjetero de piel inglesa, con monograma de plata, y se lo entregó a Asís, murmurando cortésmente:

***

Knock, knock. Two raps on the bedroom door... 'Good heavens! ... Who is it? But was I sleeping or dreaming or what?' And the lady felt the pillow. 'Damp, yes... My eyes... My eyes as well... Tears! Who's there? ... Who?'

'It's me, my dear friend Asís ... Gabriel Pardo... Am I disturbing you? For heaven's sake, please carry on with your preparations ... I met the girl. She told me you were going home tomorrow without fail ... I'm so sorry for inconveniencing you ... I'll leave, I'll go.'

'For heaven's sake ... certainly not... Take a seat ... I'll be out straight away ... I was washing my hands.'

Sure enough the sound of splashing, a quick wash could be heard. But we have evidence that the lady was washing her eyes. Then she powdered her face, dressed her hair, arranged the lace around her neck. She looked very presentable. Pardo had taken up a newspaper, *La Época*[60] I believe, and was reading without concentration and understanding: "The summer flight has begun. The Duke of Albares, and the beautiful young ladies of Amézaga will be setting off for Biarritz in the express train today..."

The two compatriots had scarcely had time to exchange a few excuses when the bell could be heard ringing and strong, manly steps echoed in the corridor. From being flushed the lady turned pale: an involuntary smile played on her lips and a brilliant light crossed her eyes. When he saw Pacheco come in, Major Pardo resisted the impulse to slap himself on the forehead.

'So that was it! Now the cause is revealed. And to think that it's not two weeks since they first met at the Duchess of Sahagún's house. Women!!'

Just as if he were intent on proving what Pardo had already guessed, the man from Cádiz had scarcely sat down than he pulled out of his pocket an English leather card case with a silver monogram and handed it to Asís with a courteous whisper:

---

60 *La Época*, a Spanish daily newspaper founded by José Ignacio Escobar in 1849, supported Canovas's conservative stance during the Restoration. Pardo Bazán sent *La cuestión palpitante* to it to be published in twenty weekly articles between November 1882 and April 1883.

–Marquesa … las señas que usted me pidió que le trajese. Las señas de la pitillera … ¿no recuerda usted? Puede usted copiarlas, o quedarse con el tarjetero, si gusta … Viéndolo se acuerda usted más del empeñillo.

¡Ay! Asís trasudaba. Era para volarse. ¡Vaya un pretexto que daba a su visita nocturna el bueno del gaditano! Si lo quería más claro don Gabriel …

Miró al comandante, que se hacía el sueco, tratando de no ver el tarjetero dichoso. No hay posición más desairada que la de tercero en concordia, y don Gabriel, notando la ojeada expresiva que trocaron Pacheco y Asís, creía estar sentado sobre brasas, tanto le apretaban las ganas de quitarse de en medio. Pero convenía hacerlo con habilidad y educación. Un cuarto de hora tardó en preparar la retirada honrosa, echándole el muerto[50] al Círculo Militar, donde aquella noche había una conferencia muy notable. Los círculos, ateneos y clubs, serán siempre instituciones benéficas, por lo que se prestan a encubrir toda escapatoria masculina –así la del que va en busca de la propia felicidad, como la del que evita el espectáculo de la ajena– verbigracia, Pardo.

Aflojó el paso al llegar a la esquina de la calle, y se puso a reflexionar acerca del impensado descubrimiento. Raro es que el amigo de una dama, en caso semejante, no desapruebe la elección. –¡Cómo escogen las mujeres! En dándoles el puntapié el demonio … Indulgencia, Gabriel; no hay mujeres, hay humanidad, y la humanidad es *así* … Esta desazón, además, se parece un poquito a la envidia y al des … No, hijo, eso sí que no: despechado no estás: lo que pasa es que ves claro, mientras tu pobre amiga se ha quedado ciega … ¡Cómo se transformó su fisonomía al entrar el individuo! La verdad: no la creí capaz de echarse un amante … y menos ése. O mucho me equivoco o le cayó que hacer a la infeliz. Ese andaluz es uno de los tipos que mejor patentizan la decadencia de la raza española. ¡Qué provincias las del Mediodía, señor Dios de los ejércitos! ¡Qué hombre el tal Pachequito! Perezoso, ignorante, sensual, sin energía ni vigor, juguete de las pasiones, incapaz

---

50 Esta frase tiene su origen en la Edad Media, específicamente en la legislación que estipulaba que si en un pueblo aparecía el cadáver de una persona muerta de forma violenta, y no se aclaraba quién había cometido el asesinato, todos los habitantes estaban obligados a pagar una multa. De ahí los vecinos más pícaros aprovechaban la oscuridad de la noche para trasladar el cadáver a otro pueblo, echándoles así el muerto a ellos y librándose de la multa.

'Marchioness … the address you asked me to bring. The cigarette maker's address … do you remember? You can copy it, or keep the card case if you like… Seeing it will be a better reminder of your little pledge.'

Oh dear! Asís was sweating. It was extremely unsettling. What a pretext good old Pacheco had given for his late evening visit! If Don Gabriel wanted it any clearer…

She watched the major, who was acting dumb, and tried not to look at the blessed card case. There is no position more awkward than that of a third party in a relationship, and noticing the expressive glance which Pacheco and Asís exchanged, Don Gabriel felt like he was sitting on hot coal, so pressing was his desire to be off. But it was advisable to do so with skill and good manners. He took a quarter of an hour to prepare an honourable retreat, pinning the blame on the Military Club, where there was a very notable lecture that evening. Circles, cultural associations and clubs will always be beneficial organisations because they lend themselves to covering all means of escape for men, from those pursuing their own happiness to those, like Pardo, who are avoiding the sight of that of others.

He slackened his pace when he reached the street corner and began to reflect on the unexpected discovery. Rarely, in any such case, does a lady's friend not disapprove of her choice. How strangely women choose! The devil must give them a kick… Don't be so harsh, Gabriel; it's not women, it's mankind and *this* is how mankind is… Moreover, this annoyance is a bit like envy and spi– … No, not that. You're not spiteful: what it comes down to is that you can see clearly while your poor friend has gone blind… How her face changed when the individual in question came in! The truth: I didn't think her capable of taking a lover … least of all that one. Either I'm very much mistaken or the poor girl is in for a let-down. That Andalusian is one of those who exemplify the decadence of the Spanish race. O Lord of Hosts, what provinces those in the south! What a man this little Pacheco is! Lazy, ignorant, sensual, without energy or vigour, the plaything of

de trabajar y de servir a su patria, mujeriego, pendenciero, escéptico a fuerza de indolencia y egoísmo, inútil para fundar una familia, célula ociosa en el organismo social ... ¡Hay tantos así! Y sin embargo, a veces medran, con una apariencia de talento y la viveza propia del meridional; no tienen fondo, no tienen seriedad, no tienen palabra, no tienen fe, son malos padres, esposos traidores, ciudadanos zánganos, y los ve usted encumbrarse y hacer carrera ... Así anda ello. Ya las mujeres ... qué diablo, estos hombres les caen en gracia ... Eh, dejémonos de clichés ... Asís, que es de otra raza muy distinta, necesita formalidad y constancia; la compadezco ... Bueno es que no se casara; no, casarse no lo creo posible. De esa madera no se hacen maridos. Como aventura tendrá sus encantos ... ¡Qué casualidad! Y dirán que no hay coincidencias ... ¡Tarjetero, tarjetero ...!

Así meditaba el comandante. ¿Era injusto o sagaz? ¿Obedecía a su costumbre de analizarlo todo, o a una puntita de berrinche? Se caló los lentes y se retorció la barba. ¿A dónde iría?

–Al Círculo Militar, ya que me sirvió de pretexto para escurrir el bulto. ¡Poco gusto que les habrá dado cuando yo tomé la puerta ...!

Tras esta ingrata reflexión apretó a andar. La obscuridad de la noche le exaltaba, y ese grupo que ve con la fantasía todo el que sale huyendo de hacer mala obra a dos enamorados, se empeñaba en flotar, vaporoso e irónico, ante don Gabriel. Fortuna que este género de visiones no suele resistir a los efectos anodinos de una conferencia sobre «Ventajas e inconvenientes del escalafón en los cuerpos facultativos».

passions, incapable of working and serving his country, a womaniser, quarrelsome, sceptical by dint of indolence and selfishness, unfit for starting a family, an idle cell in the social body... There are so many like him! And yet they sometimes thrive and look like they have talent and the typical vivacity of the southerner; they're shallow, have no seriousness, integrity or faith, they're bad fathers, unfaithful husbands, idle citizens, but you see them climb the social ladder and pursue a career... That's how it works. As for women, I'll be damned if they don't take a real shine to those men... Hey, let's forget the clichés ... Asís is of a very different race and needs reliability and constancy. I feel sorry for her... It's a good thing she won't get married; no, I don't think marriage is a possibility. Husbands aren't carved out of wood like that. As an adventure it may have its charms... What a turn-up! And they say there's no such thing as coincidence... Card case, card case!

This was what the major was pondering. Was he unfair or shrewd? Was it in response to his habit of analysing everything or a bit of rage? He put on his glasses and twisted his beard. Where should he go?

'To the Military Club, since it served as a pretext to avoid the awkward situation. They weren't half happy when I made for the door!'

He quickened his pace after these unpleasant thoughts. The darkness of night excited him, and that group imagined by everyone who avoids doing a disservice to two lovers insisted on floating hazily and ironically in front of Don Gabriel. Fortunately mental pictures like this don't usually resist the harmless effects of a lecture on "The advantages and disadvantages of the promotion ladder in professional organisations".

XXII

EPÍLOGO

No entremos en el saloncito de Asís mientras dure el tiroteo de explicaciones (¡cosa más empalagosa!), sino cuando la pareja liba la primera miel de las paces (empalagosísima también, pero paciencia). Ni Pacheco pregunta ya nada acerca de don Gabriel Pardo y su amistad, ni Asís se acuerda del baile en el merendero. El gaditano habla al oído de la señora.

–¿Pero tú te creíste que yo no sabía que mañana te vas? A Diego Pacheco no se la ha pegado ninguna hembra ... ¡Niña boba! Esta mañana ya habías dispuesto la marcha, claro que sí, y si te viniste a almorsá conmigo, fue que te di un poquillo de lástima ... Decías tú allá en tus adentros: sólo faltan horas; vamos a complacer a éste, que tiempo habrá de que estalle la bomba y dejarlo plantao ... ¡Y ahora también piensas en cosas así, muy tristes; en que ya no nos vemos, en que se acaba el cariñito y las fatigas y el verme y el hablarme ...!

22

EPILOGUE

Let's not enter Asís's little salon during the crossfire of explanations (so saccharine!), but when the couple are enjoying the sweet taste of reconciliation (equally saccharine, but be patient). No longer is Pacheco asking anything about Don Gabriel Pardo and their friendship, nor is Asís dwelling on the dance at the snack bar. The man from Cádiz is murmuring in the lady's ear.

'Did you really think I didn't know you're leaving tomorrow? No woman has ever deceived Diego Pacheco... Silly girl! You'd already arranged your departure this morning, that much is clear, and you only had breakfast with me because you felt a bit sorry for me... Just a few hours left, you told yourself; let's humour him, because there'll be time to drop the bomb and leave him in the lurch... And now you're also thinking about very sad things, such as we won't see each other again, our love coming to an end, the suffering, seeing me and talking

¡Ay chiquilla! Me quieres tú mucho más de lo que te figuras. No te has tomado el trabajo de echar la sonda ahí en ese pechito … ¡Tonta! ¡Cómo te acordarás de estos ratos, allá en tu país, entre aquella gente sosaina! Aquí se queda un hombre que te quería también un poquitillo … ¡Pobrecita, la nena!

No estaban los amantes abrazados, ni siquiera muy juntos, pues Pacheco ocupaba el sillón, y el diván Asís. Sólo sus manos, encendidas por la misma fiebre, se buscaban, y habiéndose encontrado, se entrelazaban y fundían. Callaron entonces y fue el instante más hermoso. Por el mudo diálogo de los ojos y por el contacto eléctrico de las palmas, se enviaban el espíritu en arrobo inefable. Con la nueva y victoriosa dulzura de semejante comunicación, Asís sentía que se mezclaba un asombro muy grande. Miraba a Pacheco y creía no haberle visto nunca: descubría en su apostura, en su cara, en sus ojos, algo sublime, que realmente no existía, pero que la señora debía encontrar en aquel instante, pues así sucede en toda revelación para que resplandezca su origen superior a la materia inerte y al ciego acaso, y a Asís se le revelaba entonces el amor. Poco a poco, sin conciencia de sus actos, acercaba la mano de Diego a su pecho, ansiosa de apretarla contra el corazón y de calmar así el ahogo suave que le oprimía … Sus pupilas se humedecieron, su respiración se apresuró, y corrió por sus vértebras misterioso escalofrío, corriente de aire agitado por las alas del Ideal.

–No estés tan tristón –tartamudeó con blandura mimosa.

–Sí que estoy triste, prenda. Y es por ti. Estoy de remate. Estoy hasta enfermo. No sé por dónde ando. Parece que me han dao cañaso. Es un mal que se me entra por el alma arriba. Si sigo así, guardaré cama. Después que te vayas la guardaré … Es cosa rara, chiquilla. ¡Válgame Dios, a lo que llega un hombre!

–Te pones tan lejos … Aquí, cerquita –murmuró la señora con el tono con que se habla a los niños.

–No …, déjame aquí … Estoy bien. Mira tú qué cosas más raras hace la guilladura cuando entra de verdad. Ni ganas tengo de acercarme; la manita me basta …

–¿No te gusto?

–No como me gustarían otras. ¡Ah! Ya sabes si tengo ilusión por

to me... Oh, my child! You love me a lot more than you think! You haven't taken the trouble to probe there in that dear little heart... You fool! How you'll remember these moments, back there in your region with all those dull people! And staying here there's a man who loved you a bit too... My poor little darling!'

The lovers were not hugging, nor even very near each other, for Pacheco was in the armchair and Asís on the divan. Only their hands, burning with the same passion, sought each other out, and having met, intertwined and merged into one. They were silent then and that was the most exquisite moment. Through the unspoken dialogue of their eyes and the electrifying contact of their palms, their spirits were transported in ineffable rapture. Mixed in with the new and triumphant sweetness of this sort of communication, Asís felt great astonishment. She looked at Pacheco and it was as if she had never seen him before. In his dashing appearance, face and eyes she discovered something sublime which did not really exist. But she was destined to see it at that moment, because all revelations are like this, in order that their origin, superior to inert matter and blind chance, may shine forth. At that moment love revealed itself to Asís. Little by little, unaware of her actions, she drew Pacheco's hand to her chest, anxious to press it against her heart and thereby calm the sweet breathlessness crushing her... Her eyes filled with tears, her breathing quickened and a mysterious shiver, a draught fanned by the wings of the Ideal, ran down her spine.

'Don't be so sad,' she stuttered with affectionate tenderness.

'But I am sad, darling, and it's because of you. I'm completely used up, even ill. I don't know where I am. It's like a trick's been played on me. It's a disease that's coming up through my soul. If I carry on like this I'll be confined to bed. After you've gone I'll take to it. It's a strange affair. Good God, what a man can come to!'

'You're so far off... Come here, nice and close,' murmured the lady in the sort of tone used when talking to children.

'No ... leave me here ... I'm fine. Infatuation can do such strange things when it really gets inside you. I don't even wish to come any closer; your little hand's enough for me...'

'Don't you like me?'

'Not in the same way as other women. Ah! You know full well I

ti ... Y así y todo ..., ahora prefiero callar y no acercarme, gloria ... ¡Ay! ... ¿Pero qué es eso? ¿Llora mi niña?

Puede que llorase, en efecto. No debía de ser el reflejo de la lámpara lo que tanto relucía en su mejilla izquierda ... Pacheco exhaló un suspiro y se puso en pie, desenclavijando su mano de la de Asís.

—Me voy —pronunció con voz alteradísima, ronca, resuelta.

De un brinco se levantó Asís, echándole los brazos al cuello y sujetándole.

—No, Diego, que no ... ¡Vaya una ocurrencia! ¡Irte ya! ¡Pues si apenas llegaste! ¿Cómo irte? ¿Tienes que hacer? No, irte no quiero.

—Niña ... El mal camino andarlo pronto. No tengo ánimos para más. Estoy que con una seda me ahogan. ¿A qué aprovechar unos minutos? Es la despedida. Yéndome ahora me ahorro alguna pena. Adiós, querida ... Cree que más vale así.

—No, no, no te vas ... Por lo mismo que ya es la última noche ... Diego, por Dios, mi vida ... Tú quieres sacarme de quicio. No puede ser.

Pacheco sujetó los brazos de la señora, y mirándola de hito en hito, exclamó con firmeza:

—Piénsalo bien. Si me quedo ahora, no me voy en toda la noche. Reflexiona. No digas después que te pongo en berlina. Te conviene soltarme. Tú decidirás.

Asís dudó un minuto. Allá dentro percibía, a manera de inundación que todo lo arrolla, un torrente de pasión desatado. Principios salvadores, eternos, mal llamados por el comandante *clichés*, que regís las horas normales, ¿por qué no resistís mejor el embate de este formidable torrente? Asís articuló, oyendo su propia voz resonar como la de una persona extraña:

—Quédate.

El plan era absurdo, y sin embargo, los medios de realizarlo se presentaban entonces asequibles, rodados. La Diabla, fuera de casa, por casualidad feliz; la cocinera lo mismo; cuestión de engañar a Imperfecto, que era la quinta esencia de la bobería, y a la portera, que

idolise you... And yet with all that ... right now I prefer to be silent and come no nearer, dearest... Oh!... But what's this? Is my little girl crying?'

Perhaps she was in fact crying. It couldn't be the reflection of the lamp that was shining so bright on her left cheek... Pacheco sighed and stood up, separating his hand from Asís's.

'I'm going,' he said in a voice that sounded very upset, hoarse and resolute.

Asís was on her feet in one bound, putting her arms around his neck and holding him back.

'No, Diego, no... What an idea! Going already! You've only just arrived! Why go? Have you got things to do? No, I don't want you to go.'

'Sweetheart... Let's get it over with. I haven't got the energy for any more. The state I'm in, you could strangle me with a piece of thread. Why prolong things? It's farewell. By going now I'll save myself some sorrow. Goodbye, darling... It's best like this, believe me.'

'No, no, you're not going... For the very reason that it is the last night... Diego, for heaven's sake, my love... You want to drive me mad. No way.'

Pacheco took the lady's arms and said firmly as he stared into her eyes:

'Think carefully. If I stay now, it'll be for the whole night. Think it over. Don't tell me afterwards that I'm making a fool of you. It's best you let me go. You can decide.'

Asís hesitated for a minute. Deep inside she could feel a rush of uncontrolled passion like a flood that sweeps everything away. Oh, redeeming, eternal principles, incorrectly called *clichés* by the major! Why, when you rule in normal circumstances, can't you resist more successfully the onslaught of this formidable torrent? Hearing her own voice echo like that of a stranger, Asís said:

'Stay.'

The plan was absurd, but right then the means of carrying it out looked feasible, opportune. By a lucky chance, Diabla was out of the house, and the cook as well; it was just a matter of tricking Imperfecto, who was the quintessence of foolishness, and the porter, who was

siempre estaba dormitando a tales horas. Para conseguir el apetecido resultado, combinóse un atrevido plan de entradas y salidas, de pases y repases, que hizo reír a los dos delincuentes ... Y a las doce de la noche, las puertas de la casa se hallaban cerradas, y dentro de ella el contraventor de las pragmáticas sociales y de las leyes divinas.

Si la cosa no hubiese pasado de aquí, creo sinceramente, lector amigo, que no merecía la pena, no ya de narrarla, sino hasta de mencionarla en estos libros de memorias y exámenes de conciencia de la humanidad, que se llaman novelas. Porque aun siendo el caso tan desatinado y enorme; aun constituyendo una atrevida infracción de todo lo que no debe, ni puede infringirse, bien cabe suponer que en las fiebres pasionales tiene algo de necesario y fatídico, cual en las otras fiebres, la calentura. Pero lo que me parece verdaderamente digno de tomarse en cuenta, como dato singular y curioso; lo que quizás convendría analizar sutilmente –si no es preferible dejarlo sugerido a la imaginación del lector para que lo deduzca y reconstruya a su modo– es la causa, la génesis y el rápido desarrollo de aquella *idea* inesperadísima, que desenlazó precipitada y honrosamente la historia empezada por tan liviano y censurable modo en la romería del Santo ...

¿A cuál de los dos amantes, o mejor dicho, aunque la distinción parezca especiosa, de los dos enamorados, se le ocurrió primero la *idea*? ¿Fue a él, como único paliativo, heroico pero infalible, de su extraña guilladura? ¿Fue a ella, como medio de conciliar el honor con la pasión, el instinto de rectitud y el respeto al deber que siempre guardara, con la flaqueza de su voluntad ya rendida? ¿Fue que esa *idea*, profundamente lógica (y en el caso presente tal vez expiatoria), se presenta a la vuelta del amor, tan fatalmente como sigue a la aurora el mediodía, al crepúsculo la noche y a la vida la muerte?

Que cada cual lo arregle a su gusto y rastree y discurra qué caminos siguieron aquellos espíritus para no reparar en inconvenientes, no recelar de lo futuro, cerrar los ojos a problemas del porvenir y mandar a paseo las sabias advertencias de la razón, que tiembla de espanto ante lo irreparable, lo indisoluble, lo que lleva escrito el letrero medroso: –Para siempre –y avisa que de malos principios rara vez se sacan buenos fines–. Y reconstruya también a su modo los diálogos en que la *idea* se abrió paso, tímida primero, luego clara, imperiosa y

always snoozing at that hour. In order to achieve the longed-for result, a daring plan of entrances and exits was devised which made the two law-breakers laugh... And at midnight, the doors of the house were shut, with the transgressor of social decrees and divine law inside.

If the matter hadn't gone any further, friendly reader, I sincerely believe that it wouldn't be worth narrating, or even mentioning in these memoirs and examinations of conscience called novels. Because even though this case is so crazy and outlandish, even though it constitutes a daring infringement of everything that should not and cannot be violated, one may well suppose that in the fever of passion there is something as inevitable and ominous as a temperature is with other fevers. But what seems to me to be truly worth bearing in mind, as an odd and curious piece of information, what perhaps should be analysed subtly, if it isn't preferable to leave it to the reader's imagination so that they may deduce and reconstruct it in their own way, is the cause, the genesis and the rapid development of that totally unexpected *idea*, which precipitated an honourable *dénouement* to the adventure begun in so frivolous and censurable a manner at the Saint Isidro Fair...

To which of the two lovers, or rather people in love, even if the distinction seems specious, did the *idea* first occur? Was it to him, as the only heroic but infallible palliative for his strange madness? Was it to her, as a means of conciliating honour with passion, the instinct of rectitude and respect for duty she always had with her weak, already surrendered will power? Was it that the *idea*, profoundly logical (and perhaps expiatory in this present case), presents itself after love, as inevitably as noon follows dawn, night follows dusk and death follows life?

Let each person solve it for himself, search and think up which paths those spirits followed so as not to give heed to problems, fear the future, shut one's eyes to prospective problems and wave aside the wise counsels of reason which tremble with fear before what is irreparable, indissoluble, what bears the fearful inscription 'Forever', and warns that good ends rarely come from bad principles. And also reconstruct in his own way the dialogues in which the *idea* emerged, timid at first, next clear, imperious and conclusive, then triumphant,

terminante, después triunfadora, agasajada por el amor que, coronado de rosas, empuñando a guisa de cetro la más aguda y emponzoñada de sus flechas, velaba a la puerta el aposento, cerrando el paso a profanos disectores.

Por eso, y porque no gusto de hacer mala obra, líbreme Dios de entrar hasta que el sol alumbra con dorada claridad el saloncito, colándose por la ventana que Asís, despeinada, alegre, más fresca que el amanecer, abre de par en par, sin recelo o más bien con orgullo. ¡Ah! Ahora ya se puede subir. Pacheco está allí también, y los dos se asoman, juntos, casi enlazados, como si quisiesen quitar todo sabor clandestino a la entrevista, dar a su amor un baño de claridad solar, y a la vecindad entera parte de boda … Diríase que los futuros esposos deseaban cantar un himno a su numen tutelar, el sol, y ofrecerle la primer plegaria matutina.

–Está el gran día, chichi … –exclamaba Pacheco–. Vas a tener un viaje …

–¿Y para el tuyo? ¿Hará buen tiempo?

–Lo mismo que ahora. Verás.

–¿Despacharás en ocho o diez días la ida a Cádiz?

–No que no. Y la aprobación del papá y too. Muerto está él porque me case y siente la cabeza. Le diré que después de la boda me presento diputao por Vigo con la ayuda del papá suegro. Verás tú. Para despabilar un asunto me pinto solo … cuando el asunto me importa, ¿sabes?

–¿Escribirás todo lo que prometiste?

–Boba.

–Simplón, monigote, feo.

–Reina de España.

–En Vigo …, ya sabes … formalidad.

–Hasta que el cura … –(Pacheco hizo con la mano derecha un ademán litúrgico muy significativo)–. Entretanto … me dedicaré a tu chiquilla. ¿Eh? A los dos días … te la he conquistao. Puede que te deje plantaíta a ti pa casarme con ella.

Siguieron algunas bromas y ternezas más, que ni hacen al caso, ni deben figurar aquí en modo alguno. De repente, Diego tomó la mano derecha de la señora, preguntando:

favoured by a love which, crowned with roses and clutching its sharpest, most poisonous arrow like a sceptre, watched over the door of the room, barring the way to uninitiated dissectors.

For this reason, and because I don't like being responsible for second-rate work, heaven forbid that I should enter the little salon until it has been illuminated with golden sunshine, seeping in through the window which Asís, unkempt, happy and fresher than the dawn, has thrown wide open, without apprehension and even with pride. Ah, we can go in now. Pacheco is there as well, and the two are looking out, almost tied together, as if they wanted to remove any hint of clandestinity from their meeting, give their love a bath of solar light and the whole neighbourhood a wedding invitation… You might say that the future husband and wife wanted to sing a hymn to their patron deity, the sun, and offer it the first morning prayer.

'The great day is here, sweetheart…' exclaimed Pacheco. 'You're going to make a journey…'

'And for yours? Will the weather be good?'

'The same as now. You'll see.'

'Will you make the journey to Cádiz in eight or ten days?'

'Absolutely. And my dad's approval and everything. He's dying for me to get married and settle down. I'll tell him that after the wedding I'll stand as member of parliament for Vigo with my father-in-law's help. You'll see. When it comes to dealing with a matter quickly, I'm a dab hand … when it's something that's important to me, you know.'

'Will you write as much as you promised?'

'You silly thing.'

'Simple, foolish, unseemly soul.'

'Queen of Spain.'

'In Vigo … you know … behave yourself.'

'Up until the priest…' (Pacheco made a very significant liturgical gesture with his right hand.) 'Meanwhile … I'll dedicate myself to your little girl. Eh? Within two days … I'll have won her over. Maybe I'll jilt you so I can marry her.'

Some more jokes and sweet nothings followed, which aren't even relevant and shouldn't appear here at all. Suddenly, Diego took the lady's right hand and asked:

–¿Te acuerdas tú de una buenaventura que te echaron en la feria?

E imitando el acento y modales de la gitana, añadió:

–Una cosa diquelo yo en esta manica, que hae suseder mu pronto y nadie saspera que susea … Un viaje me vasté a jaser, y no ae ser para má, que ae ser pa satisfasión e toos … Una presoniya está chalaíta por usté …

El gaditano, siempre presumido, agregó:

–Y usté por ella.

FIN

'Do you remember the fortune you were told at the fair?'

And, imitating the gypsy lady's accent and mannerisms, he added:

'One fing I can dik in vis teeny 'and, somefin'ut'll 'appen real soon, and nobody 'spects it'll 'appen... You're gonna take a trip, and it'll turn out cushty, it's gonna be to ev'ryone's satisfaction... A certain person is crazy 'bout ya...'

The man from Cádiz, as vain as ever, added:

'And you about him.'